"This is a remarkable accomplishment.
reading this deeply enriching account c
Geddes than I ordered six more copies
of book!"
James Roose-Evans, theatre director and author

"A labour of love."
Richard Holloway, chairman, Scottish Arts Council

"Frank Woods allows us deeper insights into who Gerda Geddes
was, what made her what she was, the fascinating life she led, and
how she inspired thousands to get the best they could from their
lives."
Ronnie Robinson, t'ai-chi teacher and editor Tai Chi Chuan

"I didn't want this book to end. Hers is an exciting, tough,
wonderful and life-affirming story."
Baroness Kari de Koenigswarter

"Frank Woods' moving biography is a kind of allegorical journey."
David Boadella, psychotherapist and writer

"It totally engaged me. But more than that: it has a kind of
therapeutic power."
Rhoda Michael, editor Northwords Now

"Well written and organized, and flows so well I had a hard time
putting it down. This is a must read for anyone interested in the
roots of t'ai-chi in the Western world, and is an intimate look inside
a complex human."
Michael Gilman, t'ai-chi teacher and author

Frank Woods lives and writes in North East Scotland. He was an exploration geologist, a journalist and a primary school teacher before he became a psychologist who specialized in working with troubled young people and their families. He has published short stories and poetry, as well as articles on a wide range of subjects.

DANCER IN
THE LIGHT

the life of Gerda 'Pytt' Geddes

For Julie

DANCER IN THE LIGHT

the life of
Gerda 'Pytt' Geddes

FRANK WOODS

Psi Books

First Published in 2008 by Psi Books

A catalogue record for this book is available from
the British Library

ISBN 978-0-9559181-0-0

Design and typesetting by Leopard magazine
www.leopardmag.co.uk

Printed and bound in Scotland by Bell and Bain, Glasgow

Psi Books
Foresterseat, Cothal, Dyce, Aberdeen AB21 0HX
psibooks@forseat.demon.co.uk

www.gerdageddes.com

CONTENTS

PROLOGUE 1

Part 1: OPENING 7
    Biographer's Thread 1 8
  1. The Beginning 10
  2. Norwegian Childhood 13
    Biographer's Thread 2 25
  3. Wing Spreading 26
    Biographer's Thread 3 38
  4. War and Resistance 40

Part 2: INNER AND OUTER JOURNEYS 53
    Biographer's Thread 4 54
  5. The Road to Psychotherapy 56
  6. The Road to Dance 69
    Biographer's Thread 5 75
  7. From Theory to Practice 76
  8. Drama and Movement 81
    Biographer's Thread 6 86
  9. Love and Marriage 88
 10. The Road to Shanghai 98
 11. The Fall of Shanghai 104
 12. Hostages of Mao Tse-tung 111
 13. Escape to Hong Kong 117
 14. Hong Kong Life 120

15. Treasured Guests 128
    Biographer's Thread 7 135
16. The Path to T'ai-chi 137
17. Return to Britain 148
18. Domestic Joy, T'ai-chi Disappointment 153

Part 3: TRANSFORMATION 161
19. Losing the Light 162
20. T'ai-chi Rebirth 167
21. A New Life Begins 177
    Biographer's Thread 8 184
22. The Place Where Three Strands Meet 186
23. Personal Searches 197
24. The Open Handed Teacher 207
    Biographer's Thread 9 213
25. Creative Circles 214
26. Outward Flow 219
27. Pinning Down the Golden Needle 225
    Biographer's Thread 10 234
28. Loss and Grief 236
29. The Scottish Years 243
    Biographer's Thread 11 253
30. Shooting Out the Arrow 255
31. Celebration 261

EPILOGUE 265

ACKNOWLEDGEMENTS 266
NOTES 267
BIBLIOGRAPHY 274
INDEX 275

PROLOGUE

erda 'Pytt' Geddes was a spirited and independent-minded woman who led a long, full and intriguing life. When she and I agreed her story should be recorded, I envisioned a conventional biography that would follow an ordered timeline from her birth in 1917: instead it is in three separate parts, each of which, for different reasons, begins in her childhood. And I assumed that I would systematically garner the evidence from Gerda, her family, her friends and associates, from every source I could find, and weave from it a design that would illuminate the events and pattern of her life: instead there are sections where the words are exclusively hers and it reads more like autobiography. What follows goes some way towards explaining why.

One evening in the spring of 1999 I sat in a lecture theatre at Aberdeen University, one of an expectant audience awaiting a talk and demonstration of t'ai-chi. A small, slim, silver-haired woman dressed in a black silk Chinese trouser suit entered with slow grace and stood before us in eloquent stillness. The room quietened until scarcely a breath could be heard. We were in the presence of Gerda, known as the woman who introduced t'ai-chi to Britain. For me, it was the beginning of a friendship that lasted until her death.

She enjoyed telling stories and as I got to know her I began to hear about her childhood as the daughter of a prominent businessman and politician, amusing tales involving the Norwegian Royal Family, her explorations of avant-garde dance and Reichian psychoanalysis in Oslo, her wartime escape from the Gestapo, her life in the Far East, and, more than anything, her training in t'ai-chi and the insights this had brought her. She told me of her memoir *A Norwegian Childhood* but she saw this as a private record for her grandchildren and did not give me a copy until we began working on her biography. That was when I began to uncover a story that is more complex, textured, and multi-layered than I anticipated when I set out to record the life of the woman known mainly as a t'ai-chi pioneer.

There was an important spiritual dimension to Gerda. She liked nothing better than a conversation that ranged widely over life and death, energy, creativity, art, and humanity in its many expressions. She also had an intuitive appreciation of that elusive aspect of people that hides behind abstract nouns like soul, or spirit, or essence, but apparently as tangible to Gerda as a handshake. Yet there was nothing precious or otherworldly about her. She was a practical and direct Norsewoman, a consummate needleworker and dressmaker who prized elegance and the finer things in life, a straight talker who debunked any attempt to clothe her in the mantle of master or guru. Rather, she saw her teaching as offering signposts along the way: the ultimate destination was the responsibility of each person's creative spirit.

Gerda first saw the hypnotic, dance-like ritual of t'ai-chi in 1949 when she was living in Shanghai. She was later to write:

"As I watched I had a sensation of hot and cold streaming up and down my spine. It was like 'meeting with the Holy', and I remember thinking: 'This is what I have been looking for all my life'."[1]

After many difficulties and trials, she eventually persuaded a Chinese master to teach her the secrets of this ancient art. She then brought its mysteries to Britain where, in the 1960s, she began to share her knowledge by teaching dancers in London, contemplative monks in Sussex, academics in Cambridge, inquiring minds and souls at the College for Psychic Studies, and an intriguing mixture of artists, writers, doctors, dope-smoking hippies, seekers after truth and the simply curious who turned up at her classes.

Consider the historical context: this happened at a time when

Mind, Body and Spirit sections did not exist in bookshops, and when only a handful of English translations rewarded the assiduous inquirer into Eastern thought, philosophy and culture. Gerda Geddes played a major role in changing this. In 1958 she gave the first demonstration of t'ai-chi on British television. She taught her first t'ai-chi classes in 1964, just as changes in British society were beginning to create a new openness, a willingness to look beyond our own shores and discover what light other cultures, especially Eastern ones, might throw on life's perennial questions. Almost fifty years on, t'ai-chi classes attract people across the country to their local community centres or church halls, while cities offer a wide range of t'ai-chi schools and styles embedded in a bewildering array of oriental systems of martial arts, cultural pursuits, meditation and alternative medicine.

But Gerda did much more than demonstrate and teach t'ai-chi. She delved deeper into Chinese thought to follow her intuition that t'ai-chi had an important hidden layer of meaning. She believed clues were hidden in the names of moves such as *Carry Tiger To Mountain, The White Stork Spreads Its Wings, Step Back And Repulse The Monkey, Look For The Golden Needle At The Bottom Of The Sea, The Fair Lady Works With Shuttles,* and *The Snake Creeps Down Into The Water.* When, early in her training, she had pressed her teacher for an explanation of these strange terms, he had shrugged her question aside. They were aids to memory, he had said, names used to break up the complicated sequence of movements and make it easier to learn. However her subsequent studies opened up a strange and enigmatic world overseen by the Tao, the paradoxical Chinese universal governing principle, and powered by the complementary forces of Yin and Yang and the energy known as chi. It was also a world full of references to the mysterious symbols and beings which cropped up in the names of the t'ai-chi moves. The more she studied, the more she practised, the more she taught, and the more she reflected on her own experiences, the clearer it became to her: t'ai-chi contained within the pattern of its movements a symbolic story. She called it the Allegorical Journey, and its discovery changed not just how she looked at her own life, but how she lived the last forty years of it until her death in her 89th year on 4 March 2006. Thanks to her teaching and her writing, it is a discovery that has influenced the lives of thousands of people. She summed up her insight in her book, *Looking for the Golden Needle*.

> "In trying to comprehend the whole of the t'ai-chi ch'uan one finds that moving through the three parts and thirteen sequences is like passing through life from birth to death, from beginning to end, both on the physical and philosophical plane. One enacts, through the body, the different phases of development common to us all. It is like a Pilgrim's Progress with imagery from China."[2]

Her assertion that t'ai-chi contained a roadmap of the human spiritual journey was all the more remarkable because she was describing something which, as far as is known, had not previously been recorded. In China, t'ai-chi was taught as a martial art. Beneficial effects on health were recognised, but practitioners were primarily concerned with their progress in the field of combat rather than with their inner development. The movements were practised as a form of sparring with an imaginary opponent: in his subsequent letters to her, Gerda's Master, Choy Kam Man, did not call it t'ai-chi but 'Chinese Shadow Boxing'. Now, thanks in large measure to the influence of Gerda Geddes, many people practise t'ai-chi as a path of personal growth whilst others use it to maintain health and fitness, or as a traditional martial art, or in whatever combination of these three approaches makes sense to them.

The roots of Gerda's unique t'ai-chi insight lie not just in her midlife inquiry into Chinese cultural and philosophical history, but extend far back into her Norwegian origins, her training in dance and in psychoanalysis, her wartime experiences in the Resistance, her pioneering movement therapy with concentration camp survivors, her work with the Norwegian National Theatre, and her life in China and Hong Kong. They are questing roots, constantly searching out life's meaning, seeking nourishment in an answer that she knew involved the synthesis of mind and body, and was somehow linked to the occasional numinous moments of illumination that she described herself experiencing from an early age.

As I listened to the unfolding chronicle of her long life, I began to appreciate its nuances, themes and intricacies. There was a physical odyssey involving Britain, the U.S.A., war-torn Norway, Sweden, revolutionary China, Hong Kong and Britain again. Then there was the intense inner journeying as she strove to make sense of her unique human life. It became clear that a chronological narrative could not do justice to her almost ninety years of inner and outer exploration and that a more thematic design would be required.

And I found it in her book *Looking for the Golden Needle* which in hindsight seems obvious, since it outlines her belief that t'ai-chi contains a blueprint of human development, a birth-to-death journey in three phases. According to Gerda, the first part represents early life when our task is to become independent, to accumulate our own energy, and to show the world how we can use ourselves; the second part is concerned with achievement and creativity as we journey not just through the physical world but also, at a deeper level, as we find a balance between the working of the body and the development of the spirit; and the last part contains a major transformation that opens up a spiritual path and shows us a philosophy of life which might guide us through old age and prepare us for departure from this world.

That is why this book is in three main parts: Opening; Inner and Outer Journeys: and Transformation.

Gerda was delighted by my plan to structure the book in this way. She selected the Sri Aurobindo quote that opens the first section. She died before she had selected quotes for the other two sections but she didn't leave me entirely at a loss: they are both chosen from amongst the many underlinings and margin markings in her well-thumbed copies of two books; *Sri Aurobindo or the Adventure of Consciousness* by Satprem, and *The Spiral Path of Spiritual Psychology* by Edith Schnapper. In addition, each chapter opens with a small extract from *Looking for the Golden Needle*.

Two other features deserve mention. Additional background information often appears in separate textboxes where it can be browsed as required. The Biographer's Thread is a series of observations that give the flavour of the relationship between Gerda and me as we worked on the story of her life.

Frank Woods
Foresterseat
Aberdeenshire

May 2008

Part One
OPENING

What matters most in my life is not my heredity; that only gives me my opportunity or my obstacle, my good or my bad material, and it has not by any means been shown that I draw all from that source. What matters supremely is what I make of my heredity and not what my heredity makes of me. The past of the world, bygone humanity, my ancestors are there in me; but still I myself am the artist of my self, my life, my actions.

Sri Aurobindo   *ESSAYS IN PHILOSOPHY AND YOGA*

I was driving the thirty-six miles (fifty-eight kilometres) from Gerda Geddes's home to mine, a journey that crossed some high and beautiful countryside joining the valleys of the Dee and Don rivers in the northeast of Scotland. It was a trip that I made at regular intervals. Sometimes Gerda came to visit but she was now in her late 80s and less keen to drive.

I had just taken Gerda my copy of Cheng Man Ch'ing's *Thirteen Treatises on T'ai-Chi Ch'uan*. As I left, she pressed on me a book about T. T. Liang, a Chinese t'ai-chi master who had spent the second half of his life teaching in the U.S.A. until he died at the age of 102. She had read it and was curious about my opinion. When I reached the top of the hill where the single-track road from Gerda's isolated house meets the winding road that would take me east towards Aberdeen, I turned for a last look at Lochnagar, the majestic mountain which, in the late summer sunshine, had lost some of its customary dark foreboding.

Then it hit me. I had made this journey to deliver information about one t'ai-chi person: I was returning with an account of another. Where was the biography of Gerda Geddes, known as the first European to bring t'ai-chi from China to Britain? It seemed as if the true purpose of my trip had been to allow this thought to surface.

I telephoned as soon as I reached home.

"Gerda, I had a thought while I was driving. A proposal, really, that I'd like to make to you."

"Yes?"

"But before I do, I'd like to make something clear. I don't want you to feel at all pressurised about it. If it doesn't make sense and you don't want to do anything about it, that's the end of the matter."

"Yes? Yes? Go on." She listened to my explanation of why I would like to write a book about her, why I thought it was important.

"Ah. Yes. I see. That is something I will have to think about. And talk about to my family." The measured, cultured voice had never lost an underlying Norwegian lilt which, to my ear at least, carried a hint of the Shetlands, or the Hebrides maybe. It was also very good at carrying a tone of finality: life is full of lots to do and time isn't here to be wasted. We said goodbye.

Several weeks passed and I assumed that the idea had gone nowhere. Then she rang.

"That proposal you made about a book? I would like to go ahead with it. I'm a little surprised by my daughters' enthusiasm. I sent them both some of your writing and they think you are the person to do the job."

That's how this book started.

THE BEGINNING

In the opening sequences of the t'ai-chi ch'uan, as we leave the firmly rooted standing position, we step out into a movement called Grasping the Bird's Tail. The bird is thought of as the messenger between Heaven and Earth and this grasping of the bird's tail indicates the individual's first awareness and curiosity for his wider surroundings. The bird also symbolises air and spirit, so it seems that as we become more conscious we feel ourselves as moving through air, being illumined by spirit.

Gerda Geddes   LOOKING FOR THE GOLDEN NEEDLE, p55

On a hot April morning in 1949, Gerda Geddes and her husband of four months strolled beside an irrigation canal on the outskirts of Shanghai. They were newcomers to China but had soon learned that a cool dawn walk along the paddy fields started their day well and prepared them for the oppressive heat to come. Gerda had grown up in the cool and crisp climate of Norway and was finding the clamminess especially taxing.

An old Chinese man stood silently by the water. Beside him, in a gilded cage, was a mynah bird. Then the man began to move very slowly, performing beautiful dance-like movements that were reflected in the water. He was completely absorbed in his ritual and paid no attention to his watchers. The sun was just rising and as he was flooded in its light the mesmerised Gerda had the sensation of a force creeping up and down her spine. This sense of light and energy linked her to several moments of illumination she had experienced in her life.

It stripped away the years and connected her to the first of these: a key childhood experience when, at the age of four, she propelled her little tricycle in and out of a sunbeam and, for the first time, became aware of herself as a separate human being.

This chance encounter by a canal irrevocably changed Gerda. She determined that she would find out more about the strange dance she was witnessing. And she would learn how to do it. From then on three main strands, like a Celtic design, weaved a complex but coherent pattern through her life: psychology, dance and t'ai chi.

Gerda's presence in China was itself more the result of chance than of planning. After a romantic wedding on New Year's Eve 1948 in a small Norwegian mediaeval church at Aastvedt, just north of Bergen, she and her husband David travelled to London and found a flat at 10 Pembridge Crescent, Notting Hill Gate which Gerda described as comprising

"one large, rather pretty, icy cold room, a bedroom, a bathroom and a kitchen in a cupboard. The kitchen had a sink but no water so David arranged a rubber hose from the bathroom tap!"[1]

Gerda had given up a job with the Norwegian National Theatre when the couple married and her sole means of support was a small allowance. Her new husband, the Hon. David Campbell Geddes, was a son of Sir Auckland Campbell Geddes, the First Baron Geddes. David had a mediocre ground staff job with British European Airways and his mother, Lady Geddes, had helped the newlyweds with the first three months rent on the Notting Hill flat. Beyond that the couple's plans, other than to be happy and in love, were at best vague.

Then David found employment at the Shanghai headquarters of the international trading company Jardine, Matheson and Co. As Gerda later wrote:

"David had an interview and got the job, so overnight our whole life changed. He was offered a princely salary and we headed to Shanghai, both of us completely ignorant of China and Chinese affairs."[2]

A stopover in Hong Kong gave Gerda and David the first clues of the lifestyle towards which they were heading. They stayed in a Jardine Matheson flat where Chinese servants catered for all their needs. They were later to become accustomed to the luxurious expatriate lifestyle but for the moment watched in amazement as the clothing they changed to cope with the hot and sticky weather was immediately rushed off, laundered and returned crisp and fresh in what seemed like a miraculously short time.

On arrival in Shanghai they were the guests of John and Clare Keswick while their company house was being made ready. Sir John Keswick was the head of Jardine Matheson. He and his wife lived in a beautiful and elegant house full of Chinese treasures and their garden was famous all over Shanghai. Powerful and important people congregated there on social evenings. The heads of other companies which had claimed a foothold on the Bund, the famous business street, rubbed shoulders with middle eastern bankers and colourful characters from the multinational society which had grown around, and which contributed to, the opulent, wealth-driven commercial boom that was Shanghai.

"On our first evening there we were thrown in at the deep end. The Keswick's were entertaining the upper crust of Shanghai society. Fortunately I possessed several smart evening dresses, all inherited from Tante Gerda's French couturier collection and remade to fit me."[3]

For thirty-one-year-old Gerda, Tante Gerda's gowns formed a bridge between the society she had now entered and the one she had left behind.

NORWEGIAN CHILDHOOD

Through Grasping the Bird's Tail you begin to explore your surroundings, being conscious of moving through and being caressed by air. Every outbreath finishes by Holding the Circle indicating that you are accumulating energy. When you start moving forward it is an enjoyable experience until you decide to change the situation by using your fisted hand, your Ch'uan or your free will. Once you have proved to yourself that you are capable of using your will, you return to the mountain to allow yourself to take a rest before you have to face up to the difficulties of life, represented by Pushing Away the Monkey.

Gerda Geddes   LOOKING FOR THE GOLDEN NEEDLE, pp77-78

Gerda Geddes was born Gerda Meyer Bruun on 17th July 1917 in the Norwegian city of Bergen. Both of her parents had close ties to one of the city's well-placed and influential families, the Meyers.

Although Gerda's godmother, Gerda Meyer (or 'Tante Gerda' to Gerda), was her mother's cousin, the two woman had grown up close-ly together and their bond was much more that of sisters. (See abbre-viated family tree on the following page.)

Tante Gerda's father, Rasmus Meyer, was a wealthy flour miller, busi-nessman, art connoisseur and public benefactor who lived in Krybbebakken, an impressive mansion standing above Bergen on a hill which eventually leads to Floyen, one of the seven mountains which surround the city. The house contained Rasmus' art collection, and some of Gerda Geddes's early memories were of pedalling her small tricycle through galleries hanging with paintings. Krybbebakken was a centre for other members of the extended Meyer family. It was the gathering place for Sunday lunch and a Christmas celebration; it was also home to a number of unmarried relatives.

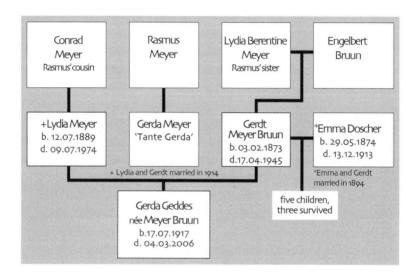

Lydia Meyer, Gerda's mother, was the daughter of Rasmus' cousin, Conrad Meyer. Conrad had, in his own right, inherited a large area of farming land and property at Aastvedt north of Bergen. Aastvedt had no school and when Lydia reached school age she spent term times living as a member of the Krybbebakken household, hence her sisterly relationship to Tante Gerda. Lydia and Tante Gerda were also related through their mothers who were sisters.

Gerdt Meyer Bruun, Gerda's father, also had familial links to the Meyers. His mother was Rasmus' sister and she, like Rasmus himself, owned a summerhouse in Aastvedt where all of the relatives would have mixed, mingled and socialised during the long Nordic summer days.

So Gerda's parents were members of a large extended and socially important family within a provincial area of a small country. It is understandable that matches might occur in such circumstances of social, cultural and geographical closeness, matches where people of similar backgrounds might find attraction and love from within their number. However family affiliation does not guarantee compatibility. Despite similarities of class and social standing, despite family links and loyalties, Gerda's parents had very different personalities. They also belonged to different generations. The disparities between them affected their marriage and Gerda's family experiences.

Gerda's father, Gerdt Meyer Bruun, and his first wife Emma, who died in in 1913.

Gerda's mother, Lydia Meyer, (right) and her cousin Gerda Meyer ('Tante Gerda').

When Gerdt Meyer Bruun proposed to Lydia Meyer he was a widower whose wife had died of cancer in 1913 when he was forty. He and Emma Doscher had married young and she had borne him five children, two of whom died in early childhood. He was the successful and wealthy owner of a family business and a man of conservative opinions with political aspirations.

He was also, in many ways, a nineteenth century man. His father owned a rope works in Bergen. In the heyday of sail, rope was in huge demand and used up by the mile as ships were built and rigged, and as Norway plied her booming maritime trade. But the young Gerdt had other plans besides easing smoothly into the family business. His sense of adventure led him, at the age of seventeen, to run away to sea with a friend and sail before the mast to Turkey where they jumped ship. After a chase through the sewers, the Istanbul harbour police captured the youths but not before shots had been fired and Gerdt had a bullet in his leg. Despite that, it was a relieved captain who took custody of his wayward crew. By this time he knew their true identities and returning to Bergen without the sons of prominent families was not an option he relished.

His rite of passage over, Gerdt was enrolled in a naval officer's training school and by the age of twenty-one he was married and a father. For the following nineteen years until his wife's death he pursued the life of a successful businessman and political aspirant while his wife bore the children and was upstairs mistress of the large sprawling house he had built for his family. It was a perfect Victorian match, tragically ended by ovarian cancer in 1913.

When Gerdt and Lydia married in 1914, she was twenty-four and sixteen years his junior. Although she had been born in the last decade of the nineteenth century, she was a young woman with her feet firmly planted in the twentieth. To begin with, she, and her three sisters, had received a tertiary education which was unusual for that time. Her aspirations to become a doctor were simply not acceptable in the early nineteen hundreds: instead, she opted for the relatively new profession of physiotherapy. And where Gerdt's teenage restlessness had taken him onto the wooden deck of a sailing ship and to the eastern edge of Europe, hers took her up the gangplank of an ocean liner heading west for the United States of America. She spent three years at a health spa in New Jersey where she lived the life of a modern young woman, wearing the styles, dancing the dances, and experimenting with the hairdos. Then, for reasons that remained a mystery to Gerda, she returned to the parental estate in rural Norway.

"She had come back from America and I don't know what happened to her there. I think she probably had a love affair that went wrong. She was very unsettled back on her father's estates and she didn't know what to do with herself. And there was my father, handsome, rich and successful. She said: 'He just wouldn't leave me alone. So in the end I said yes.' And I don't think she loved him at all when they got married. I think, as far as she was concerned, women in those days simply had to be married. And here was a wonderful opportunity."[1]

As well as her youth, Lydia had the additional problems that came with a ready-made family of three grown-up children who had lost their mother less than a year earlier.

"My father and his first wife were very happily married and were very well suited for each other in every way. They formed a happy Victorian family unit. The first wife was very musical and there was a lot of playing and singing around the piano. When my mother came in, the three surviving children were sisters aged fourteen and seventeen and a brother of twenty-one. They set their faces against my mother who wasn't allowed to be part of their little group although she wasn't all that much older than my brother. That was very hurtful. As she described it to me, she had to sit beautifully dressed in the drawing room on a beautiful sofa, ready to greet my father when he came home. And be ready for him at the wink of an eye. That was how it was for women in those days. My mother was more intelligent than the first wife but she wasn't as lively, she didn't play the piano very well, and they didn't sing songs together."[2]

By the time Gerda was born some changes had already taken place. The eldest daughter, Maria, had married and flown the coop; an event which Gerda believed may have been accelerated by her wish to escape the family home. And the family no longer lived in the sprawling house which Gerdt had built for his first wife; a place which Lydia, as she later complained to Gerda, found unwelcoming, uncomfortable and, no doubt, full of ghosts. She blamed sleeping in the huge and draughty master bedroom for the onset of the rheumatism that afflicted her throughout her life. Instead they lived in Krybbebakken where they had moved after Rasmus's death in 1916. It is not difficult to imagine Lydia's delight at leaving a house where she had felt an intruder and returning to a place which had been a second home to her as she was growing up and where, before and after her trip to America, she had acted as a hostess when Rasmus had entertained the artists, painters, architects and other people of culture who were so much part of his life.

THE RASMUS MEYER COLLECTION

Rasmus Meyer (1858-1916) loved pictorial art. His vision, backed by his substantial wealth, was to build a private collection that would be representative of Norwegian art history. Only the National Gallery in Oslo rivalled the quality of his collection.

The Rasmus Meyer Collection contains 963 works of art, primarily paintings, fine art prints, and drawings. Following Rasmus's death in 1916 it was gifted to the city of Bergen where it is housed in a purpose built museum, designed by the famous Norwegian architect Ole Landmark who also designed Storhaugen, Gerda's childhood home.

It includes 32 paintings, 102 prints and 2 drawings by Edvard Munch (1849-1929), one of the most important collections of his work which includes the seminal paintings Evening at Karl Johan (1892), Jealousy (1890) and Melancholy (1894-95). There are also important works by J.C. Dahl, Gerhard Munthe, Eric Werenskiold, Christian Krogh and Harriet Backer.

In his collection, Rasmus realised his ambition to show the development of Norwegian art from the beginning of the nineteenth century until circa 1915.

Gerdt then set about planning another family dream house to which they moved in 1922. Storhaugen, a mansion designed by Ole

Landmark, was at Fjøsanger, now in the suburbs of Bergen but then in the countryside and a desirable place to live. Down the hill from the Meyer Bruuns was the imposing sight of Gamlehaugen, the official Bergen residence of the King and Queen of Norway. By this time, Gerdt was a well-known and important figure in business, politics and society. As well as owning a booming rope works he was chairman of the Bergen Chamber of Commerce, a director of the Bergen Private Bank, head of the Corn Monopoly, and director of the Wine Monopoly. He was an M.P. for Bergen for many years, and a member of the Government (1920-23) as Minister of Trade.

And the couple were no strangers to life at the Royal court. During the years when Gerdt was a government minister they had a flat in Oslo where they lived a busy social life, and attended receptions and balls at the Palace.

"I remember my Mother getting dressed for these occasions. She had two beautiful Court dresses, both with long trains. One was in green brocade with gold flowers and shoes of the same material. The other was shimmering peach and silver. I remember her standing in front of the mirror practising her curtsey, and worrying about not being able to get up again gracefully."[3]

Gerda enjoyed telling two stories about her own contacts with King Haakon and Queen Maud during these years. One concerned the king's visit to Bergen in 1926.

"His house was at Fjøsanger, where we lived, so he got off the train at Fjøsanger station. My Father was on the reception committee, and was dressed up in his morning coat with all his decorations. He looked most impressive and a photograph was taken of the two of us just before he left for the station. I thought it might be a good idea to give the King some flowers. It was June, so I went into the fields and picked a bunch of wild flowers. I then ran down to the station where the entrance was barred and lots of people were waiting for the Royal train to arrive. I told the stationmaster that I had an important message to deliver to my Father, so he let me pass. As the train drew in and the King stepped down, I rushed forward and pressed my bunch of half dead flowers into his hand and ran away. I am sure the King did not recognise me until my Father stepped forward and explained. When my Father came home, he was very angry and said: 'You do not present dead flowers to the King when you are wearing a dirty frock and have dirty knees!' But I was mentioned in the papers the next day, as the 'sweet little girl who, on his arrival at the station, unexpectedly presented a bunch of flowers to the King and then ran away'."[4]

In the photograph taken in the garden, Gerdt stands tall and resplendent, his morning dress bedecked with the ribbons and insignia of success and recognition. He looks every inch the man of substance and position with his firm gaze, his confident pose and his head cocked proudly to one side. His collar, shirtfront and cuffs are crisp, his shoes gleam. At his right side the skinny nine-year-old Gerda screws up her eyes against the strong June sun. Her short pleated dress is pristine and, above the tops of her long stockings, her well-scrubbed knees have yet to feel the heat and dust of the summer grass.

She also delighted in telling how, on an earlier occasion, Queen Maud had put her to bed.

"In the summer of 1924 I went with my mother to stay with Tante Gerda and Uncle Otto at Fornebu. Their house was enormous and luxurious, surrounded by a big park. There were lots of Scots pine trees at the bank and in front about half a mile of beach and rocks, a boathouse, a motor cruiser and a sailing boat. One entered the house through a courtyard and came into a hall with marble pillars and a marble floor. At the far end of the hall were large glass doors leading out to the garden, on the left the dining room and the orangerie, on the right the drawing room, the rococo salon, a study, and the music room with two grand pianos and a selection of other musical instruments. There was a large marble staircase which led down to the indoor swimming pool where they had heated salt water from the Oslofjord. The stairs also led to the upper floors and had niches containing a collection of old armour.

Tante Gerda had just given birth to her first child and the Queen had agreed to be its godmother. One night there was a party for the King and Queen and lots of foreign diplomats and other 'bigwigs'. I was allowed to stay up to dinnertime and was dressed in a beautiful French white crepe de chine creation, white satin shoes, silk stockings and white kid gloves.

There was a great hustle and bustle in the kitchen and Uncle Otto was everywhere, tasting the wines and the sauces. He arranged everything, while Tante Gerda just managed to get herself dressed in time. My mother wore a green silk brocade dress with gold flowers and a long train, I though she looked beautiful.

When the guests started arriving, Uncle Otto and I stood on the front steps to greet them. I remember especially (the explorer and Nobel Peace Prize winner) Fridtjof

Gerda with her father in 1926 on the day she gave flowers to the King

Nansen, tall and white-haired with piercing blue eyes. The last to arrive were the King and Queen; the Queen dressed in grey chiffon with lots of pearls around her neck, the King very tall and handsome. Then we all went inside and the King lifted me high up in the air and said he thought I looked so sweet that he might eat me for dessert. I got very frightened and nearly burst into tears, thinking that a real king might be capable of anything.

When the guests went in to dinner, my mother rushed me upstairs, told me to go to bed, and said she would come and kiss me goodnight later. I suddenly felt very alone and neglected, in a huge unfamiliar bed, thinking there might be a ghost underneath it. Then I waited and waited and could not go to sleep so I got out of bed and went and sat on the stairs in my nightie and bare feet. At long last the dinner was over. The first people to come out of the room were the Queen and Uncle Otto. By this time I was crying and saying I wanted my Mummy, but the Queen took me by the hand and we went upstairs. She tucked me up in bed and started telling me fairy stories and singing me English nursery rhymes. She smelt faintly of violets, was very thin and gentle, and spoke Norwegian with a strong English accent. In the end I got sleepy. She told me to say my prayers and when I came to: God bless mummy and daddy and all the people in the world, I remembered to say God bless the King and Queen first."[5]

Gerda considered Storhaugen her true home and the place where she grew up. It was a handsome and imposing house at the top of a steep hill. The encircling wall with its entrance gate enclosed a courtyard where the arches of the main doors were echoed in an arched and pillared loggia.

"My father was very generous and did things on a grand scale. The house he built for his first wife came out about double the size it was meant to be. That was typical of him. The second house, Storhaugen, where I grew up, wasn't all that enormous. But everything had to be absolutely tops. So all our curtains and hangings were bought from Liberty's. And everything from England was very much appreciated. My father had all his clothes made in Savile Row, not by Norwegian tailors."[6]

The reality of life indoors at Storhaugen is charmingly captured in a playbook made for Gerda by her older half-sister, Emma. It survives today, tattered but intact despite its many years as a favoured plaything of Gerda and later her own two daughters. Inside its dog-eared covers, life is depicted in a series of clear, detailed crayon-coloured drawings with cardboard cut-out characters whose changeable sets of clothing are designed with folding tabs in the style of Victorian scrapbooks. Many different scenes can be recreated: children play in the nursery under the watchful gaze of a nanny; the family sits around the drawing room with a tray-carrying maid in alert attendance; the chauffeur takes the family for a drive.

And it was a life that Gerda could evoke in rich anecdote:
"The bullet from my father's Istanbul adventure had remained in his leg for many years, until it was dug out in a botched operation. The wound was not properly stitched together, they were very primitive in those days, so he had a long white scar all the way down his leg. And when I was a little girl I used to love going into his bed. I was allowed to come and lie in daddy's bed in the morning. And such were the customs in those days that the maid came in wearing her morning uniform of pale blue with an apron and a cap over her head. She brought a cup of coffee and cakes. That was how you started the day if you belonged to that class. She came in with a silver tray and I was allowed to have two cakes before breakfast. Sometimes I asked to touch my father's bullet scar and my imagination went wild with how brave he was."[7]

Beneath the surface, however, all was not well in her parents' marriage. Children often intuitively sense such things without understanding them, or see evidence which, through their innocent and unknowing eyes, they misinterpret or find mysterious and frightening. This certainly happened to the young Gerda and left her with a legacy whose resolution in adulthood was one of the defining signposts of her life. With the hindsight of her own long life, she put it together thus:

"So she married into the generation before her, really, and it did cause problems…There was an sixteen year age difference between my parents. That was a mistake in a way. I don't think they ever really got together. They never, ever shared a bedroom in my life, and those were the days when wives would lock their doors against the intruding husband, like an Ibsen drama. The thing was, my father was a very prominent man in Norway for the better part of his life, but he wasn't intellectual, he was much more practical about things. And my mother was an uneducated intellectual. So they had different interests altogether, and that was quite difficult for them.

She was only five years older than my half-brother. And her group of friends were really his group of friends and my father was the wise old statesman. He had all the money and everything else. I couldn't understand it. She could never explain the relationship very well, and a child doesn't know what goes on in their parents' marriage when they are very young.

I've always tried to visualise if they could ever have been young and happy and gay together but I can't. It must have been a miserable marriage. And I can remember the many, many times I asked my mother, 'Why on earth did you get married? What is it all about?' "[8]

No doubt, in those more formal times, appearances were kept up as Gerdt and Lydia performed their social round, maintained their important extended family contacts, made their marks as businessman and minister of state and his attractive young wife, and generally played their parts in the culture to which they belonged. But underneath there was a disharmony, a turbulence through which Gerda swam towards her adolescence and her own emerging independence.

We had to make decisions about two names The first was relatively straightforward: from the several options available we settled on the spelling t'ai-chi to maintain consistency between the body of the book and the quotes from Gerda's *Looking for the Golden Needle*.

The second was more complicated. Most people called Gerda 'Pytt'. She told me as much the first time I visited her but throughout the seven years of our friendship she never encouraged me to use anything other than Gerda.

I puzzle about it now that she's gone. My theory is that she liked the way my Scottish accent dealt with the 'r'. I can remember many times picking up the phone, hearing "Hello Frank, it's Gerda" and noticing how the underlying Norwegian accent gave a good burr to the r's in both of our names. So it's comforting to speculate that maybe something in the way I said it reminded her of her roots. I wish I'd asked her.

We discussed what she wanted to be called in this book. She thought through the options and the consequences for a bit. I knew how much she had valued her husband's judgement and I tried to be helpful.

"What did David call you?" I asked.

"Puss," she said. Then twinkled, then chuckled.

She finally decided on Gerda "because that is my real name". So Gerda it is, except for some instances in the later chapters where people who knew her as Pytt use that name in a direct quote.

WING SPREADING

Then we have Crane or Stork Spreads Out Its Wings. The crane and the stork represent longevity and communication with the divine. The figure of the crane with outspread wings and uplifted foot is placed on a coffin to convey the soul, riding on the bird's back, to the Western Heaven. In the T'ai-chi Ch'uan, 'spreading the wings' prepares one for a new clarity of thought.

Gerda Geddes   LOOKING FOR THE GOLDEN NEEDLE, p56

The growing Gerda was a sensitive girl, easily affected by life's twists and turns.

"One of my weaknesses in childhood was my inclination to burst into tears. If something moved me, I just could not help myself, and burst out crying. There was a poem about a little goat which was eaten by a bear, and the mother goat looked for it in vain. Every time my Mother read me this poem, I burst into tears. Similarly, the first time I went to a concert, I was so moved by the music, that I cried the whole way home. When my dog, Per, was shot by a neighbouring farmer for chasing his sheep, I cried for weeks whenever I thought of him. I would suddenly start crying in class, and I had to force myself to think of something else in order to stop."[1]

The timing of Gerda's birthday meant she was almost a year younger than many of her classmates; perhaps some of her sensitivity in the classroom stemmed from her relatively young age. Nonetheless, she was a happy, if not entirely industrious, pupil.

"On the whole, I loved my school days. For the first three years I was top of the class, but after that my genius subsided and I slid down to be a comfortable middle of the road scholar. I was very often the teacher's pet, because I was very attentive and always eager to impart invaluable information to others! That tendency, I think, was handed down to both my children, and David seems to have suffered from the same character trait."[2]

When Gerda had finished her compulsory primary education - six years at the folkeskole, or people's school, followed by three years at middle school - she was still just fifteen and was considered too young to begin her abitur studies at the gymnasium, as the final school was called in Norway. When her headmaster suggested that she go somewhere for a year to learn a language, it was a perfect opportunity for Gerdt to indulge his enthusiasm for the English way of doing things: in 1933 his daughter was shipped off to board for a year at Mrs Fleetwood Varley's Academy for Young Ladies in London. Gerda did not immediately share her father's passion for the culture on the other side of the North Sea.

Gerda in 1931 aged fourteen

"I was a full boarder at that school. It was very beneficial although I hated it to begin with. I really hated it. But once I managed to say a few words it got better. I had been learning beginner school English at home but it hadn't enabled me to speak. I was completely dumb. I pointed. It was my first time away from home and I was very homesick. It was terrible. But it was just a phase, and once I learned to speak the language I fitted in. I learned to speak English quite quickly."[3]

And, by the spring of 1934, her performance drew plaudits in a letter to her mother from the headmistress who describes Gerda as '...a splendid girl and I am very pleased indeed with her. She tackles her work in a most business-like way and is very happy and contented. I am pleased to say that she is making great progress in English. She goes to many classes with the English pupils and that is the way to learn... (She) is very popular with all the students and has made many friends in this short time.'[4] Spring and summer term reports from the school detail a hardworking, responsive pupil who is making excellent progress and has special interests in history, needlework and dressmaking, and French.[5]

Later in 1934 Gerda, now a fluent English speaker and a wiser and more confident youngster, enrolled in the local gymnasium in Bergen. But her educational ups and downs were not yet at an end. When preparation for sitting the abitur, the final year examinations and the key to university entrance, was at its peak, ill health struck.

"Unfortunately, I never passed my final exams, the equivalent to the present day 'A' levels, because in the last year I became very ill. I had to have my appendix removed and I caught measles at the same time, and very nearly died. After that, the doctor said he did not think I would be strong enough to stand up to the pressure of the last few months' preparation for the exams, so I was sent to a Domestic Science school instead. Although I was very disappointed, I did in fact learn a great many practical things at that school which have stood me in good stead all through my life. My Father was not at all keen on a classical education for girls. I thought him dreadfully old fashioned and resented him at that time. He said; 'A girl must know about housekeeping, about how to manage servants, she must know about babies, and about how to manage money. When she has acquired these skills, she can do what she likes'."[6]

There is an evident tension here. Disappointed by the consequences of unforeseen illness, Gerda was prepared to find the positives in a tertiary education which met neither her own aspirations nor reached the levels which her mother had attained. But there is also growing indignation at her father's attempts to shape his cherished daughter in a mould not of her choosing. The domestic science school she attended was a superior establishment aimed at young women who would marry into big farms and know how to run the household. Interesting though Gerda found it to learn to prepare menus, to cook, to slaughter animals, to sew and to weave, she had other ambitions and plans for her life. And they did not match those of the father she had grown up adoring.

"I worshipped my father until I came up into the age of protest. Then, in my early twenties, I rather rejected him: 'You're no good, you're too old fashioned, I don't want to be like my mother, I want to go and study.' And he said, 'Well you can't do that until you learn how to be a proper housewife, and a proper mother and a proper manager of a household.' So he forced me to go through all these courses. Once I had completed them I said, 'My time has come, now I am a proper lady but I'm not going to marry the chap you want me to marry.' That was the way it was supposed to be in those days, but I became independent."[7]

Two unforeseen events, both originating in the U.S.A., contributed to that route towards independence.

The first was financial. The Wall Street Crash of 1929 rocked American capitalism to its core and by the early 1930s the waves it had created were beating on the economic shores of Europe. Although the depression of the 1930s was milder and shorter in Norway than in most western countries[8] there was, inevitably, financial impact on individual businesses and their owners. In Gerda's school alone, three of her friends lost their fathers to suicide. As far as her father's business, Gerdt Meyer Bruun A.S., was concerned, other factors were also at work. The end of the sailing ship era reduced the demand for rope and, in addition, traditional hemp fibre was being replaced by nylon thread. Gerdt responded to the challenge with acumen and business vision.

"He took the initiative to relocate the rope works, which was down by the harbour so as to be close to the sailing ships that came in and it had been there for over a hundred years. He moved the whole thing lock stock and barrel up into the countryside. And that was the beginning in Bergen of the factories moving away from the harbour.

And once my father had moved his factory up there, other people started doing the same, so eventually the first big industrial district in Bergen developed.

He also diversified and began to produce hemp fabric and carpeting."[9]

But as well as having a forward-looking vision, he was a benign nineteenth century gentleman and a generous, paternalistic employer.

"My father was loved by his workers. When the labour unions were established in Norway, everybody was saying, 'Join the labour union; the workers are going to take over the country'. But all my father's workers refused to join. They said: 'Our life is so comfortable and we love our master so much that we don't want to go against him.' And they never wanted to retire, that was one thing. So in the end his whole factory was full of octogenarians!"[10]

It is likely, therefore, that a combination of factors: the Great Depression, the decline in sailing and the shift away from hemp rope, and Gerdt's gentlemanly style of ownership, all contributed to the financial predicament which was beginning to intrude upon the comfortable elegance of family life at Storhaugen.

"So slowly, slowly the great money supply dwindled. And I can remember very clearly one morning when my father came down for breakfast. He said: 'You know the situation is very, very severe and we now have to start having less staff.' And he said to me: 'Your mother will have to look after the upstairs.' And I thought: 'Gosh, how can she do that? She'll have to make the beds!' 'And also, we can't have so many newspapers anymore. We must stop having that newspaper and that newspaper so we can make savings.' And this was what I always remembered; the main saving was two less newspapers a day. (Laughs). And it was very difficult for my father who was born with a silver spoon in his mouth and had really been a very successful man from the start."[11]

However amusing the young Gerda, rapidly emerging into womanhood, might have found her father's fussing over the daily newspaper delivery, the crisis was a real one. In 1937 Storhaugen was sold. The family moved to Aastvedt, north of Bergen and to the farm complex, Aastvedt Gaard, where Gerda's mother Lydia had grown up and where her mother, Gerda's grandmother, still lived. It was a typical 18th century Norwegian farmstead with several buildings surrounding a courtyard. The large main building was flanked by a visitors' house. There was also servant accommodation and a range of storage outhouses. For Gerda, it was a place packed full of the happiest of childhood memories.

"I loved visits to my Grandparents at Aastvedt. In their eyes I could do nothing wrong and I was always welcome. A new bus service had just started to Aasane County, and the bus terminus was just below Krybbebakken, so my Mother used to take me there and hand me over to the driver with strict instructions for the bus to wait at the Aastvedt stop until my Grandmother arrived to pick me up. I was very small, only three-and-a-half to begin with, so it was a great adventure. The bus in those days went over the mountain, and if we got stuck behind a horse and cart it would take ages and the motor regularly boiled, so the driver always carried a large bucket of water to replenish the radiator.

At Aastvedt I had my own room. The furniture was painted white with blue decorations and a pale blue hand-woven bedspread. There was also a wood-burning stove which was lit every morning by the maid. The washing water was heated on the stove. The linen sheets on the bed smelt of lavender, just like my Grandmother. She smelt of lavender too. I felt very safe and cosy in that room, and I often go back to it in my dreams.

Aastvedt was the perfect place for a child. In Krybbebakken we had no animals, but my Grandfather kept dogs, pointers and retrievers, and they often had puppies. There were geese and hens, ducks and cats. The farm animals, horses, cows and pigs were kept further from the house in big farm buildings, torn down before the war. There was also a perfect Wendy house at the bottom of the garden by a stream. My Grandparents had had four daughters, so the Wendy house was well equipped, and I played there for hours and hours with Martha, a neighbouring tenant's daughter. There was a deadly dangerous old Primus stove on which we made blueberry jam, and we had tea parties for the grown ups, serving home brewed dandelion tea.

Aastvedt had no bathroom, just a cold tap in the kitchen, and there was a privy across the courtyard where my Grandfather used to retire to read the newspapers. He would always sit there with the door open. One day, Martha and I wanted to play ball against the door, so we locked it from the outside, and after a while went off to play somewhere else. My Grandfather was locked in, and it took a long time before anyone heard his cries for help. Eventually my Grandmother came to his rescue, and she had to bear the brunt of his fury."[12]

But now her childhood was behind her, her beloved grandfather was dead, the house she had considered her family home had been sold because of financial problems. Her aging father continued to nurture plans for her future and the gap between their disparate views was widening. For her part, Gerda claimed as her studio the Borgstue, a turf-roofed house no longer needed for servant accommodation, and she set about enjoying her new life.

"My parents thought the move to Aastvedt was going to be a big social drop. In a small community your social standing is very, very important. And the big question was whether moving so far out into the country would reduce my social standing and my possibilities of finding a suitable young man to marry. But little did they know that when we moved out to Aastvedt, I just blossomed. I though it was so lovely out there. And all this feeling for nature, which my grandfather had instilled in me when I was a small girl, flourished and came out. So I didn't care two hoots about social standing. It meant nothing to me and I just loved being in the country."[13]

The repercussions of the American financial crash had pushed the conflict over Gerda's future out into the Norwegian countryside. Now another arm stretched across the Atlantic, this time one which would separate father and daughter and take Gerda to the United States, following in the wake of her mother who had made the voyage twenty-six years earlier. In the autumn of 1937, the year that Storhaugen was sold, she sailed for America to take up a one-year scholarship at a college for women in Pittsburgh, Pennsylvania.

"It was a scholarship that was offered by an American woman who was married to a Norwegian called Mr Ruud. This scholarship was for a young woman to come over from Norway for one year.

At that time I had decided to go to France in order to learn French. You learnt German first and then you learnt English and then you had to learn French. I had been booked in with a family for a year in France, then the American scholarship came along. I went up a big mountain for a day and thought about it. I thought:'Well I can always go to France next year but I'll never have an offer like this to go to America.' And America in those days was far, far away. You couldn't fly there at that time. And I thought:'I'll never have a chance to go to America again. So I'll take up this scholarship.' And that was how I went to America."[14]

After the ship had set sail Gerda, with the farewells and good wishes of family and friends still echoing in her mind, unpacked her cabin trunk. She found between her clothes a small envelope, just eleven centimetres by five, containing a letter from her mother. Lydia had carefully attached a four-leafed clover to the top left hand corner. Beneath it she had written:

"My dear little darling, when you open this, it is just a little greeting from me. You know that my good thoughts and wishes will always be with you, over the sea and on the sea and wherever you find yourself. You know that I am proud of you and I believe in you, my little Pytt. I am so grateful for all the good times we two have had together. I only hope that things go well for you and that nothing bad will happen to you. Remember that everything comes from yourself. I have often told you that, it must come from yourself. I have told you so often.

"Throw this overboard when you have read it. Lift your head you lovely girl and understand that life is sometimes difficult and sometimes wonderful. Remember Ibsen, that a person's nature is his destiny. Your nature is good but you are a bit quick at giving up. I hope and believe that your destiny will be good. Remember now and again about your sister Emma and all the good times you had together. God preserve you from all danger. That will be my only prayer for you. Live and be happy. XXXX Your only mother." [15]

Gerda's psychology education began during the year she spent as a boarder at Pennsylvania College for Women. She took it as her main subject and also studied English, English Literature and French. And there was much more to catch the eye and the interest of a young, well-bred Norwegian woman.

"The other students were all American and to me they all looked like film stars: so pretty and well-dressed and well-everything. I was very very impressed." [16]

But in the meantime, Gerda was making her own mark. She was young, vivacious, and the only European student who, despite studying in a foreign language, was earning impressive grades. And her father's earlier insistence that she attend the domestic science college was bringing unexpected benefits.

"Before I went to America I had made an extremely smart skirt and coat. That tweed, a very beautiful tweed, I had woven myself then a tailor had made it up. It was beautifully made. Everybody came up and said:'Did you really make this? How did you make it?' That put me slightly apart from the others." [17]

PENNSYLVANIA COLLEGE FOR WOMEN, PITTSBURGH

The college that Gerda attended as a boarder in 1937-38 was chartered on December 11, 1869, under the name Pennsylvania Female College, and was founded to provide women with a college education comparable to the best which men could receive at the time.

The introductory tone of Gerda's copy of the 1938 yearbook emphasises what is, in American terms, the college's antiquity with references to buildings that are 'stately, impressive…as of old…with tapering, legend-filled tower…pointed gables…ivy-covered walls…and stone steps leading to Gothic-arched doorways….' And there are clues to the life-styles of the boarders who lived within the college's walls: 'Dormitory life…where college fun is centred and spirits are high in the spring…and on cold winter evenings when the snow is deep on the hill…"tray-riding"…surprise packages at the Christmas dinner…corsages arriving…afternoon teas and midnight spreads…signing out to leave the campus…' There are also hints here and there of more worldly and sophisticated pursuits: '…equestrian-minded students ride in a tan roadster to the north Park riding stables during favorable (sic) weather in the fall and spring. (Note Winnie Bliss and Gay Hays in boots and breeches) The students on horseback are Kay Rockefeller…and Ada Lee Mangum.'

Gerda, the Pennsylvania College student, in 1938

The book contains pages and pages of society-style portraits including one of a relaxed and smiling Gerda. Several friends have annotated their pictures with a personal note such as 'It has been swell knowing you and we all hope you come back so we can see you again. Lou'

It is now known as Chatham College and is one of four original eastern colleges founded for women that still admits only women as undergraduates although its postgraduate programmes are co-educational.

Despite the economic depression from which the U.S.A. was recovering, there was still a lot of wealth in Pittsburgh, the City of Steel and of Carnegie. And if the wealthy sent their daughters to one of the oldest women's college in America, then it was certain to exert a magnetic pull on their sons. Amongst those who hung around the gates and the soda fountains was a Cadillac-driving young man called Red. Gerda fell in love for the first time.

"One of the boys had a wonderful motorcar. I fell flat on my face for him. He was number one, I thought. Then after a year I came back to Norway with good exam results and I said: 'I'm going to get married now. I'm going to get a ring sent to me and I'll go back to America and live with this American man.' And my father stood there and said: 'Well ok but who is he?' And I said: 'His name is Red and he owns a wonderful motorcar.' Then my father said: 'Do you know what family he comes from? Have you met his parents?' And I said: 'No, he never took me to meet his parents.' My father said: 'You cannot marry somebody if you haven't met his family because you marry into a family and you don't know them. I won't let you do that.' My father made all kinds of investigations behind my back. Then he came to me and said: 'You know I don't think he is suitable. But if you really want to know, you must go back and see him again and make up your own mind.'"[18]

In the summer of 1939, Gerda made a return journey across the Atlantic.

"I went back to Pittsburgh and spent my inheritance. I had some money and I spent it all. I met Red's parents and I didn't like them one little bit. That influenced me quite a lot. And I broke it off. It was a very painful business. My father sent me a telegram every other hour saying: 'Come home, come home, there's going to be a war in Europe and we're not going to be able to send any money to you. So come home'. And Red stood on the other side saying: 'Stay here, stay here. I will look after you. You'll be perfectly all right in America'. Oh dear! But eventually my father won, why I don't know but he did. I got the last ticket on the last boat going back to Norway. While I was on that boat, Germany walked into Poland and so I went home. My father said:'Thank goodness! Now you're safely home' and I said: 'Oh but I don't really want to be here! I want to be in America!'

I spent a very, very unhappy six months being torn in twain, not knowing what to do with myself and then eventually my father got me a job in the Corn Monopoly where he was a director. I was miserable, absolutely miserable."[19]

One of Gerda's photograph albums has detailed and annotated coverage of this period. She was in the U.S.A. from 20th September 1937 until she arrived back in Norway on 2nd July 1938. She returned to Pittsburgh in June 1939. One of the final photographs shows a serious-looking, darkly handsome man in highly polished riding boots and breeches. Beside it Gerda has written "C'est fini!"

The primary source for this book was Gerda herself. Between October 2005 and her death on 4th March 2006 I interviewed her at length on twelve occasions. The tapes run to around twenty hours and transcribed out to over seventy thousand words. Sessions were planned in advance and she was always thoroughly prepared for the focus of the day's interview. This no doubt in part accounts for the clarity of what she had to say. On the tapes she speaks with a crispness and an immediacy all the more remarkable considering she was in her 89th year when they were recorded. Such is their quality that I have usually chosen to quote them directly, with a minimum of editing, rather than convert them into a third person account. I hope this gives the reader a sense of also being a listener as Gerda unfolds her life's tale.

She was the author of two written sources: her t'ai-chi book *Looking for the Golden Needle* and *A Norwegian Childhood,* an unpublished fifteen thousand word memoir which she prepared as a Christmas gift for her five grandsons in 2003. I have drawn heavily on both of these.

As expected in writing the biography of an octogenarian, I was unable to interview any direct participants in her early life. Many people were generous with their time and their recollections of the later stages, especially following her return to the UK from Hong Kong in 1958. A list and an acknowledgement of my sincerest thanks appear at the end of this book. In particular I have valued the input of her two daughters, Jane and Harriet. After Gerda died, they became the prime witnesses to the realities of life within the Geddes family and to the details of Gerda's own journey as understood through their childhood experiences and recollections and in the close adult relationships they both had with their mother. When relevant and possible, I sought corroboration or further background detail from external written and Internet sources.

But ultimately a biography is not an academic treatise. It's a story, the story of a real life with all its joys, woes, uncertainties, loves, aspirations and disappointments. From the perspective of the person living it, a life isn't always clear, or consistent, or understandable. But he or she always knows more, has a better grasp, than someone looking on. Third party views, important and enriching as they are, do not carry the authority of the first person account: the details of a life are best known to the person who has lived it. So I have always let Gerda's voice carry more weight than any other. She was, and remains, the greatest expert on Gerda Geddes.

That said, discrepancies were few and far between, usually relatively inconsequential, but always an interesting opportunity to theorise about their cause. Take the origins of Gerda's pseudonym Pytt.

Gerda said: "My father wasn't very good with small children. But when I was a baby, he discovered I would smile at him if he poked me in the chest and made a noise 'pittie-pittie-pittie-pittie' so the name stuck."

Daughter Jane said: "There was another version too. That her half brother wasn't exactly delighted at the appearance of this noisy little baby and called her Pytt, which in Norwegian is a sloppy puddle."

In Gerda's shoes, which story would you tell?

And couldn't both be true?

WAR AND RESISTANCE

The first part ends with Carry the Tiger in Your Arms and Return to the Mountain. The tiger, in China, is an ambivalent animal; it can be either Yin or Yang. When it is Yang the tiger depicts authority, courage, bodily strength and military prowess. It is often painted on warrior's shields to frighten away the enemy. It terrifies demons and spirits.

Gerda Geddes   LOOKING FOR THE GOLDEN NEEDLE, p57

The Corn Monopoly job took Gerda to the Norwegian capital, Oslo, where she seems to have thrown off her lovelorn feelings with customary energy. Within a short time she was attending classes at Oslo University and had embarked on a two-year dance course. Then, an hour before midnight on April 8th 1940, a Norwegian security vessel Pol III, on patrol in the Oslo fjord, discovered unidentified ships on the horizon. A few minutes later it was shot at by a German torpedo boat. The German invasion of Norway had begun.

OPERATION WESERÜBUNG APRIL 1940

Operation Weserübung was the first major operation where an army, navy and airforce operated as a combined and co-ordinated force. It was the brainchild of General Nikolaus von Falkenhorst who, in February 1940, was given the task of preparing a plan for the swift invasion of Norway and Denmark. In five hours he had made a rough sketch of the invasion, presented it to Hitler, and was given the order to develop his plans. By March preparations were complete and on 8th April the invasion began with co-ordinated attacks by the Navy on six Norwegian cities including Oslo. By 9th April there were about 16,000 German troops on Norwegian soil and by the end of the invasion the air force had participated with 1,082 aircraft.

The German aim of surprise and quick surrender went largely to plan. After some initial confusion, the Norwegian Army was thrown into the fighting but the superior training and equipment of the Germans made them unstoppable. Allied forces attempted several counterattacks. There were significant engagements between the Royal Navy and the Kreigsmarine with losses on both sides. By mid-April allied troops had landed at several locations and joined up with Norwegian forces. But the speed and efficiency of the German advance was overwhelming, the role of the RAF was limited because of the long ranges involved, and there was an increasing risk of British troops being cut off in Norway, a loss which would have had serious miltary and psychological consequences so early in the war. The campaign in Western Europe was also unfolding and, at the end of May, the British Cabinet decided on a withdrawal from the whole of Norway. Although armed resistance had been militarily unsuccessful, it had won time to allow the Norwegian government, including the Royal family, to escape to Britain and form a government-in-exile.

On June 7th 1940 King Haakon, to whom the muddy-kneed Gerda had once handed a bunch of wilting wild flowers at a train station, and Queen Maud, who had once sung her lullabies, climbed the gangplank of the cruiser Devonshire at Tromsø and sailed for London. Norway was under the heel of the Third Reich.

"The whole of the population of Norway was seething with anger about the Germans, saying 'Who are these bastards who come to my country and pretend that they own it? Why should we accept their regime?'"[1]

The immediate impact on Gerda's family was the requisitioning, by German officers, of their home at Aastvedt. And it was events here, rather than in Oslo, that led her to join the Resistance movement. "… the reason why I got so angry or so irritated by the Germans was several personal experiences. At Aastvedt the houses were all around a big courtyard. The Germans came and said: 'Get out of here in twenty-four hours. Get out of here. We want to put some officers in your house. Get away from here altogether.' My mother put her foot down and said: 'I'm staying here.' My father was already slightly senile by that time, so it was my mother who was in charge. In the circle of buildings there were different houses with different purposes. The Germans installed themselves in the main house and my parents moved into what was called the guesthouse. They moved in there within twenty-four hours and buried all their silver in the ground. When the war was over we had a hunt. We found it."[2]

Occupied Oslo 1941. She joined the Resistance the following year.

In the winter of 1941 Gerda arrived to spend the university Christmas break with her parents and found Aastvedt swarming with German officers who were living in what had been her family home and were lounging around the courtyard. As far as her father was concerned, the realities of the situation were lost to his encroaching senility and he happily practised his German on the interlopers. They, in their turn, expected his attractive young daughter to follow suit.

"My father didn't quite understand what the war was all about by that time and he enjoyed talking to these rather cultured officers. My mother and I and the rest of the Norwegian population just wanted to spit on them. They walked around in the courtyard and tried to talk to me. I was in their eyes probably quite an attractive young girl. I didn't respond to their approaches at all. I turned my face the other way around and avoided them in every possible way. Then some of these officers came up to my father and said: 'Why is your daughter so unfriendly? Please tell her to be friendlier towards us. We know she speaks German so why does she avoid us?' So my father came and told me what they had said. I said to my father: 'They are now our enemies. And why should I associate with the enemy? I don't want to.' Then the officers again went back to my father and said: 'Now you tell your daughter to behave herself or you can't rely on what we will do with your family.' And they threatened me, saying: 'Unless you are friendly towards us we might put you in prison.' So I totally refused any kind of communication with them because that was what one did. But I felt threatened so I talked to my parents and we decided it was probably better if I went away."[3]

Gerda did not immediately implement this plan. She hadn't just come home to see her parents. This was where she had grown up and nearby Bergen had attractions which she wanted to share with her old friends. However a night out led to an encounter with a German soldier that could have ended very badly.

"One evening I had been to the theatre with a friend. To get home to Aastvedt I had to go over the high mountains, across the plateau and down the other side, north of Bergen. It was late after the theatre when I caught the bus. I sat down by a window, and a German soldier came and sat next to me. I stared out of the window. It was pitch dark. When the bus started moving, he began to press himself closer and closer towards me, trying to squeeze me. And he got a hold of my thigh and I turned myself completely away from him. When we came up to the top of the mountain, he suddenly stood up, ordered the driver to stop and told him 'Throw this woman out of the bus'. The other Norwegian passengers were seething with anger but they were also very frightened. So I was thrown out of the bus on the top of this mountain, in the middle of the night and in the middle of the winter with snow and everything else. I had to walk home. It was a long way, down the mountain and along the valley. I also had to go through a German camp which was very frightening. I was really, really scared, wondering what all those soldiers would do. But anyway I managed to get myself through the camp and down the valley. Nothing did happen to me, nobody touched me. But of course I went through the nightmare of thinking that they might.

When I arrived home in the small hours of the morning I said to my mother: 'I'm leaving tomorrow. I can't stay here.' I went back to Oslo. Those two incidents made me feel that I had to do something, and that was why I joined the Underground. I was then put into a unit of six people, four boys and two girls. We were all part of a university clique in Oslo and were very, very intimate friends."[4]

Gerda had no difficulty making contact with the Resistance movement although to the end of her life, as a matter of principle, she remained reticent about giving details of the process. Opposition to the German invaders was well established within the universities and, for that matter, within the wider Norwegian education system. German plans to use the education system to bring about the Nazification of Norway foundered on the principled opposition by the country's teachers, 1,100 of whom were sent to concentration camps in spring 1942 where they were subjected to several months of very harsh treatment. Later, in the autumn and winter of 1943, hundreds of students at Oslo University were rounded up and sent to a special camp in Germany for 'indoctrination'. Gerda was not amongst them, because by that time the dangerous work she was doing for the underground press had led her to flee her beloved Norway.

RESISTANCE AND THE UNDERGROUND NEWSPAPERS

Two notable examples of Norwegian unwillingness to do the bidding of their German occupiers were teachers' solidarity in the face of pressure to involve them in a programme of indoctrination, and the independent actions of trade unions and professional associations. In September 1941, the Germans responded to an unofficial strike which was disrupting milk deliveries in Oslo by declaring a state of emergency, rounding up trade unionists and executing two young trade union leaders. All radios were requisitioned and possession thereafter carried the death sentence. "The most interesting result of the decision to requisition the radios was the flourishing growth of an underground press. From its modest beginnings a year earlier, this activity now grew into a veritable industry, which in its heyday was to count over three hundred different newspapers and kept thousands of people busy. Some papers appeared regularly, others irregularly, and many died an abrupt death, as the highly dangerous work of distributing the products as widely as possible took its toll. But the value of these 'illegal' newspapers, with titles such as 'Whispering Times' or 'London Radio', their contents sometimes concealed inside such innocent wrappers as 'Potato Growing in Your Garden', can hardly be over-estimated. Besides offering a welcome antidote to the heavy-handed Nazi propaganda, they provided links in the growing barrier of patriotic solidarity…with the courage and leadership of the few, and the means by which they could reach the many, a unity was created whose strength withstood the test."[5]

In 2003, Gerda wrote a detailed account of her wartime experiences for her grandchildren.

"Of course the German occupation of Norway in April 1940 changed the lives of everyone. It was almost impossible for a young person not to become involved. Various incidents built up my aggression against the Germans and made me decide that I had to do my bit for my country. So I joined the Resistance movement.

There was a death penalty in Norway for possessing a radio. No one was allowed to listen to news bulletins from abroad. We were only allowed to read German propaganda newspapers. The Norwegian Government had escaped to London and every night at midnight the BBC would send a news bulletin in Norwegian, telling what was happening on the various battle fronts. I joined a group of four boys and another girl. We had a radio and a small printing press, and every night the boys would print out the news on sheets of paper, and the girl and I would distribute these papers to 'safe' houses.[6]

It worked well for several months and we really felt that we were doing a good job, but one day in January 1943, when the temperature was −28C with lots of snow, I went, in the evening, into a little dairy shop opposite the building where I had my digs, hoping to obtain a bottle of milk from the lady. Only old people and babies were allowed milk, but sometimes there would be a bottle left over at the end of the day, and the lady would give it to me. On this particular evening, as I entered the shop, she pointed out to me a Gestapo car parked outside my house, and she said: 'I think you should wait here until the Gestapo come out.' So I stood at the back of her shop and saw four officers get into their car and drive away. I then ran up to my flat and discovered that that was where they had been. Everything was turned upside down, all the papers from my desk scattered on the floor, but I knew they had found nothing incriminating. We had been told what to do if such a situation should arise. We all kept a packed rucksack with warm clothes and food, dried biscuits and tins of corned beef. We were all given secret addresses which we had to memorise. We had to go straight to the address without trying to contact anyone. So I went to an unknown part of Oslo and found some big apartment buildings and a flat where I rang the bell. A nice lady opened the door and when I told her my name, she said she was expecting me, and she would give me a bed until I would be collected by someone from the secret Norwegian army which operated inside the country. I stayed there for three days, feeling very isolated and lost, but I knew that I must on no account try to contact my friends. On the third evening an unknown man appeared. He told me to go to a special road on the outskirts of Oslo late that evening, and at midnight a car would come and the driver would say a pass word, and he gave me a pass word with which to reply. In fear and trembling I found my way to this road. It was long and straight and had pine forests on both sides. It was very cold and there were mountains of snow on both sides of the road. At midnight a car came driving very fast, and the driver shouted out of the window: 'Run for your life, the Germans are after us'. So I ran into the forest and just managed to hide behind a tree when I heard the German car racing along. As there was a curfew in Oslo, no one was allowed out until seven in the morning and all buildings were locked, so for the rest of that night I just wandered around in that wood, feeling frozen, terrified and utterly alone.

When I returned to my hiding place the lady was not at all pleased to see me and she said: 'It is too dangerous for me to have you here, but we have a little trunk room in the cellar.' So she put a camp bed down in the cellar among all her boxes and junk, and there I stayed for three weeks.

Those weeks must have been the longest in my life. I had very little to eat and I thought I had been forgotten by everyone. At last another strange man came along and told me that he was going to try and get me across to Sweden that night. He also explained the delay. The party I should have joined had been overtaken by the Germans and imprisoned. Their leader, under stress, had revealed their escape route and it had taken three weeks to work out another safe place from which it would be possible to cross the border to Sweden.

This second time I was also instructed to present myself at midnight in a factory yard on the outskirts of Oslo, there I would see a truck loaded with timber and I would meet with a party of people. Amongst the people, as it turned out, was the most wanted man in Norway, the head of the Resistance. He was a judge and with him was his wife, his three small children aged four, three and six months and also his wife's sister. Then there was a lady who had been smuggled out of a hospital still with stitches in her tummy from a hysterectomy! – and a journalist with his wife.

They were both partially blind so we made a fairly decrepit party.

The truck was loaded with timber, but a space had cleverly been made at the bottom where we had to creep in. The three-year-old child was thrust into my arms, and I was told to keep it quiet at all costs, even if it meant smothering it. Fortunately all three children were heavily sedated, so they did not stir all through the night. After having driven for about two hours, the truck stopped and we heard German voices. A soldier said: 'Halt machen! Ihre Papieren bitte!' We all held our breath and hoped that no one would cough. After another hour or so, the truck stopped again and we were told to get out. We were in the middle of a thick forest. Meeting us was a wood cutter with a horse and sleigh and two armed soldiers who were going to be our escort. The lady with the stitches, the sleeping children and our rucksacks were put on the sleigh and we all started to walk. Only the soldiers had skis. We stumbled along in deep snow, sometimes crossing lakes, in complete darkness, for there was no moon.

At about 8.30 in the morning we suddenly saw lights in the distance. That was Sweden, and safety, at long last. As we stood at the border, we all turned our faces towards Norway and sang our National Anthem with tears streaming down our faces. We felt like rats leaving a sinking ship. Then we had to give ourselves up to the Swedish border patrol: two great burly Vikings who lived in a little warm hut. We all piled in and were told to divide up, women to one side of the room, men to the other. Then we were ordered to strip naked and stand with our feet wide apart and arms over our heads, and we were all sprayed with a very itchy delousing powder, and all our clothes were sprayed as well. It was a fairly humiliating procedure but also very funny. There was at that time an epidemic of typhus among the refugees, so it was a wise safety precaution.

After that we were interrogated by the police. They were especially keen to find out which route we had taken, but we had been told beforehand not to answer any questions until we were in the hands of the Norwegian authorities. Next we were taken to a Swedish farm where we were given real coffee and newly made white buns with jam. That was a treat I think none of us will ever forget. From there we travelled by train to a Norwegian refugee camp which was organised from London by the Norwegian authorities. At this camp we were instructed to tell our full stories. I was very lucky to be examined by a policeman from Bergen. He happened to know my Father so I was very well treated. At the camp we slept in dormitories with forty women to each room and four people to each bed unit. With the temperate outside below −29C, no windows were open and with all those unwashed bodies, it was not very comfortable! We all had to be examined by doctors and dentists and we were given every injection under the sun. In fact I got so ill from my smallpox vaccination that later on I had to have plastic surgery to remove the scar.

Those of us who were lucky enough to have friends in Sweden who were willing to vouch for us were then free to travel. The rest of the people spent their time in refugee camps until the end of the war.

I had my Mother's friends, the Cloumanns, who received me with open arms in Stockholm. Stockholm in 1943 was full of refugees, foreign agents, spies, couriers, traitors etc. It was quite a dangerous and exciting place. Many people lived as if each day was his last. One night I went to a party and I was dancing with a charming young man. He was a courier and was making constant trips back and forth to Norway. It was through this young man that I was able to send a letter to my poor parents who had not known my whereabouts for six months, so I was grateful to him. As we were dancing, he suddenly said to me: 'Put your hand in my pocket'. I touched something cold and clammy and discovered that it was a hand. I was just about to scream when he kicked me viciously on the shin and said: 'If you so much as utter a word about this to anyone, I will kill you'. It was clear to me that he had reached breaking point and that he needed treatment and a rest from his dangerous job, so the next day I reported him to the Norwegian medical centre and never saw him again. But I heard that he recovered, returned to Norway after the war and led a normal life. He and his gang had killed a Norwegian collaborator, and hacked him to pieces, and taken parts of his body as souvenirs!

Only when I arrived in Stockholm did I find out what had happened to my Resistance worker friends. Our little group had all been captured by the Gestapo who surprised them in the cellar where we kept our radio and printing press. They were all there on that evening when I stood in the dairy shop. The other information I got was that the wood cutter who had been our guide to the frontier had been shot two days later when he was taking another party through the woods. The woodcutter left behind a widow and eleven children. All the members of his party were imprisoned."[7]

NORWEGIAN RESISTANCE CASUALTIES

"According to official sources, the Resistance lost 2,091 men and women during the five years of occupation: 366 were executed; 162 were killed in open fight (sic) with the Germans; 130 died in prison in Norway, many of them either as a result of torture or because they committed suicide. In the concentration camps in Germany 1,340 Norwegian political prisoners lost their lives, among them 610 Jews, and the escape route across the North Sea took 93 lives. In addition comes an unknown number whose health had been ruined for life because of torture or maltreatment in prison."[8]

Gerda knew the following about the fate of her comrades. The other woman was broken by imprisonment and died soon after her release at the end of the war. One of the men drowned when the ship taking him to Ravensbruck concentration camp in northern Germany was torpedoed. Another was tortured and died in prison. One of them survived relatively unscathed: Gerda had indirect contact with him in 2004 when he was 95. She was unsure what had happened to the fourth man.

Such experiences inevitably leave their marks; the indelible finger-prints in the moulds which shape us. In Gerda's case the enduring lega-cy had less to do with the bravery of her actions than with what she saw as the near miracle of her escape.

"It was a remarkable time. What I did wasn't remarkable at all. Lots of other people did similar things and risked their lives in the same way. The remarkable thing about my story is the way that I wasn't caught - three times. In that dairy shop, if I hadn't gone in to look for my milk I would have gone into the arms of the Gestapo. I actually saw them leave the building; it was that close (gestures across the width of her sitting room). And the second time was when the Gestapo came driving along that road out in the countryside. I just managed to get myself into the woods and heard the car coming. That was also a matter of minutes and if I hadn't had my wits about me I would have been caught then. And the third, and maybe the worst was the woodcutter who guid-ed us through the woods and got us safely over to Sweden: the next lot of people he took over were caught and he was shot.[9]

It was an experience which made a deep impression on me. Three times I had escaped imprisonment and possible death by a hair's breadth. I kept on asking myself: 'Why me? Why should I be the lucky one? Is there a meaning behind it?' I felt as if I had an obligation, as if I had to repay a debt. But how?

For quite some months after I came over to Stockholm I walked on the street and looked behind me, seeing if I was fol-lowed. I felt very frightened then. Maybe that wasn't necessary but it was written into the situation. Eventually that fear went away. I was there for two years until the war was over."[10]

And it was during her time as a refugee in Sweden that two of the streams running through her life, psychology and dance, merged into an important river.

Part Two
INNER AND OUTER JOURNEYS

Joy alone is true. Because the one real thing in us is the 'I' which embraces all existences and all possible contraries of existence. We suffer because we put things outside us. When all is within, all is joy, because there is no hole anymore, anywhere.

Satprem: Sri Aurobindo or The Adventure of Consciousness n 1939, Gerda began a psychoanalysis that continued for several years. She cherished this experience and readily acknowledged her debt to the therapists involved. Psychology was a major formative strand of her life and, along with dance and t'ai-chi, made a vital contribution to the creation of the person she became.

Psychoanalysis involves a confidential relationship. Before I became a full-time writer, I had a long career as a practising psychologist so the boundaries and responsibilities of this relationship are very familiar to me. Because of my background, I was hesitant about inquiring into the details of her analysis as I began to learn of the important part psychotherapy played in her young adult life. For her part, she did not invite me in.

Then, during our meeting on 12th January 2006, she asked if I felt I was making sense of the story of her life. Could I see the overall picture, could I see the forest and then the trees? When I described the structure I was evolving, she was very approving, and she also seemed encouraged by my plans for exploring the multifaceted and many-themed path she had followed. She resumed our discussion that day with a new vigour and wanted to revisit certain aspects, to clarify the details of some events, and to talk about particular features of her childhood and early experiences until we ran out of time.

A few days later, after I had transcribed the tape, I wrote a note with suggestions for our next meeting. I mainly listed the topics which we had been unable to explore fully the previous week, added one or two more, and put at the end of the list: "And could you talk about the details of what actually went on during your analysis?" Then I deleted it. It seemed an unacceptable intrusion.

We next met on 24th January. I took along a draft structure for the book. And I explained to Gerda that until she had told me everything she thought I should know, I couldn't make some final decisions about it. Within a short time she began to talk about her psychoanalysis in considerable detail. Here is how that part of the interview ends.

Gerda: Yeah. Well…(sighs, sounds tired)

Me: That's been great. That's exactly what I had been focussing on…

Gerda: Well, talking so straightforwardly about what goes on in an analysis is not what one does every day. But I think in order to understand it you have to know what happened.

Me: When I first drafted that letter to you, I put in a question asking you to go into the analysis but I took it out because I felt it wasn't a question to ask. But indeed that is what you chose to do. Thank you.

Gerda: If it comes into the book, you have to make it a little less personal.

And I have.

THE ROAD TO PSYCHOTHERAPY

The second part commences with a sequence called Step Back and Repulse the Monkey. The Monkey Fairy, in Chinese mythology, represents human nature and, although human nature is basically good, the monkey is very easily tempted into whatever distractions may come across its path. In China they talk about 'Monkey Thoughts' which go flashing through your brain. Whenever you want to concentrate or be still, these monkey thoughts come in to disturb you, so you have to push them away in order to become clear...When you have repulsed the monkey and emptied yourself of intruding thoughts, you repeat the movement of Holding the Circle in order to regenerate your energy...

Gerda Geddes   LOOKING FOR THE GOLDEN NEEDLE, pp57–58

Before the invasion of Norway, Gerda was already in the early stages of a psychoanalysis in Oslo with Dr Ola Raknes, a disciple and friend of the famous, and sometimes notorious, Wilhelm Reich.

WILHELM REICH 1897–1957

Reich was one of the psychoanalysts who emerged from under the wing of Sigmund Freud's groundbreaking work and went on to develop psychoanalytic ideas and personality theories of their own. Reich focussed on the human body and the links between physical and psychological development. His early work as a sexologist, combined with his Freudian experience, led him to the conviction that neuroses stemmed from a damming-up of sexual energy instead of it being released in sexual orgasm, ideas that he elucidated in one of his early books *The Function of the Orgasm* (1927). In Vienna and, later, in Berlin, he did not restrict himself to psychotherapeutic work: he also took an active part in the social and political education and organisation of young people and he organised clinics and advisory centres for mental hygiene and sex counselling. Another publication *The Mass Psychology of Fascism* (1933) seemed to offend, in equal measure, the Communists, who excluded him from their party, and the Nazis, who tried to imprison him shortly after coming to power. In 1933 he escaped to Denmark where his presence and ideas caused unease and a year later he moved to Norway where he had been invited to become Director of the Institute of Psychology at the University of Oslo. During his years in Oslo, Reich began a series of what he called biophysical experiments where he was trying to identify the sexual and orgasmic energy that he was convinced played a major role in his psychological theories and possibly also in the genesis of cancers.

On 19th August 1939, just two weeks before the Germans marched into Poland and triggered the Second World War, he sailed for New York where he had been offered a post teaching Medical Psychology. In *The Cancer Biopathy* (1948) he announced his discovery of a hitherto unknown energy form which he called Life Energy or Orgone for which he claimed many roles and functions including its release in the course of human orgasm. Applications of these ideas included the development of the orgone accumulator, a box-like device in which patients lay to increase their orgone level, and the cloudbuster, a gadget which he claimed could be aimed at the sky and used to bring rain by manipulating available orgone concentrations in the atmosphere.

By now his unorthodox theories and treatment methods had put him on a collision course with the US authorities who were also suspicious of his Communist past. In 1954, and following a complaint by the Food and Drug Administration, an American Federal Court declared, in a Decree of Injunction, that orgone energy was non-existent and therapeutic practices based on it should not be used. Reich refused to obey the injunction and in

May 1956 he was sentenced to two years imprisonment. He died of heart failure in jail on 3rd November 1957, one day before he was due to apply for parole.

Several factors in Gerda's life had encouraged her to seek psychoanalysis. On the surface, most obvious was her first physically passionate affair: at Oslo University she had met, and fallen madly in love with, a young psychology student.

"He introduced me to sex in the most wonderful way. Absolutely. And that is not all that common because girls can have a terrible time when they first become women. And I just jumped up and down for joy and thought gosh, what a wonderful life this is! (Laughs) And I was always grateful to him."[1]

Her new lover was himself undergoing a Reichian analysis to try and untangle a traumatic childhood, but that wasn't why he recommended the therapy.

"He thought that I was too shy; that I wasn't able to let myself go in our lovemaking; I was always holding something back. Even Ola Raknes said something similar to me. He said: 'You're too much of a lady, just let go of that ladylike exterior of yours and you'll be ok.' That was obviously from my background."[2]

Two major factors in her background contributed to her active interest in psychology, which she had already studied at college in America and which had led her to enrol in psychology classes at Oslo University: she had witnessed madness within her own family; and some of her childhood experiences had left psychological scars.

"A great tragedy that hit our family was when my half brother became a schizophrenic. It happened when I was twelve years old. My brother was only five years younger than my mother, and they had many friends in common. He was my father's pride and joy. He was going to carry on the business of rope making, just like my father had taken over from his father. In the nineteen-twenties rope making was still very lucrative and my brother had a good, secure future ahead of him. His troubles started when his engagement was broken off. He was engaged to a charming English girl and he had just finished building a house for them to live in when things began to go wrong. He started hearing voices and receiving messages from some unknown guru in India who told him what he should do. My brother was obviously very distressed. He could not sleep, and wandered restlessly about the house by night, drinking endless bottles of beer, leaving empty bottles all over the place. My brother was very fond of me and he would often come and talk to me. One night he woke me up. He leaned over my bed with a bewildered expression on his face and said: 'I am a hero. I have just saved the lives of all the people in this house. My guru told me that all the wine in the cellar was poisoned and I have broken all the bottles'.

I can remember being terrified, not so much by what he said, but by the way his face seemed contorted, and I ran to tell my mother.

The wine cellar had a special double lock, and only my father had the key, but somehow my brother must have got a hold of it. When we went down there, the whole cellar was flooded by the most expensive wines. We had a great deal of wine in those days because of my father's job as a Director of the Wine Monopoly. The next morning a famous psychiatrist arrived with two male nurses to take my brother away to a lunatic asylum. The nurses appeared with a straitjacket – there were no calming injections in those days – but my brother went quite willingly with no resistance. He said goodbye to me and told me to be a good girl and remember my English table manners. But what I shall never forget was the expression on my father's face. He almost became an old man in front of my eyes.

As it turned out, my brother spent only a few months in the asylum, but the doctor advised that he must lead a protected life and never be put under stress, so his future in the business was finished. A house was built for him in Hurdalen near Tante Anne, whom he loved very much, and he lived there for many years, most of them seemingly perfectly normal, but every now and again he would get attacks and go into great rages which he afterwards was unable to understand or explain. He spent a great deal of time reading, and he boasted that he was probably the only man who had read the Encyclopaedia Britannica from beginning to end.

My brother's illness profoundly influenced my life. My interest in what makes people tick developed out of that tragedy and put me on a path I have followed all my life."[3]

Another reference to family madness surfaced from Gerda's papers after her death. Two pages of typescript contain a warm and informative description of Rasmus Meyer, written by Gerda's mother and headed "Written by Rasmus's niece, Lydia, who knew him very well. Translated by Pytt." (ie Gerda). It contains the following addendum:

"Added by Pytt: In 1915 Rasmus was certified and in 1916 he committed suicide. As he could not be buried in consecrated ground, his ashes were kept in the larder in Krybbebakken for several years until finally permission was given for the urn to be placed in the wall of the old family cemetery at Aastvedt."[4]

As her psychoanalysis unfolded, Gerda began to make sense of troubling aspects of her own childhood experiences and to achieve valuable insights which lasted until the end of her life.

"It is quite easy when one looks backwards into the past to remember only the good things, and to look through rose coloured spectacles, trying to forget the hurt and the suffering, but it is quite often the painful happenings which make us grow and develop.

All children suffer from the inadequacies and insecurities of their parents. During the process of growing up and becoming independent one has to try to shake off most of the tensions and restrictions which have developed over the years. Eventually, one has to see one's parents objectively, and forgive what one sees as their mistakes and realise that they did their best at the time, and that they did not want to hurt us.

I was very fortunate to go through a most beneficial and successful psychoanalysis in my early twenties. It enabled me to come to terms with many problems at an early age. Most people have to wait much longer before they find a solution, and many carry their 'grief accumulators' through most of their lives. In this respect my mother was a great help. She had a guilty conscience about her behaviour towards me in early childhood, and wanted to make amends, which she certainly did.

When I was five years old my mother fell passionately in love with a very remarkable man. He was highly educated, very artistic, and he wrote the most beautiful poetry, much of it to my mother. He spoke fluent English, German, French and Italian. He was handsome and elegant, a man of the world. My mother was totally swept off her feet, to such an extent that she was prepared to throw everything overboard, to make a complete break, leaving her old life behind, abandoning my father and me. To avoid too much scandal they planned to leave Norway and settle in Sweden. My mother left us and went to Paris where they had agreed to meet. When she arrived at the hotel and went up to their room, she found him with a bullet through his head. As he was an internationally well-known figure, it was a catastrophic situation for her.

While all this was going on, my father and I stayed at home. I was extremely worried about my mother not being there. I had nightmares and could not sleep at night, and had difficulties in breathing. I had a feeling as if a great big bear with green eyes and big sharp teeth was sitting on my chest, just ready to bite my throat. My father sat patiently by my bed and held my hands, and sometimes when I pretended to be asleep, I heard him cry. A very strong bond was formed between us at that time. I felt that he was the only person in the world whom I could trust. He came down with a very severe attack of asthma, so there we were, both of us, struggling for breath. During this period, I became very insecure. I never dared to go and spend a night, even with my best friends because I was afraid there would be no one in the house when I returned. Of course, I never really understood what was going on at the time – only many years later did my mother explain.

One day, my father came and said that my mother was coming back. He said she had been very ill and now I had to be very kind to her to make her better. We drove to the station early one morning to pick her up from the night train from Oslo. When

she came off the train, I could hardly recognise her, her face seemed all blotchy and swollen. I sat in front with the chauffeur, and my mother cried most of the way home. We drove past a baker's shop and I asked if we could stop to buy some hot croissants for breakfast, thinking that this might cheer my mother up.

As I grew older, my admiration for my father grew. How could he take her back after what she had done to us? I tried to put myself in his place and realised what strength of character and what kindness he had displayed. As a human being, he grew from his misfortunes. In fact, towards the end of my father's life my parents became very good friends, and when he died in 1945 she was quite devastated. But she never apologised for her actions. She said that the experience which she had gained from the affair with her lover, although so tragic, had lifted her whole life up to a higher level and had given her an understanding of other people's suffering which she would not otherwise have known. And she was indeed very

Gerda's portrait, painted in 1923, a time of confusion

wise. Most of my friends came to her for advice, and when I left home, and she lived alone, her house was always open to young people."[5]

Gerda had clear, conscious memories of these dramatic and stressful events as seen through a child's eyes. Some of the other material that surfaced during her analysis was from earlier, pre-verbal times and emerged via the specific theoretical Reichian approach being used by her therapist.

INVOLVING THE BODY IN PSYCHOTHERAPY

Reich's move away from Freudian psychoanalysis was based on his conviction that the body and its sexual energy were fundamentally involved in human psychology and its problems. One of his first major books, *Character Analysis* (1933) argued that the cause of a person's neurosis lay in repression of their libido, and that the aim of therapy should be the restoration of a person's capacity for joy in their love life and in their work. The conflict between the two approaches can be summed up in their different interpretations of the defence mechanisms which patients brought to the therapy room. Just as Freud was moving away from the libido theory in favour of an interpretation that saw the person's resistance to therapy as part of their 'death wish' or thanatos, Reich was becoming more interested in psychosomatic factors, in the links between psychology and physiology. In his view, the route to overcoming patients' resistance was through the understanding of their 'muscular armouring', a correspondence in the body to their psychological defence mechanisms. As Ola Raknes put it:

"It soon became clear to Reich that the muscular armour,which consists of spasm, cramps and tensions, is nothing but the bodily expression of the repressed emotions and ideas, and the somatic anchoring of neurosis...This discovery led to another innovation in psychotherapeutic technique, namely attacking the neurosis from the bodily side, partly by calling the patient's attention to the chronic tensions, partly by making him (sic) feel them by direct manipulation...Not only repressed emotions and memories came to light, however, but also things that nobody had thought of before or paid any attention to, and that should prove to be of the utmost importance for therapy as well as for further discoveries. These new and unexpected experiences were feelings of streaming in the patient's body, streamings that to most of the patients were formerly unknown and which to most of those who knew them had been of little or no significance. Such streamings were pleasurable, usually soft and rather weak, but occasionally so strong that the person felt they overflowed him...These streamings seemed to stem from the vegetative or autonomous nervous system, and Reich therefore called them vegetative streamings."6

The resulting therapeutic approach was called Vegetotherapy which relies on the theory that emotions are stored in the structure of the body and build tensions that can be seen, for example, in posture or stiffness or facial expression. The therapist worked directly on this 'muscular armour' itself to release the pent-up feelings which were causing it. This was the approach Raknes used with Gerda.

"The therapeutic technique was a combination of verbal and physical but very much stress was put onto the breathing: you should feel your breathing, and it should give rise to the sensation of an energy flowing through you. If you felt the energy flowing, you would also have this sensation of something warm coming into your body: a lovely, wonderful, warm feeling. Lying there on the couch in a session, you started feeling that your breathing went down through your hip joints and down into your thighs, your thighs started slightly vibrating and it was wonderful. In one way it was a very strong sexual feeling but it was more than that. It wasn't just a desire to feel an orgasm. It wasn't like that because it came by itself. You didn't think about it, you just thought about your breathing.[7]

The analysis was very much a process of rediscovering events from my past which made sense in my present situation. I think that in one way the healing part of an analysis is the smoothing out of events that you've got stuck on because they've been too horrendous to take in rationally. You can get stuck on something special and your thoughts go back to that point all the time. In a Reichian analysis you work your way through these blocks and leave them behind. That is one of the things that gives you freedom, you don't have to keep going back to that bad incident all the time, harking back. And you have to work through it not only mentally, you also have to work through it physically. All the time in a Reichian analysis, the physical and the mental go hand in hand because you say to yourself: 'How do I feel in my body when I'm thinking about this?' You can say that an analysis has come to its fulfilment when you really go back as far as you can. And for many people you go back before you have any rational thinking. You go back to the physical memory.

You said you would like me to talk about my early happenings and for me, the conclusion of my analysis was when I came back to what I think was my first trauma that I had any feeling about. It was of being more or less force-fed by this nanny who had been engaged because my mother wanted to stop breast-feeding me. A stupid doctor said the only way that could be done was by my mother going away altogether. She told me later on that she had such a lot of milk that she could have fed an army of babies and that every time she came anywhere near me, the milk came gushing out. This stupid man, who was a fashionable doctor at the time, said six months is the maximum amount of time that it is good to breastfeed a baby: after six months the baby can start eating other food.

So she went away and left me with a nanny who was recommended by this wayward doctor. She turned out to be an alcoholic, and when my mother came back from her holiday with no milk she found me lying there dirty and smelly with sores on my bottom and not having been looked after at all well. And when she came to lift me up, I did like this, (mimes a pushing motion with both hands). I pushed her away. I pushed everyone away from me.

That came back to me in my analysis. It was very, very strong, and it had caused me to develop an attitude towards people: I wanted to push them away. The nanny had force-fed me with porridge: when she pushed the stuff into my mouth I spat it out, she put it back and we had this battle together. And because she only gave me horrible porridge, I put on a lot of weight. I became too fat. I have a picture of that. The doctor then said: 'Oh, she's had too much porridge, she has to have some vitamins. She must have carrots.' So, as a slimming cure at six months old I was given carrots in order to get some vitamins because I was developing signs of rickets. Lots of babies had rickets in those days.

That was as far back as I reached in my analysis. After that, because it was such an emotional upheaval for me when I was in my twenties, Raknes said: 'Well I think you and I should have a holiday now. You go away and see how you're getting on with your life.' And that was more or less the end of my analysis. Except in those days people who were in analysis, whenever life became difficult for them and whenever there were new problems coming up they would go back to their analyst. Endlessly they would go, for ten years to lie on the couch. But I got married at that stage and I went to Shanghai where there were no psycho-analysts so I didn't have an opportunity to go back when life was jolly difficult out there. And many times I wished that I had Raknes to go and cry on his shoulder. But he wasn't there so I had to cope, I just had to cope and that weaned me of my need for an analyst."[8]

Those last few sentences oversimplify the unfolding and the length of Gerda's analysis in two ways. Firstly, her treatment by Raknes was interrupted during the war by her 1943 flight to Sweden where she spent two years and where she found another Reichian therapist to continue the work. On her return to Norway she recommenced with Raknes and maintained occasional therapeutic contact with him until her marriage in 1948. Thereafter they remained friends and he had a great interest in her development into a t'ai-chi practitioner and teacher. Secondly, her analysis evolved into what is known as a training analysis, where, through the experience, the patient learns the skills to practise as a therapist herself. These were skills that Gerda was able to draw upon during her exile in Sweden, and for that matter, throughout her life. And they were skills that were based on a theoretical approach that made an intimate link between human psychology and human anatomy.

"It was a very strange sensation to go back to that state with no words. But it was all in the muscle. You see we do have a physical memory which maybe we are not enough aware of but it is there. And when you learn to read that, and Reichian analysis is very much a training in how to read a person, that knowledge is very very helpful when you want to judge people. It's a knowledge that you keep to yourself mainly. You don't go around saying: 'Look at him, he's got tension in his shoulder so maybe somebody hit him on the shoulder.' You don't do that. But your understanding of other people becomes very much clearer if you have been trained to do that. And I think one of the reasons why I became such a good teacher was because I had trained myself and I did see quite a lot. And I was able to give little hints to people which I didn't direct at them but still they hit home and sunk in. I think that was one of my secrets."[9]

And what was the fate of the passionate love affair with the young student that opened this chapter and propelled Gerda onto Ola Raknes' couch? It ended in tears, on Gerda's side at least.

"He ended the relationship. Left me heartbroken, I can tell you. But I think many young people go through a devastating period when their first love collapses, it's the end of the world. I thought I wanted to end my life at that time. I thought it wasn't worth living. So I went out in the middle of the winter in Norway, got myself drunk, and tried to bury myself in a snowdrift. I dug a hole, crept into it, and I stayed there for a little while. Then I got so darned cold that I thought no, I can't stand this cold any longer so I went back home again. That was my only attempt at suicide. I was twenty-two."[10]

Despite her tongue-in-cheek self-mockery when recounting these events sixty-seven years later, Gerda also identified a positive legacy, a guiding principle, which she had taken from the relationship and held onto:

"My first lover was the one who said: 'If you really want to be successful and positive in this life you must find something in your life that you enjoy doing.'"[11]

And another emerging passion in Gerda's life, which was to prove less fickle and more enduring than young love, was dance.

THE ROAD
TO DANCE

*When…you have repulsed the monkey and emptied yourself of intruding
thoughts, you receive a blessing from the phoenix which enables you to Look
for the Golden Needle at the Bottom of the Sea. The Golden Needle
represents the creative force. Perhaps it may also be described as looking for
inspiration in one's own sub-conscious. When we find it, we bring up the
Golden Needle, and whatever we are able to create with it, we then show it to
the world in a movement called Opening the Fan or Fan Through the Back.*

Gerda Geddes   LOOKING FOR THE GOLDEN NEEDLE, p58

Oslo in the late 1930s had become a meeting place for several strands
of radical thought including pioneering work in psycho-physiological
therapies; avant-garde developments in movement, dance and theatre;
and liberated, experimental life-styles. Wilhelm Reich lived there
from 1934 and was a key figure in what has since been called 'The
Golden Age of Body Psychotherapy in Oslo'.[1] In addition to his conventional medical and psychiatric training, he had acquired an impressive array of anti-establishment qualifications. He had been kicked out
of the Communist party, denounced by the Nazis, and expelled from
the International Psychoanalytic Association. He was a renegade sci-
entist and a militant for sexual freedom and liberation, who sometimes
encouraged his therapy patients to strip to near or complete nudity. In
Oslo he lived openly with dancer and choreographer Elsa Lindenberg

while his wife and two children remained in Austria. Lindenberg not only participated in the development of Reich's Vegetotherapy but she also created her own form of dance psychotherapy that continues to be taught in Norway. Amongst those who were drawn into the Reich/Lindenberg circle were A.S. Neill, the Scots-born educational pioneer who went on to create Summerhill, the *laissez-faire* 'free' school in Suffolk where children made their own decisions about their education. Other members of the circle were Ola Raknes, Gerda's therapist, and Gerda herself.

"The analysis certainly released my pent up energy. I threw myself into a two year dance course and attended every lecture at the Faculty of Psychology at Oslo University, read anatomy and philosophy, took singing lessons, and attended seminars with Reich's girlfriend, Elsa Lindenberg. I also fell in love again, this time with a beautiful dancer, painter, and dress designer. Life was really singing.[2]

I had lots of lessons with Elsa Lindenberg. She taught movement, not exactly dance although she was a dancer and came from the Berlin Opera. She had been in the Berlin Opera Ballet. She was trained in ballet but she changed it into Reichian ways of movement. It was also very avant-garde and I was in the front of this movement."[3]

A co-pupil at Lindenberg's classes was an artist called Ingeborg Rudi who painted a large, striking, full-length portrait of Gerda, which is on the front cover of this book. In it her powerful presence dominates the front left of a plain geometric room. She is dressed in dark blue leotard and tights and is perched lightly on a round seat, as if ready to move off and dance at any moment. A taut, authoritative gaze has replaced the puppy-fat smile of her teens: this woman is in command of the space around her and, one guesses, the thoughts and feelings within.

Gerda's involvement at the cutting edge of modern progressive Oslo served to emphasise again the differences between her nineteenth-century father and twentieth-century mother. When she first told her parents about wanting to go into psychoanalysis, her father had dismissed the idea after which it became a secret between Gerda and her mother who found an irregular way of paying for it partly, Gerda believed, as a way of compensating her daughter for her childhood experiences.

"I told her that I wanted to go in for this analysis and it was very expensive. I didn't have the money. She said:'I will pay for your treatment. I owe you that.' That was in '39. I can remember we had just moved away from Storhaugen, the wonderful big house that we lived in, and there were lots of antiques that were going to be sold. She took some of those antiques and sold them without my father knowing so that she had enough money to pay for my analysis. Because it wasn't cheap, it was very expensive in fact."[4]

Psychoanalysis was also proving popular in some parts of Oslo society and Gerda was in no doubt about its potential as an agent for change. She cited the cases of two prominent women who underwent analysis by Reich himself and experienced a release of their own energy which led to transformations elsewhere.

"One was a doctor, a psychiatrist; she changed a lot about the way patients were treated. Her own energy was unstoppable....The other woman was an actress, Gerda Ring, who was very popular at that time. And she managed to change the theatre. She was the one that I worked with later." *(in 1945. See Chapter 8)*[5]

Gerda's connection with these circles came to an abrupt halt when she fled to Sweden in 1943. She was determined to continue her training, however, and two of her priorities after arriving in Stockholm were to find both a dance teacher and a Reichian analyst. First, though, she had to find a way of supporting herself, but it was important to her to find a way of doing this that did not compromise the new directions her life was taking.

"I was offered a very good job as Secretary at the Norwegian Embassy in Stockholm. It would give me security and enough money.

Reich's teaching suggested that there were two things one

ought to get right in this life in order to be happy and fulfilled. The first was to find work that was creative, where one's potential would be challenged, where one could grow and develop. The other was to find a partner with whom one is able to express love and tenderness. To me, the job at the embassy did not seem very creative, so much to the distress of my friends, I turned it down. I decided to continue with my studies. Like a miracle everything fell into place. An old man appeared on the scene who turned out to be my grandfather's cousin. He offered to loan me enough money so I could just survive – the money to be repaid after the war. Then a Reichian therapist, Dr Tage Philipson, arrived in Stockholm from Denmark. He started teaching, and giving seminars, and I was able to join his group and continue my studies. I also met a very talented Swedish dancer, Birgit Aakesson, and carried on my dance training for two years."[6]

Birgit Aakesson 1908-2001

Birgit Aakeson was a dancer and choreographer who is considered a founding mother of Swedish modern dance. She was trained in Germany in the Dresden school of Mary Wigman but turned her back on these Expressionist roots and concentrated on developing an experimental and uncompromising style. She specialised in pure, rigorous and hypnotic solos in which she would mould herself into sculptural shapes, assembled as parts of her body took on the forms of independent planes. Critics extended their vocabularies and their references in their efforts to represent her work. She was described as the Picasso of dance, and the development of her body forms was compared to the flow of images in the poems of Dylan Thomas.

Ecstatic reviews of her 1955 New York debut commented on her stark simplicity, her sculptural and dramatic lines drawn from nature (comparison was made to Henry Moore), and her liquid convolutions.[7]

Birgit Aakesson, right from their first meeting, was to have a deep and lasting influence on Gerda.

"The most wonderful thing she did was to make me into a professional. I had my dance training from Norway and I met her and showed her what I had done. She said: 'Well you can't call yourself a trained dancer with a body like yours.' She was very sharp and very demanding. And why she offered to train me I don't know, she must have seen something that I had not yet discovered. So I went to her and she said: 'I will train you and you can pay me after the war.' Because this was when I was a refugee and I didn't have any money. She was very generous with her teaching but expected a lot in return.

I can remember once when I came to a class she held early in the morning for a group of architects. They went to her class before they went to work in the morning. I had been out on what you could call a rather debauched night and when I came to her class I don't know whether I was still drunk…I probably was fairly far gone anyway. I didn't do very well and all of a sudden she turned on me. I was sitting on the floor. She stood above me like this (gestures with raised fist) and she said: 'It's about time for you to make up your mind. Do you want to be a dabbler and an amateur all your life or do you want to become a real professional? If you don't want to be a professional you can go away because it's not worth my training you.' She really forced me to work. She just absolutely remorselessly forced me to work.

And she taught me something very essential, which I might not have been able to develop otherwise, and that was to have endurance. I had to work through my pain and I had to just make up my mind that I'm going to stick to this. And I did. I can never thank her enough for that."[8]

Embedded in the above account is a strong hint that Gerda was sometimes finding life difficult. As an adolescent and as a young woman she had spent time away from home, first in London and then in Pittsburgh, but both times as a supervised boarder. Latterly she had embraced the freedom of student life and radical interests but within a city she knew well and in the company not just of pals but also fellow members of the Resistance, with all the camaraderie and emotional attachment which that implies. Now, at twenty-seven, she was more alone than she had ever been, a refugee and out of touch with friends, comrades, and family. It is likely that she benefited, not just as a dancer, from the support and the example of the strong and purposeful Birgit who was nine years her senior.

Gerda the dancer

And, thanks to Dr Philipson, she was able to put her developing skills to very good use and to experiment with the power that lay in combining psychological thinking with body movement: she was about to put theory into practice.

THE BIOGRAPHER'S THREAD 5: Reading People

Throughout her life, Gerda maintained a deep interest and curiosity about what made people tick and she enjoyed making swift and accurate assessments by observing their posture and movement. As the following excerpt from an interview with her daughters Jane and Harriet shows, it brought an added frisson to home life.

Harriet: It was quite terrifying in some ways that aspect of her nature, looking at people. She got their core almost instantly. And it was terrifying when you were bringing anyone home. She'd say: 'He bites his nails. Have you seen his shoes? They're not very clean. Have you seen how stiff this side of his face is?'

Jane: Yes! 'Frozen tears, frozen tears.' 'The tight throat.'

Harriet: Yes. 'Tight Throat.' 'Tight bottom.'

Jane: How could you have boyfriends? Or even girlfriends? When they went through this mangle?

Harriet: It wasn't criticised. It was just observed.

Jane: But once you'd been told about the diaphragm, it was impossible: you couldn't see anything else.[1]

I was easy meat. I came to t'ai-chi relatively late in life and attended my first class in 1999, the year I turned fifty-seven and also the year I met Gerda through a t'ai-chi connection although I was not learning her style. By then, I had been living a professional middle-class life for many years but, I now realise, my posture and my walk betrayed the legacy of an industrial Clydeside childhood and adolescence. In particular my way of carrying my upper body, especially my shoulders, was probably based on James Cagney, as modulated via Elvis Presley, Gene Vincent, and the attempts of a skinny youth to make the most of the padded shoulders of a cheap 1950s suit. All of this was self-evident to Gerda who was also kind enough to comment on my gradual progress as the years went by and as the relaxation I was learning slowly went deeper and my shoulders and arms began to slough off the tension they had held for decades. She was able to take my hand and make an accurate appraisal of my state of relaxation simply by gently palpating the fleshy area at the base of my thumb. I liked that.

FROM THEORY
TO PRACTICE

*There is a lovely story about an old Taoist monk who made the most
wonderful embroidery with such beautiful shapes and colours that people
came from far and wide to admire his work. They asked him how he was
able to create such beauty. He replied that it had only been made through
the use of the Golden Needle, and those who want to do likewise must find
the Golden Needle for themselves.*

Gerda Geddes   LOOKING FOR THE GOLDEN NEEDLE, pp58-59

As part of her psychology studies in Oslo, Gerda had already done some
work in an asylum. She had combined her psychological knowledge,
her dance training, and what she had learned from Reich's girlfriend,
Elsa Lindenberg, to help the mentally ill people there.

"Ten patients were selected. I gave them a long thick rope which
they all held onto with one hand. We then walked slowly round
in a circle. To begin with the patients walked as if in their sleep
with completely expressionless faces, but little by little they
seemed to get a feeling of the rope and a feeling of doing something together with others. After a while a drum was introduced and simple rhythms were beaten like 1-2: 1-2-3: 1-2-3-4
and they were told to walk and emphasise the hard beat. This we
did for a long time and I could see that some of them started to
pay attention to their neighbours. They even went as far as to

correct each other if someone stepped hard on the wrong beat. The doctor with whom I was working thought this a great improvement. The next step was to remove the rope, but I still made them walk in a circle because it seemed to give them a sense of security. By this time six of the patients showed a real interest in what was going on and the nurse in the ward told me that they were asking all the time when they were having their next dancing lesson. With the four others we could discover no reaction so they were left out of the class. But lessons continued with the six. A big ball was brought in and they threw it to each other. We played simple tunes on a piano and they were told to move around the room to the rhythm of the music. This they particularly liked and they looked very sweet, like little children – one almost forgot that there was something the matter with them.

After five months, these six patients were moved to another ward and were given simple work to do like wood-carving and making wicker baskets. They were unlikely ever to leave the asylum but at least their lives would not be spent in utter darkness and misery."[1]

During her exile in Stockholm, she was able to develop this work further.

"Early in 1945 a group of political prisoners were brought to Sweden by Count Bernadotte. He had secured special permission from Himmler for their release. Most of the people were in pretty bad shape. They were all in a hospital being given proper food and counselling treatment, only being released when they were considered fit to 'face the world' again. Dr Phillipson became very much involved with this group, and asked me to come and help him. He said: 'You have a special advantage with your combination of dance training and psychology. Use your movements to free these people.' And that is what I did, and from then on my theme became 'Where dancing and psychology meet!' Most of our patients recovered rapidly with good food and secure surroundings, and my work was to train their muscles so that they could rely on their bodies again. But there were cases which needed more help. One example is a woman called Miss Haabet. She had been a political prisoner in Sachsenhausen concentration camp for three years. During her time there all the women had been made to sew mailbags. The material was so hard that they all got infected fingers from pulling the needle through. They worked in a shed where the ceiling was so low that they could not straighten up. They always had to have their heads bent, and after three years Miss Haabet had become bent. She could not straighten her spine and therefore never looked anyone in the eye. We started out by doing gentle swings with the arms. To begin with there was very little movement. All her movements were done with her staring at the floor.

After several sessions I asked her if she could swing her arms all the way around. She resisted for a long time until suddenly her arms made a full circle and she straightened her back, and as her back straightened she also looked up and she looked me in the eye. And that was her breakthrough. As she stared at me her face started to contort, and the most awful expression came onto her face, alternating between hatred and fear – and then her tears started coming and she also started to talk. Once she had started she could not stop. She stamped her feet and screamed: 'I hate the Germans. They had no right to treat us like that. I am terrified. I don't know what they are going to do to me'. All I had to do was to listen.

We continued working on her back both with exercises and with massage, until one day she said she thought she could manage on her own. Of course her trauma was not a long lasting condition. It had been directly produced by the circumstances, and was therefore easier to get rid of. I learned a lot from Miss Haabet."[2]

Perhaps most poignant of all is her account of work she did around the same time with the daughter of a traumatised Resistance worker.

"Anne was a twelve-year-old refugee who had escaped from

Norway with her mother who had worked for the underground.

Anne's mother was nervous and upset and they were living in Sweden under difficult circumstances with very little money. In Norway Anne had been a happy and contented girl but when they came to Sweden she became more and more withdrawn. She did not want to play with other children, she refused to go to school, and she only wanted to sit by herself or to lie in bed. Her mother went from one doctor to another; Anne was being filled with pills and health tonics, but nothing seemed to help.

When she finally was brought to me I discovered that many of her difficulties were caused by the mother who was impatient and irritable with her, saying all the time that Anne was so stupid and so naughty. Anne herself had a sweet face but with a still smile and a very frightened expression. She looked as if she might burst into tears at any moment. The first thing was to try and make friends with her. I talked to her and tried to get her to talk to me. But that was impossible: she only answered with 'yes' or 'no' or 'I can't do that' and all the time she had this pathetic smile on her face.

I tried to teach her some simple dance movements but she was very awkward and clumsy and did not know what to do with her long thin arms and legs. She seemed to have no coordination or harmonious rhythm in her body and whenever she could, she squeezed herself into the corner of the room. She was frightened of everything and was always saying;' I can't do that because I am so stupid.' After about four lessons, where no progress had been made, I one day drew the figure of eight on a sheet of paper, put it up on the wall, and asked if she could make that figure with her hand. She said she could not possibly do that, but I told her to try and then I left her by herself for half-an-hour.

When I came back, I asked if she had anything to show me. She smiled and looked very shy and said she could show me something. Then she turned her back on me and, with one finger straight in front of her nose, she drew a tiny figure of eight. I told her that was all right but she could make a bigger one: and all of a sudden a change came over her. She started to swing figures of eight with her arms and legs and danced around the room and cried in a loud voice: 'I did it myself, I did it myself. I am not so stupid, I am not so stupid.'

After that we made wonderful progress. She came to me every day and I taught her the most complicated dance steps and rhythms and she worked like a slave and enjoyed herself tremendously. After about a month she was able to go back to school and made friends with other children, but she still kept coming to me and I sometimes helped her with her prep and talked to her about school and her friends.

Then one day she said: 'Please tell me about when you were a little girl'. She sat down on my lap and I told her that I had half-sisters and brothers and she said that she also had four half-brothers. I knew that one of them had been killed in the war and stupidly I asked which one it was. She looked at me with great big eyes and said that it was not true, no one had been killed. When she had gone home I telephoned her mother and told her what had happened. The mother was furious and said that Anne was not to know about the death of her brother until the war was over. She also said that Anne was never to come back to me because she had now quite recovered and she hung up the receiver with a bang.

Early the next morning my doorbell rang. When I opened the door there was Anne, flinging herself into my arms saying: 'Oh, I love you so much, more than anyone else in the world, because you are the only grown-up who does not lie to me. Now I understand everything. Whenever I came into the room Mother was crying and I thought she cried because I was so stupid and that she did not love me any more. But naturally Mother cries because my brother is dead and maybe I can help her instead of sulking all the time'."[3]

DRAMA AND
MOVEMENT

Next comes Waving Arms Like Clouds. Your arms perform circular, wave-
like movements. By waving your arms like clouds you make yourself
invisible and invincible; you merge with the environment, feeling yourself to
be part of everything around you, realising that although you are unique in
yourself, you are also an integral part of everything else. This experience of
being part of the great whole is both humbling and comforting; one no
longer has to feel isolated and alone.

Gerda Geddes   LOOKING FOR THE GOLDEN NEEDLE, p60

The war ended two years after Gerda's flight to Sweden and she was
able to return home at last.

THE LIBERATION OF NORWAY 7TH MAY 1945

There was nervousness on the Norwegian side about what might happen
to their country as the end of the Third Reich approached. Norway was
well fortified and had an occupying force of around 350,000 well equipped,
well-trained and seasoned Wermacht soldiers under the command of
General Böhme. The Norwegian Government in Exile, and Milorg, the
secret army within the country, feared a catastrophe if any military move
was made against the German force. And if the Wermacht in Germany
surrendered would an undefeated army in Norway follow suit? Even after
Hitler had committed suicide and his successor, Admiral Dönitz, declared

an unconditional surrender on all fronts on 7th May, there was still doubt over whether General Böhme would obey the order. And there was concern about the actions and influence of the German commissioner (Reichskommissar) and Nazi hardliner Josef Terboven who was the country's real ruler and who was associated with talk of fighting to the last man.

The anxiety was misplaced, however. Admiral Dönitz dismissed Terboven and handed his powers to General Böhme. On 8th May an Allied military commission under the command of a British Officer, Brigadier Hilton, landed at Lillehammer and travelled to Oslo to deliver its conditions for capitulation, which were accepted in full by Böhme. At the time of the German surrender, the total Allied force in Norway was Brigadier Hilton's small party. Within a few days the German forces had carried out their orders to withdraw from all fortifications and hand in their weapons although they could not have been forced to do so had they resisted. In the event, there were hardly any casualties except the suicides of a few Nazi die-hards, both German and Norwegian. Amongst those who took their own lives were Josef Terboven and his police general Wilhelm Rediess. The Norwegian Nazi and puppet president whose name is now synonymous with 'traitor', Vidkun Quisling, was arrested and later sentenced to death by a Norwegian court.

Norwegian celebrations continued throughout the month of May and reached a climax on 7th June with the return of King Haakon to Norwegian soil, exactly five years to the day he fled Norway for England.

Gerda never saw her father alive again: Gerdt died at the age of seventy-two on 17th April 1945, two months before her return. It was a loss that she felt very keenly. She loved him dearly and Gerdt, for his part, had doted on her, but their relationship had experienced some strain as she developed into a liberated and self-reliant young woman. His death in her absence created in her a sense of something unresolved.

And there was unfinished business involving her mother too. Lydia had played a prominent role in many of the childhood events and feelings that had surfaced in the course of the five years of analysis that

Gerda had by now undergone. She had spent over two years living in a foreign country and largely out of contact with her parents. Although this was a consequence of her own bravery in joining the Resistance then fleeing for her life, and although she had made very positive use of her time in Sweden, it is also likely there were times when she felt lost and alone, even abandoned. Furthermore, her first reaction on learning of her father's death was that she would never be able to put things right with him. Perhaps her reaction was to try and clear the air with Lydia. Whatever the reasons, she made it a priority to confront her grief-laden mother about their past. The effect was cathartic for them both.

"Looking back, I think that was very cruel of me. But it had to be done; it just had to be done. We had been apart for two-and-a-half years when I was in Sweden and she was in Norway. When I returned my father had been dead just two months and my mother was deep in sorrow. And I went for her. I told her how difficult she had made my life during my upbringing because of how she had treated me. Then both of us dissolved into floods of tears. We just cried and cried and cried. Eventually the tears wore down the barrier between us. And we became friends. Not so much mother and daughter but more like friends. We had a wonderful relationship for many, many years. I thought she was my best friend. Absolutely."[1]

Gerda did not stay long with her mother because she landed a job with the Norwegian National Theatre school, a job that again drew on her unusual combination of qualifications in dance and Reichian therapy

"I started off teaching the actors how to move with ease on the stage and also getting them in trim. The importance of physical fitness for an actor was just being recognised then. But the job quickly developed to a point where I would work with the producer and take actors separately to analyse their part. 'What do you think you would look like if you were going to portray that character? How would you carry your body? How would you move, sit down, stand up?' This is something a very talented actor has in him intuitively. But not everybody has that particular gift and it very much helps if they can be made aware of it. So that was what I did. I found it fascinating. My Reichian analysis and my training in observing people's bodies came in very useful."[2]

Once again the Reich effect was bearing fruit for Gerda. Actress Gerda Ring was now director of the National Theatre and was introducing psychoanalytical thinking into the world of drama. She was also a friend of Gerda's mother who, although she had not personally undergone psychoanalysis, had been attracted to the intellectual and cultural energy of Oslo.

"My mother had all these very modern intelligent friends. That was the way she was. She had a very inquiring mind and asked lots of questions. And through being like that she made contact with these people and made friends with them."[3]

And that was not the end of Reichian connections and coincidences contributing to the unfolding of Gerda's life. Her new and exciting job meant that she had to find a place to stay amid the post-war housing crisis that Oslo was suffering. The problem was solved courtesy of Miss Haabet, who had been one of her patients in Sweden.

"She and I then became quite good friends. When the war was over and we went back to Oslo there was a tremendous housing shortage. Miss Haabet had quite a big flat and she said to me: 'You can have a room at my place.' I stayed with her for quite some time and I very often heard her getting up in the middle of the night and walking around the other rooms and going to the kitchen and eating. I think she felt she could never be full enough again. So she was disturbed for quite some time, and was a quite difficult person to stay with. But she gave me shelter."[4]

By now Gerda was almost thirty. She had survived the war, turned her exile in Sweden into a constructive opportunity that had furthered her development both in dance and in psychotherapeutic skills, and had worked through the problems with her mother in a way that had enriched and deepened their relationship. Her job at the cutting edge of contemporary drama was fulfilling and used her abilities to the utmost, and she had private patients with whom she practised her psychotherapy. Life was almost complete. Then, in 1947, she met The Honourable David Campbell Geddes.

So far, this biography includes abundant references to psychothera-py and, in particular, to Reichian analysis. And for good reason. Throughout her life Gerda, while tut-tutting at the less accepted and more outlandish aspects of Reich's thinking and behaviour, acknowl-edged her debt to him and to her two therapists, Ola Raknes and Tage Philipson. She was fond of quoting her version of Reich's claim that there were two keys to the achievement of human happiness: finding challenging and creative work; and finding a partner with whom one could express love and tenderness. Gerda's expression of the second part of this recipe for fulfilment glossed over Reich's meaning: explicitly, he saw a satisfactory sex life as an essential condition of lasting mental health, a sex life which included a complete, convulsive discharge of sex-ual energy in orgasm.

I had a problem. It is very acceptable to talk, or be questioned in detail, about our creative pursuits. Discussion of our romantic life, love life, sex life, call it what you will, is another matter, usually reserved for our closest intimates, or savoured within the pleasure of our own memories. It is not normally on the conversational agenda with eighty-nine year old friends of the opposite sex, no matter how dear.

A combination of factors contributed to easing my way towards an appreciation of the young Gerda's love affairs. First, both of Gerda's therapists, in their writings, had put a softer face on Reich's starkly orgas-mic model. Philipson shifted the emphasis towards human love: "Here then are two of the most important characteristics of love: it fills peo-ple with pleasure, happiness, life, and movement: and it reaches into the depths of a person, filling the whole of his (sic) body and the whole of his soul. A third characteristic is the expression of love through sex-uality. Love, on the one hand, gives rise to a tendency between two people who have fallen in love with each other...to unite in sexual love-making which usually leads to a mutual fusion in the supreme pleas-ure of an orgasm. On the other hand, love can lead to the strongest possible sense of relatedness between the two lovers."[1] For his part

Raknes, whose doctorate thesis was entitled *Meeting the Holy: an investigation into the psychological foundations of religion* speculated that the psychophysical feelings reported in accounts of religious ecstasy might equate to the 'vegetative streamings' released in Reichian therapy.[2] So, in their different ways, they created a wider context for discussion and inquiry.

And Gerda's own reportage includes frank evidence of herself as a sexually liberated young woman. Her memoir *A Norwegian Childhood* makes reference to three passionate affairs before she met and married her husband David. In the course of our interviews together it became clear that, as student in Oslo, a refugee in Sweden, and when working at the National Theatre, she was no stranger to the attractions of men and the delights of Venus.

But, most of all, there was her enjoyment of an occasional saucy memory. As with all other areas of her life, she conducted herself with taste and refinement when talking about the men she had met and the impassioned, sometimes tempestuous, affairs she had embarked upon in her twenties. Sometimes, as she reminisced, she would treat herself to a throaty chuckle or perky turn of phrase. When talking about the one-time lover who features in the opening of the next chapter she said: "I was passionate. I don't think I've ever been so physically in love with anyone. Some days I didn't know which foot I was standing on."[3]

LOVE AND
MARRIAGE

*We in the West, in our fairy tales, always have to kill the dragon in order to
win the princess or find the treasure, whereas in the east, to kill one of these
supernatural animals would be catastrophic; it would upset the whole
balance of the universe. The Chinese say that the wild horse, and also the
dragon, must be tamed or neutralised. This is achieved by giving them a
mate who is gentle and loving, such as a docile mare, and through her
intervention harmony will be re-established.*

Gerda Geddes   LOOKING FOR THE GOLDEN NEEDLE, p61

In recognition of the pioneering theatre work she was engaged in,
Gerda, in 1947, received two grants, one from the Norwegian National
Theatre and the other from the British Council. They funded a four-
week trip in London to research the use, within British theatre, of psy-
chophysical techniques similar to those she was helping to develop in
Norway. She arrived in early June, dropped in on classes at all the
famous theatre schools, and quickly decided she could learn most at the
Old Vic.

"At that time the Old Vic was just soaring up to fame. There was
a woman who taught movement called Miss Pisk. She gave
wonderful classes to the actors, rather in the same style as I did but
with more energy and more experience and more everything.

So it was the Old Vic I concentrated on. There I met

people who later on became the great actors of the period, like Laurence Olivier. And Ralph Richardson, and various others, all on their way up. I learned a lot in that month."[1]

LITZ PISK 1909-1997

Litz Pisk was born in Vienna where she studied stage architecture and 'Kineticism' at the State Arts and Crafts School. In 1932, when she was in Berlin as a student of the theatre director Max Reinhart, she designed, at the age of 23, Bertolt Brecht and Kurt Weill's first producton *The Rise and Fall of the Town Mahoganny*. During her first visit to Britain in the early 1930s she taught at RADA. In 1937 she settled permanently in England. She taught movement at the Old Vic Theatre School in 1947 and later taught at the Central School of Speech and Drama.

She choreographed for the Old Vic Theatre, the National Theatre and the Royal Shakespeare Company amongst others. She also choreographed for television and film including *Isadora Duncan* starring Vanessa Redgrave.

In 1970 she moved to Cornwall where she wrote *The Actor and His Body* which explores the emotional and psychological impulses that motivate actors to find their roles. She was also a talented artist whose work was shown in several exhibitions.

It is no surprise that Gerda found Litz Pisk at the Old Vic within a short time of her arrival in London. Throughout her life she showed an unerring ability to seek out and find quality.

She also attended the theatre as often as she could and took in performances by Donald Wolfit, Laurence Olivier, Ralph Richardson and John Gielgud. Her appointments diary for the time records the programme of a woman buzzing with energy and drive: daytimes and evenings packed with appointments and engagements. And she also managed to fit in a tempestuous romance.

"I had rather a passionate love affair at the same time so my life was very full at that stage and I was open for anything that happened. I really took every opportunity when I was over here. I could afford to stay in rather a good hotel in South Kensington and I had this intense boyfriend who was an Englishman that I'd met in Stockholm during the war. We already had a lively connection but he had so many girlfriends. He was one of those Don Juans who looks at a girl, falls for her, and she falls for him. But he became rather serious when I was over here and thought that marriage might be a good thing.

Then towards the end of these precious four weeks a crisis turned up. I had been buying some wonderful gramophone records; it was Mozart and Handel I was into. I came back to this boy with wonderful records and said you must sit down and listen to this, it's absolutely divine. He sat down and tried to listen to my records but wasn't in the least bit interested. And I thought, 'Well something is wrong here. I can't marry someone who is not interested in music.' And that did it."[2]

Considering he had recently been contemplating sharing his life with her, her lover seems to have taken her explanation of his incompatibility with remarkable equanimity. There are brief hints, simply a word here and a word there in her small appointments diary, that, for all its passion, their relationship might have been running its course. There may have been a recognition on both sides that the pleasures they were sharing were insufficient to sustain a lifetime's commitment; thus the issue of loving or not loving classical music was more of a last straw than a prime cause. In *A Norwegian Childhood* she describes the decision to end the relationship as a mutual one because it had become 'rather painful'. And she goes on to tell of an offer of help that changed her life:

"When I was leaving London my old flame said that he had an acquaintance who was working at Stavanger airport as a trainee officer for British European Airways. He would tell his friend to look out for me as I had to wait for a plane to Bergen. So when I arrived in Stavanger there was a young man greeting me at the bottom of the steps. He looked up at me and the first thing I noticed was his warm and friendly smile. He was very handsome in his navy blue uniform. I also remember precisely how I was dressed. I wore a very smart grey flannel suit with a grey and white striped cotton blouse and a dashing light brown hat with a big bow at the back in the same material as the blouse. Brown alligator shoes with platform soles (almost impossible to walk in, I had to walk with my knees bent) and an alligator handbag to match. I had quite a lot of self-confidence! His name was The Hon. David Campbell Geddes. David invited me out for dinner, but first he had to go home to his flat to change out of his uniform. I came with him and while he was changing I was sitting in his living room and I started looking at the books that were lying around and I discovered to my delight that they were the sort of books that I would read. I also opened a folder of drawings which at first sight seemed rather strange, but then I came across a painting of circles and those circles went straight to my heart. All summer I had been working with circles in my dancing, thinking that a curved line was the beginning of everything and feeling how the body was full of spirals and circles. By this time I really started to get excited. Our dinner was a tremendous success. We talked about art and music and literature with the greatest of ease. It felt as if we had waited to meet each other all our lives. I was totally swept off my feet and completely forgot about my plane to Bergen. Well, that was it, love at first sight!

David came to visit me in Bergen two weeks later and I invited him out to Aastvedt to meet my Mother. It happened to be my birthday, 17th July. I was thirty. Although I had had several boyfriends during the war, it had never been the same as this. David and I seemed to have so many interests in common including an all-absorbing physical attraction for each other.

Aastvedt on a perfect summer's day is probably one of the most dramatically beautiful places in the world (at least in my eyes) and David was duly impressed. We went swimming in the fjord and I dragged him up a very steep mountain and nearly killed him. I should have seen a little warning sign. David never became a willing mountain climber and for me that was a little bit sad.

Although I was determined that David was the man I wanted to marry, it was not plain sailing. I had my contract with the National Theatre in Oslo for another year and a half. David was involved with two other women at the time, in fact he had a new born son by one of them. He also had no money. In October of that year David returned to London to work at Northolt and I went back to my job in Oslo. We wrote long, passionate love letters. One slight drawback was that I had great difficulty in reading David's writing so I had to get my best friend to help me interpreting and sharing all our secrets!

The following summer, in June 1948, David came back to Norway to see me and we got engaged under an apple tree in Tante Gerda's orchard and David gave me, not a ring, but a beautiful Victorian bracelet which still is my favourite piece of jewellery. We were blissfully, irresponsibly happy."[3]

**David Campbell Geddes
self portrait aged 23**

David was the fifth child and the fourth son of Sir Auckland Campbell Geddes, the first Baron Geddes; doctor, professor, soldier, cabinet minister and ambassador. Gerda's introduction to the family went very well. Firstly, David's elder brother, Ross, visited the Meyer Bruun's in Norway, then Gerda and David were invited to stay with him in Malleny House, a handsome eighteenth-century building with famous gardens at Balerno, near Edinburgh, which is now owned by the National Trust for Scotland.

"I got on well with Ross and his wife, Enid. We liked each

other at once and then David's mother came too and we also made friends. In fact after a few days, Mama, (that is what the family called her) said how relieved she was that I was going to be her daughter-in-law. 'You should have seen some of the girls David brought down to Frensham last year! The only thing wrong with you is that your hips are too narrow. You will have difficulties in producing many children'.

When my visit with Ross came to an end, I did not want to return to Norway. I travelled to London where I got a room in the London Musical Club in Holland Park where David had stayed before the war. David at that time lived out at Northolt where he worked. It was an unsatisfactory arrangement, we did not see much of each other. Eventually David's brother, Alexander, took pity on us and lent us his pied-a-terre in St John's Wood where we lived 'in sin' secretly. Lady Geddes was not supposed to know but I think she had a pretty shrewd idea. I made some money treating patients recommended to me by Dr Doris Howard who was a friend of Wilhelm Reich.

We finally decided to get married although David was most reluctant. He thought it was irresponsible because we had so little money, but I assured him that I would be able to support myself. 31st December was going to be the date because on the 1st January 1949 a new law was being passed. A foreign woman who married a British man would no longer automatically become a British citizen.

In November I went home to prepare for the wedding. In 1948 there was still rationing on many things. For instance, a bride was only allowed to buy three single cotton sheets for her trousseau. The idea being that you changed one sheet at the time and put the upper sheet under and the clean sheet on top! A few years earlier there had been a terrible explosion in Bergen and a big fire and people had been asked to give everything they could do without to help and my Mother had given away all her spare sheets so there was nothing left for me. Good material was also

impossible to buy, so in the end I was married in David's sister Peg's beautiful wedding dress."[4]

FIT FOR A PRINCESS: THE TRAGEDY BEHIND THE WEDDING DRESS

Gerda was married in a dress that had been made ten years earlier for David's sister Margaret ('Peg') but had not been worn because of a disaster. On 17 November 1937, Margaret was due to be married to Ludwig, a member of the German ducal family of Hesse and the Rhine. Ludwig's brother, the then title holder Hereditary Grand Duke Georg Donatus, was married to H.R.H. Princess Cecilia of Greece and Denmark, the Duke of Edinburgh's sister. The wedding was to be held in London at St Columba's Scottish Presbyterian Church in Knightsbridge and was to be a big social event followed by a reception at Claridges. The night before the wedding, Margaret and Ludwig received shocking and dreadful news. The plane carrying Ludwig's relatives from Germany had crashed in Belgium and all on board had been killed. The dead included Grand Duke Donatus, Princess Cecilia, two of their children and the late-term baby which Cecilia was carrying. All wedding plans were cancelled, and, before flying to Belgium to help identify the bodies, the couple married in a short ceremony at 8.00am in which Margaret became a princess by a route she would never have wished for nor could have glimpsed in her darkest nightmares.

At last the dress was worn for the sort of joyous occasion for which it had been created years earlier. On this occasion, it was crowned with a beautiful Brussels lace veil, lent by a friend of David's mother.

There had always been a very close bond between David and his sister Margaret. From now on, Princess 'Peg' and Prince 'Lu' were important people in Gerda's life.

"There was also severe food rationing and many travel restrictions so the wedding had to be small. I was so excited about everything that I did not think much about my mother. She was heartbroken because she was going to lose me to a foreign country. I was incredibly selfish at that time and have many times regretted that I did not pay more attention to her feelings. Now that I am a mother myself I know very much how she must have felt.

David and I were married in the small medieval church at Aastvedt. When I was dressed up in all my finery the old woman, Oline, our laundress and bread maker came along with a branch of myrtle leaves and she said that I had to put the myrtle on my head. She had been given the plant by my grandmother and it would bring me good luck. As we were setting out for the church suddenly a tremendous thunderstorm blew up with sleet and snow falling on very slippery roads. All the electricity went out. The church was lit only by candles and it was bitterly cold. I was shivering with panic and cold as I went up the aisle on the arm of my uncle Finn and there was David and his best man, Douglas Grey. He was the man who had introduced us. They both looked as if they had a bad hangover and they had!

After the ceremony we drove back to Bergen to the Bristol Hotel where the dinner was held. There was still thunder and lightning and drifting snow on the last day of 1948.

My mother had worked terribly hard to produce the food. The hotel would cook everything for us, but we had to produce the raw material. A beautiful salmon was a gift from my father's firm, we managed to buy some ducks and butter, eggs and cream we gathered from several farms around in the district. I remember having to climb up to the highest mountain farm begging for the eggs. But in the end the hotel managed to put together a fantastic dinner and all went very well.

After dinner there was dancing. David and I left the party just before midnight. We looked out of our bedroom window and at 12 o'clock all the church bells started ringing and down below us the square filled with people. They all had umbrellas because of the terrible weather and suddenly they all started dancing. This is a sight I shall always remember.

When we went to bed we found that the hotel had provided us with their bridal sheets. The pillow cases were embroidered and had lots of starched frilly lace and the same with the top sheet, everything in the finest Irish linen.

In the meantime the party went on downstairs and Lady Geddes danced non-stop till 2am really enjoying the giving away of her youngest son. I thought quite a lot about my own parents and was very sad that my Father was dead because I knew that he and David would have liked each other. I also thought about how much I loved my own mother and wondered where my new life would take me.

The next day we boarded the old ship Jupiter and had a very stormy crossing over to Newcastle. David and I were both dreadfully sick. We arrived back in England on 2nd January 1949 looking pretty green to start our married life which was to last for 48 years.

On arrival we gave a large party for David's family and friends which consisted of leftovers from our own wedding dinner, lots of delicious smoked salmon.

Our future looked rather bleak. We had hardly any money. David's mother had paid our rent for three months and that was as far ahead as we dared to look."[5]

Up to the time of her marriage to David, Gerda's path had led her to a point where she was an independent and fulfilled woman of thirty-one, with an exciting and artistic job. She was a living example of the twin-principled dictum for happiness which she had embraced, thanks to the Reichian influence: she had found someone to love and share her life with, and she had found a creative focus for her energies. She and David settled down into their chilly London flat to begin their life together and to ponder their next move. Then a major change occurred not because of events in Gerda's life but because of a development in her new husband's. David found a job in Shanghai.

THE ROAD TO SHANGHAI

Finding an answer to my third question: "Where am I going?" is not easy.
Maybe there is no answer!"

Gerda Geddes   Looking for the Golden Needle, p75

The early months of 1949 flew by in a whirlwind of activity. By
April, the newlyweds were en route to China, an adventurous trip by
flying boat with several overnight stays. They usually stayed comfort-
ably in BOAC hostels. In Calcutta they were put up at the Grand Hotel
where Gerda, unaware of the risks, enjoyed a large delicious salad. The
result was her first encounter with dysentery. By the time they arrived
in Hong Kong she was exhausted, drained and ill prepared for the very
humid and sticky April weather. The mysterious East was letting her
know that life might not be without its problems. Then on to Shanghai,
a city which was a distant enigma to Gerda.

"All I knew about Shanghai was that it was an international settlement and that my Uncle Clement, who was captain of a
Norwegian cargo boat, had jumped ship in Shanghai and was not
heard of for ten years. When he returned to Norway he was in
disgrace and he looked all shrunken and yellow. I found him very
mysterious and exciting. I was told that he was picked up down
and out in an opium den, more dead than alive, riddled with
unmentionable diseases. He was given a small cottage on the

estate and shared the rest of his life with a very kind, fat lady who owned a sweet shop in Bergen."[1]

SHANGHAI: GODDESS OR WHORE?

The disparity between two of its nicknames - 'Paris of the East' and 'The Whore of Asia', - is a measure of the contradictions and paradoxes of 1949 Shanghai. Its very origins barely a hundred years earlier grew out of the murky and ambiguous practices of British traders, including William Jardine and James Matheson, who provoked a war by smuggling banned opium into China then extracted from the defeated Emperor the 1842 Treaty of Nanking. It gave them rights to establish a city and trading port which allowed access to the hitherto unavailable and extensive markets and to the raw materials of the Chinese Empire. They were granted a 'concession', which was to remain outside Chinese jurisdiction, on mudflats close to where the Huangpu River meets the Yangtze. There, they raised a city upon a foundation of timber piles, pounded into the mud by the muscle-power of armies of Chinese coolies. A muddy towpath began its transition into The Bund, perhaps the single most famous street in the East, the economic centre of Shanghai, which housed its banks and the headquarters of its biggest trading houses.

Shanghai's growth was spectacular as American and French traders joined the British, and major trading firms bought their own muddy spots to develop a foothold. Ownership of land brought potentially huge returns. By 1935 the price per acre had increased twenty-one thousand times compared to what was paid by the first British settlers in 1843. It was one of the world's spectacular boom stories and attracted a colourful and sometimes exotic cast of characters: traders, investors and speculators; sea captains, shipmates, shipping suppliers; bankers, builders and entrepreneurs; gamblers, chancers, wheelers and dealers; Chinese people drawn by the magnet of the opportunities and, sometimes, the relative safety that awaited within this foreign place; Jewish bankers from Baghdad; White Russians; club owners, merchants, whores, boors, and opium dealers; water carriers, peddlers, beggars and itinerant cooks: a

stunningly varied population of human moths attracted to the blazing
flame of Shanghai.

And at the top sat the mainly British Shanghailanders who also included
a goodly number of Americans and French, plus a few other Europeans.
Some were descendants of the original traders or had links to the trading
houses. Others followed the tradition of young men going east to make
their fortunes. Today it is China's largest city and the world's busiest port.
It remained an International Settlement until 1945 when power of
administration was handed over to the Nationalist Government.

The couple's introduction to the higher echelons of this society
occurred during their first week when they were the guests of David's
new boss, Sir John Keswick, head of Jardine Matheson. At one *soirée*,
they met a woman, famous for giving elaborate parties.

"She engaged David to draw some huge posters *à la Toulouse
Lautrec* and she persuaded me to dance. I choreographed a dance
about my first impressions of the sounds and rhythms of the Far
East, which left everyone puzzled! Slightly embarrassing, but the
result was that David and I were taken up as 'that gifted young couple', an asset to the extremely narrow society.[2]

After a week we moved into our mansion at Granada. Granada
was a compound of Spanish-looking houses built for Jardine's
departmental managers with one much bigger house which was
for us. In three months we had moved from a tiny rented flat in
Notting Hill to a mansion in Shanghai. It seemed almost like a
fairy tale. We had eight servants. Ah Dee, the number-one boy,
Missie's amah (maid), cook, coolie, gardener, garden boy, night
watchman and chauffeur. The house had basic furniture. We only
had to supply our personal bits and pieces. All our wedding
presents and my trousseau were on their way by boat."[3]

They had become Shanghailanders. Gerda's previous knowledge of
China was limited to schoolbook accounts of brave Christian mis-
sionaries, women with tiny bound feet, and baby girls who were
unwanted and thrown in the river. Now she found herself in the

midst of an exotic hubbub that assaulted her senses, her sensibilities, and her health.

"Everything seemed so different, and what fascinated me at first were the different rhythms. Life on the main road that passed our house started about five o'clock in the morning when the so-called night soil workers came out of the town with their human excrement. They took great big barrels out of Shanghai along this road, and then they dumped them onto the fields further out in the country. And you could hear these barrels going out of the town. Once they had gone, movement started in the other direction, vegetable sellers and farmers coming into town to sell their products. They carried vegetables, live chickens, live dogs, everything that they had to sell. They usually had a bicycle with huge baskets on each side. The man of the family led the bicycle and the wife or children steadied baskets, and they were always singing. It woke us in the morning. The man would sing 'rumm, rumra, rumm' and the wife and the children 'rimm, rimm, rimm'. The rhythm of all this singing merged into one main voice, the chorus of the family. They went into the town.

And then a little bit later when that stream had gone, all of the vendors came out of the town again with big bamboo sticks on their shoulders. There was a charcoal burner at the back of the bamboo stick and whatever they were going to sell hung from the front. They set up their shops along the side of the road to sell hot dumplings and tea and all sorts of things. They beat two pieces of bamboo together in a special rhythm to advertise their wares. One person beat out: 'This is tea, this is tea, I'm selling tea,' and somebody else: 'Dumplings, I'm selling dumplings'. And all the time there was a stream of people going this way and a stream going that way. I was fascinated.

As a special treat we also had an old, blind Chinese flute player who came, and we paid him some money. He came every morning and played his flute outside our bedroom window for about half an hour. Now you can imagine, we were just newly married and tremendously in love, and everything was very romantic. We listened to these ancient Chinese folk tunes, and I thought, 'Where am I? This is like a dream, it's like a sort of Aladdin's cave.'

Then of course there was the noise of the crickets, and at night there were fireflies all over the trees and hedges.

At the bottom of our garden we had a great big container filled with night soil. One day I opened it up and it was just full of maggots. The whole thing was moving with maggots. And I thought, 'Oooh, how awful! This goes onto the salads, the lettuce that we eat.' And my stomach got full of those worms as well.

So it was such a tremendous contrast, all the wonderful sounds and rhythms and all these awful things. We got so ill! I had sunstroke, and I had worms, and I had miscarriages. Everything! Everything! And out of all this I made a choreography, I made a dance, which was about Shanghai.

There were lots of beggars out there. One day a beggar woman came and threw her dead child onto my lap and said, "Missy help! Missy help! Missy help!" and I had to throw the dead child out of the window. So there were these terrible extremes. Then it got hotter and hotter and hotter, and in those days there was no air conditioning and we sweated away and I got prickly heat all over my body and mosquito bites swelled up like balls on my legs, and it was altogether very strenuous."[4]

The headquarters of Jardine Matheson, where David worked, was a prominent building on The Bund, the famous business street which towered proudly above the cramped hubbub in the old centre of Shanghai. The Granada compound where they lived was in Hungjao, an exclusive area some eleven miles (eighteen kilometres) southwest of The Bund. A main road joined The Bund to Hungjao. In the city centre it was called Nanking Road, at that time described as a cross between Broadway and Oxford Street, where the rich shopped by day and dined and clubbed by night. Near the old racecourse, now a sports ground, Nanking Road became Bubbling Well Road, then

Yu Yuen Road, as it pointed west towards the fashionable opulence of Hungjao with its golf course and its villas sprawled in their spacious gardens. Along this artery David was driven to and from his office while Gerda stayed at home to organise the staff of their large house at 222 Hungjao Road and to learn the lifestyle expected of a young woman in her position. The newlyweds rose early to enjoy the cool riverside dawn and to prepare them for the stifling and oppressive heat of the day. During one of these excursions Gerda had her spine-tingling first experience of tai-chi.

"My first meeting with the t'ai-chi ch'uan was on a summer's morning in the paddy fields outside Shanghai in 1949. It was very hot in Shanghai in the summer so, in order to get some exercise, my husband and I often went for walks at dawn. The soil around Shanghai is very fertile (they often crop the land three times a year), and with the crops, the nature of the landscape changes. The fields are surrounded by drainage canals, and it is very flat, but when they grow gaw-liang (cattle fodder) which looks rather like maize and is very tall, the landscape suddenly becomes rather secretive and mysterious, the canals become hidden and at dawn there is a slight mist. On one of these hot misty mornings, my husband and I went out, and, as we turned a corner where there was a bend in the canal, we saw an old Chinese man by the water. Beside him, in a gilded cage, was a mynah bird. He was moving very slowly, performing some incredibly beautiful dance-like movements which were reflected in the water of the canal. He seemed so totally absorbed in what he was doing that he paid not the slightest attention to us. We just stood there watching, quite mesmerised."[5]

A prosperous, exciting, interesting, if sometimes physically uncomfortable, life was beckoning in this strange and enigmatic land. And below its mysterious surface, certainly below the awareness of the young couple who had gaily flown off from their roots to this enclave of east-west trade and business, was a country in the grip of a civil war. The pattern of Gerda's life was once more about to be affected by military conflict.

THE FALL OF
SHANGHAI

The mythical wild horse was a ferocious, saw-toothed animal, capable of tearing a tiger to pieces, often associated with the Tartars and the Mongols who invaded China from the north. In the context of Tai-chi Ch'uan, one learns the need for great gentleness if one is to approach this fierce creature close enough to part its mane.

Gerda Geddes   LOOKING FOR THE GOLDEN NEEDLE, p60

Gerda and David watched the old man doing t'ai-chi by the canal in April of 1949. By then, Mao Tse-tung's Communist army already controlled Northern China and was massing on the north bank of the Yangtze River.

CHINESE CIVIL WAR APRIL 1927-MAY 1950: TECHNICALLY STILL ONGOING

This long and complicated conflict was waged between the armies of the Chinese Nationalist Party and the Communist Party of China. It began life as a cooperative venture when, with Soviet assistance, the large Nationalist Party and the fledgling Communist Party formed an alliance in 1923 to defeat the warlords who had seized control of most of Northern China. However by 1926 the Nationalists had divided into left- and right-wing factions and in 1927 Chiang Kai-shek, the right–wing Nationalist leader, initiated hostilities by purging Communists in Shanghai on April 12 when he arrested and executed hundreds of people.

After Chiang's Nationalists captured Beijing from the warlords in June 1928, he was in charge of most of eastern China and his government was internationally recognised as the sole legitimate government of China. The Communist cause seemed in decline, although a new potential figurehead was emerging in Mao Tse-tung who had led a peasant insurrection in Hunan province. During the early 1930s, the Nationalist army carried out several campaigns against the Communists, with mixed success. The Communist heartland was in several 'Red' areas in south eastern China and in 1931, with the connivance of the Soviet government, a 'Red' state had been declared, based in the town of Ruijin in Jiangxi province, under the rule of 'Chairman' Mao, although it was not recognised by any other country including its sponsor, the USSR. By 1934, Chiang's Nationalist army had encircled the Jiangxi 'Red' region with a system of blockhouses and was preparing to tighten the noose on the Communists. Instead, Mao walked his way into the history books. He slipped out of the trap and set out on the Long March, a year-long four thousand mile (six thousand kilometre) retreat to Shaanxi province in the far north of the country where there was another Communist base. Only one-tenth of the army of 80,000 made it to Shaanxi.

Both sides in the Civil War attempted to create an alliance during the Second Sino-Japanese War (1937-1945) but it was at best half-hearted and ended following a clash in 1941 when the Nationalists defeated the Communist army. Generally, though, Chiang Kai-shek's troops suffered greater losses than Mao's during the Japanese war and when, in the last month of World War Two, Soviet forces invaded Manchuria and took the surrender of 700,000 Japanese troops, they handed all of their armaments over to the Chinese Communists. Although the Nationalist army subsequently received substantial aid from the United States, their morale did not match that of the Communists and the country under their control was suffering from rampant corruption, political chaos and hyperinflation.

By late 1949 the Communist People's Liberation Army had swept north-south through the country and, on October 1st, Mao Tse-tung proclaimed the People's Republic of China. Chiang Kai-shek had fled to Taiwan (taking with him the large gold and silver reserves from the vaults of the Bank of

China in Shanghai¹) where he proclaimed the city of Taipei the temporary
capital of the Republic of China. The fighting ended with the Communist
conquest of Hainin Island in May 1950.

With hindsight, it seems remarkable that Gerda knew so little about
the military and political background of China but not so strange
when put into the context of post-war Europe. Matters much closer
to home had dominated her life as a student, dancer, Resistance member and refugee during the war. Since then, she had thrived in a creative and stimulating job which had consumed her interests, consolidated
and developed much of what she had learned, and taken her to London.
She had met David, fallen in love, and got married. His finding an
exciting and well-paid job in the Far East had seemed like the greatest of good fortune, an answer to the question of how they would now
spend their lives together. Why would anyone offer such a job and
transport them around the world if there were any problems, any dan-
gers in Shanghai? And, compared to a Europe which was struggling to
recover from the destruction of war -the losses, the hardships, the
rationing, the austerity and lack of non-essentials - Shanghai seemed
like a haven of luxury, abundance, style and wealth.

So for the Shanghailanders living in comfortable opulence, a civil
war that had been rumbling away for decades seemed of little interest
or significance. It was difficult to understand the twists and the com-
plexities of a tangled struggle in which the two sides had sometimes
been allies and sometimes deadly enemies; who seemed at one point
in history to have shared aims and at another to kill one another in large
numbers. And, to the Shanghai elite, the city existed to allow them to
make money through the day and to wine, dine, and enjoy their leisure
at night. Shanghai was their creation: it had grown and developed inde-
pendently of the China which seemed to be eternally in the throes of
a civil squabble.

And there was a particularly British attitude towards the approach
of China's civil war to Shanghai's doorstep. Late in 1948 when the
Americans were urging women and children to leave, the British

advised people to stay.[2] For her part, Gerda was too excited by her remarkable first contact with t'ai-chi to pay much heed to the storm clouds.

"For me it was the discovery of the t'ai-chi which was my main interest, not the political situation. The t'ai-chi was like a flame of excitement that happened when I first saw the old man."[3]

Furthermore, Shanghailanders with links to the large trading and financial houses and access to foreign currency were largely immune to the consequences of hyperinflation which was threatening the country with economic collapse because of Chang Kai-shek's reckless printing of paper money. In 1944, notes for one hundred and eighty-nine billion Chinese dollars were put into circulation. By the end of 1946 that figure had increased to more than four-point-five trillion Chinese dollars. Inflation spiralled until bank notes were literally worth less than the paper they were printed on, and in 1948 a paper mill was reported to have bought up eight hundred cases of notes ranging from hundred-dollar to two-thousand-dollar bills which it used as raw material in the manufacture of paper. Sometime in 1948, the conversion rate for an American dollar to a Chinese dollar passed the one million mark, and by early 1949 it reached six million. Stalls were erected outside banks so that people could spend their large bundles of Chinese paper money before prices went up again.[4]

For David and Gerda, literally paying each of their staff millions of Chinese dollars a month, the total monthly cost of their domestic retinue was equivalent to only a few pounds sterling.

On the morning of 20th April 1949, Communist artillery on the north bank of the Yangtze opened fire on a British frigate. HMS Amethyst was making its way upriver to Nanking, the Nationalist capital, with supplies for the British Embassy and to replace HMS Consort as guard ship. The timing of the Amethyst's journey had raised a few eyebrows in Shanghai where there was some knowledge of the Communist's declared plan to cross the river in force at midnight on the 20th unless the Nationalists accepted a surrender ultimatum including the handing over of Chiang Kai-shek. Was it a piece of misplaced gunboat diplomacy or, as with the Shanghailanders, was there an unwillingness to accept the military and political reality that was taking place? Sadly, the outcome of the 'Yangtze Incident' was all too real: before it was over three other Royal Navy ships had been involved and a total of forty-two British sailors killed. The Communist army crossed the river and quickly captured Nanking. On 23rd April the retreating Nationalists declared martial law and a 10.00pm curfew in Shanghai. The city, which traditionally had acted as a haven for civilian refugees at times of unrest, had until now been spared a large-scale military presence. Now it swarmed with restless, nervous Nationalist forces under the command of General Tang En-po, a hard-line supporter of Chiang Kai-shek who had by this time 'resigned' and fled to Taiwan with the gold reserves.

The city descended into disorder and brutality. Nationalist officers requisitioned family homes for themselves and their entourages. Businesses of all kinds, from offices to bars, were forced to close as their premises were taken over to billet the troops who roamed the streets. Under the martial law conditions Nationalist soldiers were allowed free and preferential access to public transport and to cinemas and were ready to hand out punishment or death to anyone unwise enough to protest. Robbing and looting were commonplace. Suspected Communists were rounded up and had their brains blown out in public street executions watched by large crowds.

Mao Tse-tung spent the next month consolidating his position and was content to leave Shanghai as it was for the time being. Then, on Tuesday 24th May, a major Communist advance began from the direction of Hungjao where Gerda was at home.

"I experienced a moment of great panic. The fight for Shanghai was moving nearer. We could hear the guns and the shooting from our house. I was alone there with the servants. We got a message on the telephone from David, saying: 'Drive at once to Shanghai to the ICI compound where you will be safe', so the driver, Ping Liang, and I set out. We drove to the Bamboo

Curtain at the railway crossing into Shanghai where we were stopped by a crowd of thousands of hysterical Chinese carrying all their belongings on their backs or in wheelbarrows or bicycles, saying that they were told that Shanghai was going to be bombed and that they had to get out of there quickly. Ping Liang panicked and tried to get out of the car to join them. I panicked and thought I would be trampled to death, but then I clung to Ping Liang and said that Master's orders were to bring me to the ICI compound and if he did not do that, he would lose his job."[5]

The 'Bamboo Curtain' at which Gerda and her driver had arrived was a wooden palisade that had been hastily built, supposedly to guard the inner city but the rumour was that it was more a means of expanding the fortunes of local timber merchants. It was unlikely to halt an army which was inexorably 'liberating' the whole of China. It did however create a serious bottleneck against Gerda's progress in the face of chaos exacerbated by conflicting advice.

"The Bamboo Curtain was the boundary. There was one main road coming into Shanghai and there was a gate that everyone had to get through. There was terrible congestion as six million people tried to get out of Shanghai and one hundred thousand people tried to get in. Conflicting news bulletins were broadcast. The Chinese were urged to get out of Shanghai and take with them as much chattels and goods as they could. The Europeans were told to get into Shanghai because it was said that Shanghai was not going to be bombed and the Europeans would be safe in Shanghai. And outside Shanghai it was totally lawless. Our house was outside; we were on the wrong side of the Bamboo Curtain. That was an awful moment. I can remember feeling so exhausted inside myself because it wasn't all that long since I had been a refugee myself and gone into Sweden. That was something that had made a big impression inside my body. And then when we were trying to get inside Shanghai I could remember thinking: 'Not again, I don't want to do this again!'"[6]

Whether in response to the threat of losing his job, or in response to his mistress's plight, Ping Liang stayed with her, but not without some persuading:

"The awful thing was I couldn't drive at that time and I had to make the driver do what I said. I managed it. When he heard all the Chinese had been told to get out of Shanghai he wanted to get out as well with his people. And I almost had to take him and hold him and make him go into Shanghai. Somehow or another our servants didn't want to go with the mass of the Chinese out into the countryside, they wanted to come with me. They weren't in that car but somehow or another they managed to get themselves into Shanghai. That was quite a moment."[7]

Gerda and her driver eventually reached the safety of the ICI compound. David however was still at Jardine Matheson's headquarters on the Bund. It was clear that the Nationalist army was in full retreat and a general exodus by sea had already begun. A rearguard action to fight for more time was based on the Garden Bridge which crossed Soochow Creek at the far end of the Bund, and which was overlooked by the Jardine Matheson offices where several senior staff were trapped but had a grandstand view of the final skirmishing. One of the watchers was Gerda's husband, David. Another was his colleague David Middleditch whose dramatic account, reported in Noel Barber's *The Fall of Shanghai*, contrasts the chaos of mortars and machine guns in the street with the opulence of John Keswick's office living quarters where houseboy-served cocktails and meals were occasionally interrupted by stray bullets whistling through the window.[8]

Shanghai had fallen to Mao's People's Liberation Army, in such a short time and with so few casualties that it was difficult to escape the conclusion that the Nationalists had been more concerned with escaping it than defending it.

HOSTAGES OF
MAO TSE-TUNG

Later, talking to my friends about what I had seen, I tried to get some information, but was told that it (t'ai-chi) was one of those strange things that the Chinese did. They called it 'Shadow Boxing', and it was not for foreigners. I came across Shadow Boxing again in the parks of Shanghai, but it was not anything like as common then as it is now, and I do not recall seeing a single woman performing.

During this period in China the Communists were taking over, and they were not very friendly towards us, so most Chinese stayed well away from us.

Gerda Geddes: LOOKING FOR THE GOLDEN NEEDLE, p28

For the next two years, Gerda and David were effectively hostages in a Shanghai that changed very quickly under Communist rule. From the first day there was a clampdown on bribery, corruption, black marketeering, prostitution, and other practices that had been features of the city's richly chaotic life-style.

Change was effected by a carrot and stick approach. Initially a Communist soldier or official would patiently explain the errors of the offender's ways but a brutal fate could await those disinclined to listen. Persistent profiteering black marketeers were taken to the racecourse for public execution by the 'Watch Chiang' method. The offender was hoisted by pulley to the top of a high pole. The Communist holding the rope shouted "Can you see General Chiang?" Then, on receiving a faint "No!" he released the rope and the wretch undergoing the ordeal plummeted to the ground. If the first drop was not fatal, the ritual was repeated. News soon spread. Black marketeering disappeared and incredulous Shanghailanders suddenly found that prices had stabilised.[1]

The foreign community, not always aware of the techniques being used, was intrigued by the methodical way in which Shanghai's ideology changed. Gerda watched the changes with interest.

"There were certainly things that you could approve of. The first and most important was that the corruption, which was absolutely phenomenal, disappeared very quickly. And in the beginning the Communists were very law abiding and they put law and order into lots of very difficult and complicated situations."[2]

Despite the apparent casualness with which the Communist advance had been viewed, significant numbers of the British colony had left before the fall of Shanghai. Those remaining now faced a different life. Movement was restricted, exit visas denied and, sometimes, homes requisitioned. Gerda and David were not allowed to return to their home initially because of a strict 7.00am to 8.00pm curfew which also banned Westerners from travelling more than five kilometres beyond the Bamboo Curtain that surrounded Shanghai. Then, after many weeks in the ICI compound, they were given leave to go back to 222 Hungjao Road.

"Soldiers had been stationed in our house. We found lots of hand grenades and other kinds of weapons when we returned at last. I simply can't remember what happened to our belongings in the time we were out of the house but we got them back. Somehow or other the Chinese must have removed most of the things and looked after them."[3]

Although they were back within the house that had seemed such a dream home just a few weeks earlier, circumstances were now very different. Curfew and travel restrictions remained in place and two armed guards were mounted outside at the gates to control movements to and from the exclusive compound in which they lived. Life indoors had also changed.

"There were many subjects that David and I couldn't talk about, because we never knew who could be listening on the other side of the door. Or whether they would say to the authorities that we were against Communism. If you said anything against the regime people could report you to the authorities. And then they would quite quickly come and lock you up. I remember clearly feeling: 'Gosh this is too soon after the Second World War for me to find myself in the same position again'. Because it had been the same in Norway. If you worked for the Resistance you were always looking behind your back to see if there was anyone following you or anyone was listening to what you said. That was very much what happened in China as well. And I thought that I had certainly had enough of that kind of existence."[4]

One paradox was that Shanghai, in keeping with its glittering reputation, contained huge stocks of imported luxury goods. Gerda could buy unlimited amounts of best quality wines and spirits, caviar was available at knockdown prices, while many basic foodstuffs became hard to find. The Chinese do not share the European dependence on dairy products and supplies of milk, cheese and butter effectively dried up following the large scale slaughter of dairy herds by the Communists.

Fundamental changes were occurring within the business realm where the freewheeling capitalist boom that was Shanghai did not sit easily with the Communist ethics of the new city rulers. And the new relationship was an unequal one. Where once the taipans, the heads of the large business houses, had been all-powerful, now they had to bow the knee to diktats that included new and heavy taxes as well as employment laws which forbade the sacking of workers and allowed those previously sacked to re-enter the payroll whether there was a job for them or not. Workplace trade unions became compulsory and there were mandatory wage rises to levels much higher than previously. The methods used to obtain compliance with the new regime were often heavy handed.

"The huge firm of Jardine, Matheson & Co was taken over by the

Chinese and endless, difficult negotiations were taking place in which David was very much involved. If the English did not agree with the Chinese terms, they were not sent to prison, but were locked up in their offices very often without food and water. When David left in the office car early in the mornings (all the directors and senior staff had to share the same car because there was very little petrol) I never knew whether I would see him again in the evening. Often he had to spend the night in the office. I was pregnant at the time and had visions of being abandoned in China and walking down to Hong Kong carrying a baby!"[5]

To make matters worse, Chiang Kai-shek had placed the Yangtze estuary under naval blockade and his warships prevented shipping from entering or leaving Shanghai. High-powered businessmen, used to spending their day negotiating important deals, twiddled their thumbs, watched their reserves dwindling, and cabled back to head-quarters for more cash.

"Many people obviously left Shanghai at this stage. But for some it was not straightforward. If you had any debts or outstanding business arrangements you were not permitted to leave, and we heard many sad tales of people jumping out of windows or taking their own lives in other ways."[6]

The prohibition on leaving applied to people like David who were in the higher echelons of large businesses. And so Gerda sat it out in the Hungjao mansion whilst luckier friends and neighbours were allowed to leave. To make matters worse, the naval blockade meant that incoming and outgoing mail was very patchy but the sense of being isolated and forgotten provoked a typical response in the British community.

"All entertainment came to a standstill, so we had to rely on our own resources. We had two friends who worked for the British Council and they were a great inspiration. They got books out of the library and we had many sessions together when we arranged play readings and read poetry. It was very rewarding and most enjoyable. We really had a go at T.S. Eliot, Shakespeare, Ibsen and others, so something good came out of the situation."[7]

Gerda made her own unique contribution to the community's cultural life. In a talk entitled 'Where Dancing and Psychology Meet' she spoke to the British Woman's Association about her work with mentally ill patients and traumatised war victims in Norway and Sweden. And it was not her only creative activity: on 26th April 1950, after almost a year of living as a hostage, Gerda gave birth to her daughter, Jane.

"Towards the end of April 1950 our baby was due to be born. I had a German doctor in Shanghai, some distance from Hungjao. One night I started having contractions. We rang the doctor about 10pm and he said: 'Go back to sleep! Don't panic. First babies always take a long time in arriving. Because of the curfew I cannot come to you until the morning'. By three o'clock my pains became much worse and we rang him again and he said we had to try and break the curfew and he would try and get himself to the hospital. So we set out in the car and took Ah Dee with us as interpreter. As we drove out of the gates we were stopped by the guard who told me to open my window. He put his bayonet on my tummy and told me to get out of the car and go back to the house. Brave Ah Dee came to our rescue and said: 'This Missie just now have the baby, must go hospital!' so much to our relief the soldier let us go. When we came to the Bamboo Curtain we were stopped again, but again Ah Dee's magic worked and we eventually arrived at the hospital. After a long and painful struggle on my part a healthy daughter was born."[8]

By now, even the most committed and fervent Shanghailander hoped for the rare and elusive exit visa, which was often conditional upon their company arranging an exchange for an employee of similar status. When a visa was granted, the lucky recipient was given a rollicking, if slightly envious, send-off. Gerda's family archives contain a comic celebratory postcard dated October 1950. In it, the Jardine Matheson hostages, their real faces pasted onto cartoon bodies, peer around the Bamboo Curtain as Sir John Keswick and his wife Clare fly over it to freedom. In the bottom left hand corner David is waving while Gerda looks on enigmatically.

The British community had dropped from four thousand to twelve hundred people by Christmas 1950. It was the second Christmas Gerda and David had spent under Communist rule. And it was to be their last.

ESCAPE TO
HONG KONG

It is as if the T'ai-chi Ch'uan says 'Always remember that as long as you are in this life you must live through the wholeness of yourself, not just the body in one place and the spirit in another.'

Gerda Geddes   *LOOKING FOR THE GOLDEN NEEDLE*, p64

In January 1951 Gerda, David and their nine-month-old daughter Jane were granted exit visas, a development made possible because another Jardine Matheson employee agreed to swap places with David. The family now faced a rail journey of more than seven hundred and fifty miles (twelve hundred kilometres) under the watchful, and unfriendly, eyes of armed guards: a journey which could have gone seriously wrong had it not been for Ah Dee who had been allowed to leave with them.

"For nearly two years David and I were kept as hostages in Shanghai. We were not allowed to leave unless someone else would come in and take our place. Eventually a Jardine director from Hong Kong was willing to come. He was an elderly man with a wife and no children. So we packed our bags and prepared to take a train to Canton, which in those days took two days and two nights. We were told to bring our own food for the journey and food for the baby and I was allowed to bring the baby in a cot.

On a cold and sleety morning in January 1951, about 5.30am, we arrived at the railway station. We were inspected by guards and the first thing they did was to empty the baby's cot where I had put all her food and big thermoses filled with boiled water and all her clothes and nappies for the journey. The guards took the nappies out one by one, threw them on the filthy, muddy ground and stepped on them. Then they emptied all the water out of the thermoses and took both the food and the cot away. They also took all our food and luggage away, so we eventually entered the train with absolutely nothing. Fortunately our beloved Ah Dee had been given permission to come with us and he entered the train unnoticed.

It was a very long train. We were the only Europeans on the train and had a whole carriage to ourselves where the most excruciating Chinese music was played non-stop. It was too loud for us to carry on a conversation; we could just hear the baby screaming!

Eventually Ah Dee found us. We had nothing, no luggage, no food, no clothes, no nappies. Fortunately Ah Dee's wife had given him plenty of provisions for the journey so he shared everything with us, even his shaving brush!

I asked the conductor if I could boil some water for Jane but he said: 'Not allowed, get water from tap on station', so at the next stop I managed to get some rusty water from a tap on the platform which I had to give her and we also managed to buy some bananas and that is what she lived on till we reached Hong Kong. Fortunately Jane suffered no ill effects from her sparse and unsterilised diet, but the experience left me utterly exhausted.

When we eventually reached Hong Kong safely and were met by a Jardine representative at the border, we felt truly liberated. We had escaped from a real nightmare."[1]

Fifty-five years later, Gerda could vividly recall the feelings this journey had provoked.

"I still remember every single nappy being taken up by the

soldiers, put down onto the muddy floor and stepped upon. Then they were thrown away. People with guns and in uniform; it was very frightening. But the worst thing was how Jane was treated, because a mother with a baby becomes like a lioness. I would have put a rifle to the hearts of those Communist soldiers if it had been possible. I was hopping mad. And having to give her polluted water was terrible."[2]

Arrival at the Hong Kong border did not bring an end to their hostile treatment. Given the summary way in which their personal effects had been taken from them before they boarded the train, they were initially delighted to see some boxes of treasured belongings being unloaded from the freight section. Their pleasure was short-lived.

"Before the Communist takeover we had already bought some artefacts in Shanghai at what was called the Thieves' Market. At that time it was possible to find some real gems. We had found quite a lot of figures like that (indicates a life-sized Chinese painted pottery head on a shelf) in the Thieves' Market, grave figures made of mud. These belongings had been professionally packed and the packer said: 'This will travel anywhere, it will never break.' Then at the Hong Kong border everything which was beautifully and carefully wrapped up was unpacked again. The border police took it all out, threw in on the ground and then threw it all back into the packing cases so that when it arrived in Hong Kong it was pulverised. David had a very big and treasured collection of gramophone records, classical music. They were all broken and I think he was more worried about that than about the Chinese treasures. So we lost most of our belongings."[3]

The exhausted couple, their trusted and indispensable Ah Dee, and baby Jane, smelly but none the worse for her ordeal, crossed the border into Hong Kong and another new life.

HONG KONG LIFE

The second part…is concerned with achievement, finding your strength and your balance, and reaching maturity.

Gerda Geddes   LOOKING FOR THE GOLDEN NEEDLE, p77

After the privations of the previous two years and the nightmarish train journey from Shanghai, Gerda and David were soon once again living a very comfortable life on The Peak, the exclusive residential area high above the cramped confusion of Hong Kong.

"Strawberry Hill, our house on the Peak, was enormous. The rooms had very tall ceilings because of the heat and every room was huge. All the way around the house was a veranda with windows. A long corridor led to the large double bedrooms, each with its own bathrooms and veranda. At the end of the corridor was the nursery which was very big indeed."[1]

HONG KONG

Like Shanghai, Hong Kong was one of Britain's victory prizes from the Opium Wars. But the two places had very different status. Under the 1842 Treaty of Nanking, Shanghai was one of the treaty ports which were opened up for trade under conditions that were very favourable to British traders and businessmen. At the same time, Hong Kong Island, along with a few small neighbouring islands, was ceded by China to the British Empire and became a Crown Colony. Under the 1860 Convention of Beijing, which ended the Second Opium War, Britain was granted a perpetual lease of

Kowloon Peninsula. Britain remained uneasy about its ability to defend the colony unless the surrounding areas were also under its control and, in 1898, secured a 99-year lease of the New Territories, which significantly expanded the size of the Hong Kong Crown Colony. The lease would expire at midnight on June 30th 1997.

In 1982, fifteen years before the New Territories lease was due to expire, talks began between the British Government and the Peoples' Republic of China. Margaret Thatcher, the British Prime Minister, hoped for agreement to a continued British presence. Instead, China refused to recognise the earlier treaties which it considered unfair and unequal. It also refused to recognise British sovereignty in Hong Kong and wanted the New Territories returned to Chinese control. But, from a pragmatic point of view, the Chinese also realised that the reintegration of Hong Kong, with its free market economy, was not a simple matter. The result was the so-called One Country, Two Systems solution. On July 1st 1997, Hong Kong was handed over to China where it operates as a Special Administrative Region (SAR) of the Peoples' Republic of China.

As a Crown Colony, Hong Kong did not develop the same freewheeling and swashbuckling ethic as pre-Communist Shanghai. It was nonetheless an extremely important centre of trade and commerce and, by the time of Gerda's arrival in 1951, its economy was experiencing unprecedented growth as many foreign firms moved their offices from Shanghai and as skills and capital flooded in along with the large numbers of refugees from Communist China.

David, with considerable difficulty, had managed to negotiate exit visas for all of Ah Dee's family. Soon the Geddes's comforts within their new home were being attended to by a familiar domestic retinue, a little Chinese community which, in addition to looking after all of the families household needs, fed Gerda's hunger for understanding more about the Far East.

"I was drawn towards the Chinese, absolutely, instinctively. I was very ignorant of their culture but it exerted a pull on me. We were in the Far East for nine years and from the first day we arrived in

Shanghai until the last day we left Hong Kong we had the same servants. Ah Dee, the number one boy, was the head, like a butler. He engaged his entire family for us. They lived in servant quarters at the back of the house. He lived there with his wife and children and his wife's parents and an uncle: the whole clan settled itself down with us.

When we lived in Shanghai we had eight servants and, with their relatives, there was a little community in the back part of the house. We never knew exactly how many 'guests' there were, how many were being given free housing. I hardly ever went there: it was much better if I didn't know what was going on. I never inquired. I just thought as long as they're doing what they're supposed to do for us, I'm not going to interfere in their life or try and convert them to western ways. That worked very well.

My interest in Chinese culture came not from the upper class Chinese but from ordinary people, from these servants who had a natural grace or a natural beauty to them. Ah Dee became a friend. He was so cultured he put me to shame. The way that he used his hands when he handled precious objects, for instance, or when he arranged flowers. He was vastly superior to me and I thought: that is something that is inherited; it's in his genes, this way that he treats things. And I admired him very much.

We talked about all sorts of things, Ah Dee and I, but he was still very much a servant, so that if, for instance, we went out to parties at night we asked Ah Dee to 'look see children'. We then discovered that when the children were asleep, Ah Dee brought a little futon and slept outside the nursery door. He just slept there, listening out with one ear for the children. So I always felt they would be safe with him. They often disappeared into the servants' quarters at the back, playing with the children and eating Chinese food.

When we lived in Hungjao village just outside Shanghai the local people wanted to have dragon dances. We had an enormous lawn and Ah Dee came and asked if I would allow them to have a dragon dance there. This was in 1949 before the Communists. So we had a big dragon dance display in the garden and all the people from the village came along and danced there. That was really the beginning of my education, seeing all of these things and getting a feeling for how the Chinese people behaved.

Then the village wise woman came one day and said 'Oh, want to help missy. Give missy massage. Chinese massage.' Her massage was out of this world. Wonderful. I never had such pleasure in all my life. A lot of what I learned from her I put together as a massage course that I used to give to the dancers at The Place and they absolutely adored it."[2]

Gerda's curiosity about the life and culture of the ordinary Chinese and her benign interest in what went on in the servants' quarters was not typical of Peak housewives.

"There were a few Western women who were sympathetic, but most looked on the Chinese as servants and gave orders, so there wasn't quite that natural flow. Very often they lost their servants and then they would have to start

Gerda, David and Jane, Hong Kong 1952

with a new lot. Our claim to fame was that we kept this family for the whole time, so it was very harmonious.

We had a mutual trust, and that was because I accepted that their concept of honesty was quite different from our concept of honesty. The cook went out to market and bought all the food. Whatever he spent, he would keep a small percentage of that money for himself. He made a bill and ticked off everything he had bought. At the end of the bill there were always two items called 'doggy meat' and 'catty fishes'. Doggy meat and catty fishes was his 'kumshaw', that was his cut. Most of the time we didn't have a dog, but that didn't matter. Doggy meat and catty fishes at the end of every bill. I very much accepted that, and thought it was a wonderful system.

There's another aspect of the Chinese character which is very interesting and that is loss of face. For example, our cook was a bit of an alcoholic and sometimes his cooking suffered as a result. One night we sat there and we waited and we waited for dinner to be served and nothing happened. Ah Dee came in and said 'Dinner tonight a little bit late. Master wait a little.' And eventually he came in and served dinner. It turned out the cook had been out on the binge and was fast asleep in the kitchen. Ah Dee had to make all the food, pretending it came from the cook. Every morning the cook used to come in with my breakfast, bringing with him his little book and we would plan the day's menu.

The morning after the late dinner, the cook came in backwards. He walked through the door backwards, and walked towards my bed backwards. He said 'Very sorry, missee, Today cook no face, no face. No can look missee. Cook last night very very drunk. No makee dinner. What Mister and Missee want today?' And all the time he stood with his back to me because he had lost his dignity, had lost his face and that, to a Chinese, is a terrible tragedy. For a long time he went about with his eyes to the ground, until he managed to get his face together again."[3]

Her interest in the culture and life of the ordinary people received a boost when, on David's initiative, they chartered a traditional wooden junk for Sunday picnic cruises.

"While we were in Hong Kong we hired a fishing boat. They didn't fish on Sundays and David hired this boat. The contract was that the boat should be clean and there should be two people there to sail and steer it. Every Sunday we used to go out and sail off to empty beaches all over the place. There was nobody else there in those days, it seemed we had the whole of the China

Sea to ourselves, just David and me and the girls and a couple who were very good friends of ours who always came with us. They had a child as well. We had the most fantastic time on this boat. You had to sit on the deck. Although there was just supposed to be two crew, when the boat had taken off and we were out at sea, you would see little heads sticking up from underneath. Here we discovered a whole Chinese family. They were not supposed to be there but as we went on they all came up. We talked to them. Ah Dee was the interpreter. They lived on the boat. We brought sumptuous picnics with us and Ah Dee would come and serve like a proper butler, gin and tonic on a silver salver. Then after about a year of communicating with these boat people, we said that they had to come up and see how we lived. So we invited the whole family group; there were the grandparents, the parents and lots of little children.

They all came up to us. They came into the dining room and we were going to sit down. We discovered that none of the people could sit on chairs. We asked them to sit down and they looked big question marks at one another. Then they sat down on the chairs with their feet underneath them. They sat cross-legged on the chairs and must have felt rather uncomfortable. We took them around and they saw beds. All the children jumped onto the beds, about six or seven children, jumping and jumping, having the time of their lives. The adults said: 'No can sleep on this, so soft. Bad for back. No can sleep on this.'

We became really friendly with them and they invited us to a wedding which the whole clan attended. They were called Hakka people and they are different from the people who live on land. Their home is on their boats. So David and I were invited to this wedding which went on for three or four days. We saw all of the ceremonies which they did, how they prayed and the food they ate.

At the wedding feast, all the women were at one side of the boat and all the men were sitting on the main deck, being very majestic and in charge of everything. Ah Dee was with us because he had to interpret and when we were on board he said 'What we do with missy? She go with women over there or she go with men?' This was a major conflict. What was going to be done about me? Then I said I would like to hold David's hand, I would like to sit with David. So I was allowed to sit with him. All the other women came and they waited on us. I was in a quandary because I thought maybe I'd done the wrong thing, maybe I should have gone over to the women because I probably hindered the life of the men. It was quite difficult because I obviously didn't know the custom.

The fisherman's wife had twins which, for them, was very bad luck. How can they bring up two children? They gave the weakest twin to the grandmother to look after and feed. So one was always on the mother's back and the other on the grandmother's back. Somehow or other the grandmother managed to keep the poorly twin alive. We saw them until they were about four years old and all of a sudden it was all right because the weakest baby had survived babyhood and was now accepted as a proper child."[4]

These experiences and adventures contrasted with social life in the European community. Apart from a small number of friends - two women who were painters and a German doctor with an interest in t'ai-chi - Gerda did not form close relationships.

"Maybe it was because I was Norwegian, I don't know, but neither I, nor my husband for that matter, made very good friends with the Europeans. We didn't like this attitude of being superior and looking down on others, that didn't go down well with us.

They knew that we went out on the boat but they didn't know the experiences we had. They came round to thinking it was a good idea, actually, but by the time they accepted it you couldn't get these fishing boats anymore. So we were very lucky about that. There was something about David. He was very ebullient, very open and generous with people, warm hearted, and I think when you work from the heart it comes across. It made him very popular amongst the Chinese that we met."[5]

After her second daughter, Harriet was born in 1953, Gerda found other ways of avoiding the social round on the Peak.

"The children were my first priority in life. I was a natural mother so all of these years in Hong Kong were mainly occupied with looking after children. When my eldest daughter was ready to go to nursery school, she objected to that. I tried to put her into three different nursery schools but all the teachers said, no, this child, she doesn't fit in here. And she cried when I left her and I couldn't stand it. So I thought, the solution to this is that I start a nursery school.

So for six years I ran a nursery school in Hong Kong. And it was a great excuse for me to stay away from women's coffee parties in the morning. Women had so little to do with all their servants so they played tennis and bridge and they had coffee parties. I wasn't interested in any of those things, so I used my nursery school as an excuse. I also found a trained nursery school woman in Hong Kong who was very pleased to be offered a job. She did all the teaching and I took charge of dancing and music. We did lots and lots of songs with movement and the children loved that. I was also the headmistress!

The nursery school was held on the veranda. So little Harriet started nursery school when she started to walk. From about the age of one-and-a-half she went to school every day. It was a very popular school with about twelve children aged between three and five."[6]

TREASURED GUESTS

The danger is, if you have created a 'Masterpiece', that you might put yourself on a pedestal and feel that you are better than others. But here the T'ai-chi Chuan interferes and tries to teach you that although you are unique and special, you must never forget that you are part of a wholeness, so you must try not to get stuck in a part but always see the greatness of the whole.

Gerda Geddes   LOOKING FOR THE GOLDEN NEEDLE, p78

During their hostage years in Shanghai, Gerda and David had been cut off from family and friends. Visits from abroad were impossible and postal services in and out of China unreliable. Socially, they had been locked into the dwindling remnants of the expatriate community, a milieu that did not particularly suit Gerda and where sometimes she felt neither comfortable nor at home. But now, in Hong Kong, the wider world re-opened to them.

Early in 1951, once they had established themselves in their new home, they made a prolonged trip to Europe. The usual pattern for people in jobs such as David's was to spend three years abroad followed by six months holiday, but in the Geddes's case the leave period was brought forward. They went first to Bergen where baby Jane took her first tottering steps at the knees of her grandmother Lydia while Gerda immersed herself in the glow of friends and family. Then to London where simple family pleasures, like a visit to Regent's Park Zoo with Jane's other grandmother, Lady Geddes, were balanced by evenings of glittering socialising, dining, theatre-going. The contrasts with Communist Shanghai could not have been greater.

They returned to Hong Kong late in 1951, almost three years after the newlyweds had made their exciting journey eastwards by flying boat. This time the pace was relaxed, the style stately: a slow boat trip aboard the Glen Orchy.

Social traffic was two-way. Following the birth of their second daughter Harriet in 1953, Gerda's mother arrived to welcome her new granddaughter. She spent three months in Hong Kong and shared a family Christmas before leaving. Lydia was a daring woman, and enthusiastically took part in a trip to Macau.

MACAU (MACAO) – LAS VEGAS OF THE ORIENT

Macau was the first European possession in China and was, when handed back by Portugal in 1999, the last to return to the host nation. The peninsula, with its attendant islands of Taipa and Coloane, lies forty-three miles (seventy kilometres) across the Pearl River estuary to the southwest of Hong Kong. In the mid-1550s Portuguese sailors settled there after reputedly going ashore on the pretext of needing to dry sea-soaked goods. For many years, almost all the trade between Europe and China passed through its ports as the monsoons drove ships north-east for the spring and summer and sent them home again in the winter. It gained a reputation for opium, piracy, gambling and prostitution to rival any other world port. Hong Kong and Macao were the hubs of the opium trade which flourished in a freewheeling world devoid of taxes or trade controls. Gambling was legalised in the 1850s and by the late 19th century Macau was a European oasis beckoning those drawn to gaming, opium, girls and the gold that went with them. The 20th century brought organised casinos and the introduction of western gambling. Although it has now returned politically to the Chinese motherland, Macau has, like Hong Kong, been accorded Special Administrative Region (SAR) status which allows its free market economy to continue. Gambling, tourism and the hospitality industry fuel its burgeoning economy. In 2004 a Las Vegas company opened the largest casino in the world, the Sands Macau, and in 2006

Macau gambling revenues exceeded those of Las Vegas for the first time.
It is also a centre for offshore banking of similar status to other well-known
international tax-havens like Bermuda, Bahamas and British Virgin Islands.

"We took my mother to Macau which was the gambling and
opium den of China. It was a very racy spot and probably still is.
There was a tremendous amount of gambling going on: every
other house you looked at was a gambling house. There was also
an awful lot of drug taking, particularly opium smoking. You
could visit opium dens where people were lying. We looked into
some of them. I remember seeing a beautiful young man there
who was like a skeleton. In China it was very desirable to have
long fingernails, and he had a fingernail on his little finger which
was remarkably long and showed that he hadn't done any man-
ual work for the length of time it had taken to grow. He was
stretched out on an opium bed. There were many of these big
flat beds with carvings all around like a fence on three sides. The
fourth side was open and there sat the paraphernalia they needed for their pipes, their water and everything.

The building had several floors with balconies. As we climbed
we could see that there were many beds on the balconies. Macao
was originally a Portuguese colony and it was still very old fashioned. There were no skyscrapers then, the architecture was
Portuguese colonial with lots of balconies to keep the heat out
and help the air to circulate. It was just a couple of hours by boat
from Hong Kong and people often went as tourists but this was
our first trip. We went to the opium den with my mother
because she was very adventuresome and wanted to see everything
there was to see. And we stayed in a rat-infested hotel. In the
night David and I saw a rat in the corner by the washbasin and
we didn't sleep very well after that!"[1]

No sooner had Lydia left than Lady Geddes arrived in January 1954
to celebrate baby Harriet's christening and to enjoy three months
sharing the life of her son, daughter-in-law and grandchildren.

Then early in 1956 they entertained a group of four guests. The composer Benjamin Britten and his partner Peter Pears, the singer, had left Britain in December of 1955 for a tour of the Far East that included many concerts as well as a holiday in Bali. Their travelling companions for part of the trip were Gerda's sister- and brother-in-law, Princess Margaret and Prince Ludwig of Hess and the Rhine. Within their cultured circle of artists, musicians and friends, the couple were known affectionately as Peg and Lu, or by the combined nickname of Lupeg. Several of Britten's compositions were premiered at their home, Schloss Wolfsgarten, and they became intimately involved in the Aldeburgh Festival which Britten and Pears had inaugurated in 1948. Peg Hesse set up the Hesse Students Fund in 1959, a bursary scheme which allowed students to attend the Aldeburgh Festival in return for practical help. Britten continued to visit Wolfsgarten until late in his life, working on Death in Venice there in 1972 and resting there while ill in 1974. One of the rooms in The Red House, the Aldeburgh home of Benjamin Britten and Peter Pears from 1957 until their respective deaths in 1976 and 1986, continues to be known as 'Peg Hesse's Room'.

David had a special relationship with his sister Peg, something which Gerda had been wise enough to recognise and accept.

"She and David were very much alike; they were the two members of the Geddes's family who were most alike, actually. When David was born, Peg was six years old, and the nanny told her: 'This baby is going to be your baby, so you can look after him.' She always said: 'David, he's mine, he's mine. He's my baby.' I could see that they had this very close relationship. So I tried never to interfere. I recognised they had something special together, a closeness that had existed since David was born and had nothing to do with my life with him."[2]

As a new sister-in-law, Gerda had to overcome some initial misgivings about entry into the world of German aristocracy. One was a Norwegian trait of not respecting others just because of their station, especially if any hint of superiority or condescension attached to it.

"I couldn't bear snobbishness. My father said people who were snobbish or had similar attitudes were usually very unsure of themselves and had something to hide. This was my father's teaching coming down to me so I had difficulty with some of the people I met. In Norway you don't have anything like that, there is no aristocracy whatsoever so everyone is just plain Mr and Mrs."[3]

And inevitably the Nazi occupation and her own wartime experiences had left a legacy. But, in reality, Gerda's Norwegian education and her cultural interests made her a very agreeable companion to Ludwig.

"Over the years we saw a great deal of them. Lu and I got on well together. He was an art historian by choice. And I speak German so we had very good contact with each other. I think he felt much more at ease with me than with his other English sisters-in-law. In Norway, we were brought up with a lot of German culture at school. We had to read Goethe and Schiller and lots of German poetry. So I had a very good contact with my brother-in-law.

The socialisation started from the beginning of my relationship with David, in 1948 or 1949. Peg and Lu were always within reach, somehow. Going to their palaces was quite an eye-opener, I must say. Although I had been to the castle in Norway, these German abodes were quite different. At times I felt as if I lived two different lives.

Lu had been influenced by some awful tragedies in his life. So many people around him had been murdered or killed that he very often said: 'You know, people like us have no longer a role to play in this world. We're not needed any more.' And maybe that was true. Because you see his aunt, his father's sister Alexandra, was the last Czarina of Russia and I spent many, many nights in the bed she had slept in. I would lie there letting my imagination go haywire. And of course all those Russian prince and princesses who were killed, they were first cousins to my brother-in-law and they spent all their summers together down by the Black Sea. When they went to their brutal deaths it had a terrible impact on Lu who was himself just a child at the time.

David's sister was a very strong woman and was very influential, so you couldn't help being slightly swayed by her. She had such an incredible sense of humour. She made most situations quite ridiculous: she made you laugh."[4]

There are also echoes of Gerda's discomfort at playing the social game required within the expatriate communities of Shanghai and Hong Kong, as well as her sense that her husband made a better job of such social requirements than she did.

"I had to associate with lots of aristocrats and it wasn't very easy to find a natural rapport with them to begin with. But I got over that very well eventually and found that it was not so difficult to make friends with them after all. But David to a certain extent lived on these connections. Everybody liked him and he spoke very good German and he was totally accepted by all these kings and queens and other aristocracy. He took to it very easily but it took me some years."[5]

Peg and Lu also surrounded themselves with artistic people and these connections re-engaged Gerda in the worlds of art and creativity that had played such a major part in her life before she met David.

The Geddes's and Lupeg attended the Britten/Pears concerts in Hong Kong and in Macau. There was more socialising on the return leg after Britten and Pears had made a successful tour of Japan including their first ever television appearance.

"They came back again from Japan filled with enthusiasm for all the wonderful things they had experienced there. Ben had been influenced by the Japanese Noh theatre and he wrote an opera called *Curlew River* after he came back from Japan. And that was very very interesting for me to study because when he was he was staying with us, he was reliving this experience he'd had in Japan. You could see his musical brain working: it was as if he slipped out of contact. You spoke to him and he wasn't there, he was completely in his composition."[6]

The catalogue of Benjamin Britten's invoices and receipts for the period April 1956 to October 1956 includes an item for 'export of records to David Geddes of Hong Kong'[7]. A classical thank-you from an appreciative guest?

David's sister, Princess Margaret ('Peg') of Hesse and the Rhine

Whenever Gerda spoke of her first meeting with t'ai-chi, the story always opened, as this book does, in 1949 with an old Chinese farmer performing slow dance-like movements in the morning mists near Shanghai. She described physical sensations – energy running up and down her spine, a manifestation of inner light – which accompanied her certainty that she was witnessing the synthesis of body and mind that she had been seeking. She talked of the imperative she felt to learn this strange, tranquil and mesmeric ritual. But there were hindrances: no teacher would take a Westerner; no teacher would take a woman; the Communists invaded Shanghai. Then she moved to Hong Kong where, at last, a master accepted her and later his son continued her training.

The date of her first lesson in Hong Kong is difficult to pin down but is unlikely to have been earlier than 1956 or, more probably, 1957. She consistently said that her first teacher Choy Hawk-pang died after he had given her lessons for only a few months. His lifespan is given by various sources as 1886-1957 or 1885-1958 with the latter a better fit for Gerda's claim that he died aged seventy-four. So it appears there was a gap of seven or eight years between Gerda witnessing t'ai-chi and then beginning to learn it.

Do these details matter? Not to most of us. Errors and inconsistencies creep into the telling of a long life, notoriously so where numerical information, dates, and ages are concerned. When I interviewed Gerda on 11th October 2005, she remembered that her lessons with Choy Hawk-pang had taken place in the months before she underwent a hysterectomy; then the son, Choy Kam-man, had taken over once she had convalesced. In fact the operation took place in 1954, some years before her training began.

But precision is important to a biographer picking through the evidence to present as accurate a timeline as possible. And unravelling anomalies can enrich the unfolding story. Without doubt Gerda's life was changed by the epiphany she experienced as she watched the old

Chinese man weave his way through the mist. It also affected the lives of thousands of others thanks to her teaching, her writing, and the work of teachers who have followed in her footsteps. And the seven- or eight-year gap between seeing the old farmer and taking her first t'ai-chi lesson holds important keys to Gerda's story.

THE PATH TO
T'AI-CHI

Do not allow yourself to be swept out of balance. If you think that balance
is achieved by a pendulum swinging equally to both sides, the T'ai-chi
Ch'uan tries to help you find this balance through the 'Kicking Sequence'.
This balance has to be experienced by standing on one leg and kicking with
the other without having to make an effort. This takes years of training, but
the reward is that in the end you know you can trust yourself and your body.

Gerda Geddes   LOOKING FOR THE GOLDEN NEEDLE, p78

The climates of Shanghai and Hong Kong were exhausting for
Europeans in the 1940s and 1950s. The summer months were a pur-
gatory of torrid clamminess that had to be borne without the benefit
of air conditioning. As someone used to Nordic freshness, who loved
to lose herself on windswept mountains or walk by a pounding sea,
Gerda found the heat, the airlessness and the humidity physically and
emotionally draining. She also experienced both chronic and acute
health problems.

The stomach upset she had suffered during a Calcutta stopover in
1949 was an early warning of troubles to come. Throughout the nine
years she spent in the Far East she suffered from recurring bouts of
amoebic dysentery, which sometimes reduced her to a frail six stone
skeleton. And she was developing gynaecological problems. She had
suffered a miscarriage between the births of her daughters Jane in 1950

and Harriet in 1953. Following Harriet's birth there were further complications. And, on top of these physical problems, she was becoming psychologically drained. A crisis was inevitable.

"I wasn't very happy in Hong Kong because I very much disliked this life of the rich, wealthy, comfort-loving Europeans on top of the mountain and then six million starving Chinese living in the heat and the sweltering horrible conditions down below. That pained me. I spent all those years in the fifties resenting the position that we had; but also physically I was not well. I had great trouble with my body. It rebelled against the climate in such a way that I lived in a state of permanent anaemia so I was not energetic enough to do a lot. But inactivity was very much against my nature. I'd always been well up until then and had always been very active, but in Hong Kong I came down into a deep depression. Hong Kong was the greatest trial of my life because after Harriet's birth in 1953 I never recovered very well. I always had a low temperature and I had pains in my stomach. I only existed really. It was awful.

I had to have a hysterectomy and that was so badly done it was like a butcher's event. Everything went wrong with the operation and I nearly died because they cut into my bladder and created a major infection. They were not very clever about antibiotics in those days. They gave me the wrong doses. I went into the hospital in order to have my right ovary removed because we knew there was something wrong with that and I woke up having had the entire thing removed: my uterus, both my ovaries, everything. That created a deep depression. I was in my most active sexual life at that time and I desperately wanted more children. But that possibility had been completely taken away."[1]

The last two sentences, when put in the context of Gerda's long Reichain analysis, are highly significant. She believed that the two requirements for a fulfilled life were to be creative and to have a loving sexual partner. But the life she was leading felt vacuous and now her identity as a procreative sexual woman had, literally, been cut from her. Her daughter Harriet confirmed the problems Hong Kong life gave her mother: "There was a lot of pent up creativity. She didn't like the set-up of being a colonial wife. You had all those servants but you didn't do anything. And as you know she was a great doer. She loved making the dresses needed for cocktail party life but she found the concept of talking to other people over gin and tonics just obnoxious, very very empty. And she found that whole experience quite empty, apart from having children."[2]

The botched operation took place in October 1954. On 1st November David sent a picture of Gerda to her mother, Lydia, in Bergen. It had been taken ten days earlier. Gerda is almost in full profile, leaning against a tree trunk. Her cheek is sunken and the jawbone visible. Her hair is drawn back and her head inclined as if she is looking at the ground a pace or two ahead of where she is standing, There is a pattern of fine wrinkles below, and to the side of, her eye. She is smiling a tentative, vulnerable smile that appears to be directed inward, if it is directed anywhere. Her smart tweed coat hangs from

Gerda, aged 37, after the 1954 operation

bony shoulders and her neck is hidden behind a loosely tied silk scarf.

Gerda spent most of 1955 convalescing in Europe. Jane, her elder daughter, celebrated her 5th birthday at the home of her grandmother, Lydia, in Bergen, on 26th April. David joined them there in June and the family stayed for a time with Princess Peg and Prince Lu at Schloss Wolfsgarten before moving to a house in Dorset that they had rented for six months. There, on 17th July, Gerda turned thirty-eight.

One of her presents from her husband was a lockable notebook in which he had written: "Pytt – For your beautiful thoughts. 17.7.55 from David." She was not a natural diarist but used it intermittently until eventually it was full in 1991. The first three entries give an insight into to the turmoil she was experiencing in the wake of her operation and before she at last began to learn t'ai-chi. Three days after her birthday she wrote:

"David gave me for my 38th birthday this book to write down my beautiful thoughts. I have previously written a few pages on 'My Dream of an Ideal Life'. My longing now is not to dream about the ideal life, but to live it. I want to be filled with beautiful thoughts, to be positive & to give love to mankind & to live in harmony with my surroundings."[3]

The next entry, dated September and innocently sandwiched between a recipe for a drink called badminton cup and one for potato cake, is more focussed and has moved from the ideal towards the practical:

"We have now lived together almost continuously for seven years & I can say at once that those years have been the happiest in my life, filled with love, warmth, security & harmony.

But I feel that the time has come to stop & think & more or less make a plan for the next seven years. There is a danger. One gets so used to each other, & to the comfort of living happily together, that one's development slows down & one lives in a set routine & maybe grows rather stale. One is tied down by domestic responsibilities & it is only too easy to stay in that easy atmosphere for ever after. But if one does that one is left completely defenceless in case anything happens. One should always keep an open eye to the outside world."[4]

The family sailed for Hong Kong at the end of 1955. Fifty years later Jane, who was five years old at the time of the voyage, could still bring alive the excitement of looking through her porthole on Christmas morning, seeing three men on camels on the bank of the Suez Canal, and believing they were the Three Wise Men.[5] Childish fancy was far from the thoughts of her mother whose spirits were plummeting. The batteries that Gerda had recharged in Europe were leaking fast and as their power ebbed, so did her resolve to face another three years of humidity, health crises, and creative starvation. The third entry in her diary is dated 11th January 1956 by which time their ship has reached the South China Sea. This time she abandons the protection of the pronoun 'one'. She speaks from the heart, and is close to rebelling against her return to Hong Kong.

"The last time we came out to the Far East, I promised myself that I was going to stand it for the duration of one stay (i.e. three years) whatever happened & I did stay but I was ill for too long.

This time I will not stay. I have been ill too much & I don't think it is worth it. Life is too short & it is not fair to anyone. I don't want to be ill any more, because then the years just drag by & nothing is accomplished. It is a very serious problem to face up to because what will happen to our marriage if I go away. It is also very difficult for the children.

But here I am in Saigon and after just three days of heat I feel limp, exhausted & hopeless. I know that all my good intentions cannot be carried out. As soon as I set foot in Europe my whole constitution seemed to adjust itself and become normal, energetic and healthy. I felt there was a possibility to become creative again. The minute I come back to the Far East I feel I become full of prickles & aggression, indigestion & total helplessness. Maybe I should never have come back. Maybe I should have put up a fight for my personal existence & not just followed David willy-nilly. As it stands now I feel tied down hand and foot by an existence which is against everything."[6]

But beneath the despair and frustration something was pulling her eastwards. China held a secret treasure: the old farmer's weaving dance in the dawn light; the integration of body, mind and soul. Her determination to learn t'ai-chi had slumbered somewhere beneath her frustrations with Shanghai and Hong Kong life, the draining effects of climate and illness, and the emotional turmoil. Now it was rekindled by her growing sense that, one way or another, her time in the Far East was almost over. She could manage one more tour. It was now or never. Towards the end of her life she took a philosophical perspective. "So in Hong Kong there were lots of medical and emotional things which were deeply troubling. But as a result of this, which is what so often happens to people in life, I went down really to the bottom and I hardly knew what to do with myself but out of that came the finding of my t'ai-chi teacher. Out of unhappiness or discomfort or disharmony, something good always grows."[7]

WHAT IS T'AI-CHI CH'UAN? A BRIEF EXPLANATION

T'ai-chi ch'uan, usually abbreviated to t'ai-chi, is a generic label for an ancient Chinese martial art. History identifies Chang San-feng as the father of t'ai-chi. He may have been a mythical figure or have lived in the 13th Century. The traditional story is that he was a Shaolin monk who left the monastery, became a Taoist hermit, and, after he had witnessed a fight between a bird and a snake, developed a martial system that used softness and inner power to overcome brute force. More dependable historical information has recognisable t'ai-chi being practised from the 17th Century by the Chen family in Henan province, south of Beijing. Developed by Chen Wang-t'ing, this style was a family secret until one of the family's servants, Yang Lu-ch'an, learnt it by observing lessons as he went about his duties. His mastery was such that he is reputed to have taught Chen style t'ai-chi ch'uan to the emperor's household. In time he adapted the movements into what is now known as Yang style. One of his descendants, Yang Cheng-fu (1883-1936) was a major figure in the development of modern t'ai-chi. He was also the teacher of Master Choy Hawk-pang who visited Gerda's home in Hong Kong to begin her instruction in Yang style t'ai-chi. There are five main t'ai-chi styles. Chen, Yang, Wu, Hao, and Sun all carry the family names of the their founders. Worldwide, Yang style is the most widely practised. As well as an empty-handed form, most styles have weapons-based forms such as sword, sabre and spear. The name 't'ai-chi ch'uan' comprises two components. T'ai-chi, often translated as 'The Supreme Ultimate' is represented by the familiar yin/yang circle which is divided into black and white shapes, each with an eye of the opposite colour. It is an important symbol in Taoist cosmology (see information box on page 169) and represents the balance of energy in the universe. 'Ch'uan' can be translated as fist, or power, or self-control. T'ai-chi ch'uan therefore developed from a martial arts system based on harnessing the energy fundamental to Taoist philosophy. It is also practised as a meditation, a spiritual teaching, and to maintain good health.

Gerda enjoyed telling the story of how her t'ai-chi lessons began. "We had a Chinese friend who was a teacher at Hong Kong University. I knew that he practised t'ai-chi ch'uan and asked him if he would teach me. He said that he only practised for his own health, and that if I was really serious about learning, I had to be taught by a Master. After much searching, Choy Hawk-pang was found. He had been a student of Yang Cheng-fu. Yang Cheng-fu was the grand-son of Yang Lu-ch'an, the founder of the Yang style of the t'ai-chi ch'uan. Master Choy was a well-known teacher and performer.

I invited Master Choy to our house on the Peak, and he arrived with a friend. Master Choy was at that time seventy-four years old, and his friend was eighty-two. We had tea, and, as they could not speak much English, our houseboy, Ah Dee, acted as interpreter. They asked me questions about why I wanted to learn the t'ai-chi, and asked me to show them some of my dance movements. 'You play for us, missie, and we look see.' They did not seem very impressed. In fact, they indicated that most of what I did was bad for the body in one way or another. I then asked them to 'play' for me. The two old gentlemen stood up in their long, grey silken gowns, with black skullcaps on their heads, and performed the long Yang form. When I looked at the eighty-two year old man, whom I never met again, I had a sensation that he was transparent, like air, as if there was no barrier for him between this life and another life. His balance was perfect, and although he was old and thin, the flow of his movements and the harmony of his body seemed timeless. I have often held him up as an example for myself, and of how to grow old.

After this meeting I was accepted as a student, and Master Choy came five days a week to give me instructions. As there was a certain language barrier, he said to me, 'Missie, you look see me, you use eyes, you be like monkey, you copy my movements. You use ears, you listen my breathing, you listen my heart.' And this is what I did for a long time, and I found it very difficult. In fact, my previous dance training was more of a hindrance than a help. I had to unlearn before my body became receptive to this new way of moving. What my teacher stressed most to begin with was the importance of the foot; how it touched the ground, how each step must be soft and gentle and flowing, how I must be aware of the contact of the sole of the foot with the ground, of the energy which is drawn into the body through the sensitivity and the openness of the foot. Now this was a teaching I understood. It was as if my Grandfather's wisdom was coming back to me through this old Chinese gentleman. This was a language I already knew from childhood.[8]

All through my childhood, as far back as I can remember, my grandfather used to take me out for walks through the woods and mountains of western Norway, and fishing in the lakes and the sea. He had great knowledge of animals and plants and taught me to watch for the smallest movements in the undergrowth, and to listen to the faintest sounds. Although my grandfather was a big man, he could walk through the woods without making a sound. He would tell me to look at the ground carefully so as not to step on broken twigs if I wanted to discover the woodland secrets.

In winter he would teach me how to identify the footprints in the snow, of the fox and the hare, the deer and the elk, the mouse and the mole, and all the various birds. In the spring he would drag me out of bed in the middle of the night and make me walk for miles into the mountains to see the courtship dances of the capercailzie. We carried sleeping bags so that we could wrap up warm in the heather while waiting for the magic of the

Nordic dawn. He said. 'You must feel yourself as being part of this nature, adjust yourself to it and live in it.' This sound advice made sense when, in later years, I explored the forms of the t'ai-chi ch'uan, each of which linked readily with the patterns of natural life.'[9]

The t'ai-chi has this philosophy behind it, of nature always changing: you move with nature, and you are also changing all the time. That was one of the things I learned from my grandfather, this business of the way you walk. You have to walk continuously and be very much aware of the soles of your feet. That came from him and it was such a surprise and coincidence when I found this old Chinese teacher was saying exactly the same as my grandfather had said many, many years earlier. That was very strange."[10]

When Choy Hawk-pang died a few months later his son, Choy Kam-man (also known as Johnny Choy), took over as Gerda's teacher. "The son came to my house every single day and I had lessons with him. He was quite young and was quite new to teaching. But he was a wonderful mover, so I absorbed the teaching more by vision than by words because he didn't speak very good English. Both he and his father were very careful not to touch me. It was like two races that were new to each other. The Chinese men didn't know how to treat a western woman and probably thought, 'better stay away from her'. It was quite an unusual situation from that point of view.

But the son did touch me once, and with one finger. It was extraordinary. I can still remember: he put one finger on my buttock and said 'No back. Straight down.' And just that touch of his finger made my hips fall down into the right alignment by dropping the pelvis. So whatever he did, it was very effective. But that came later. He didn't correct anything to begin with. That was the method. They taught you the movement then left you to practise. Only when I had learnt the whole of the ritual did Johnny say 'Now you go and practice on your own' and I had to struggle with that.

It was all so new and I didn't know anything about the t'ai-chi except what I could see and what I could feel. So after three months I called him up again and said 'Help, help. Come and look at me again.' And that was the first time when he actually put his finger on my pelvis, and I understood the message."[11]

Master Choy Kam-man ('Johnny Choy'). He became Gerda's teacher after the death of his father, Master Choy Hawk-pang in 1958

The social call by two old Chinese men to the home of a western woman on the Peak contradicted the protocols of a society within which Gerda had found herself constrained and frustrated. And, much more importantly, their visit set her feet upon the t'ai-chi path that was eventually to shape her life. From today's perspective it is difficult to appreciate her achievement in searching out, and then being accepted by, a teacher. Currently (April 2008) an Internet search for t'ai-chi (and its variant spellings) finds over ten million links. T'ai-chi schools advertise in the Yellow Pages, and any decent sized town lists a t'ai-chi class in its syllabus of leisure activities. But in the 1950s it was scarcely known outside of the Far East or beyond the boundaries of a society where women were subservient.

"These Chinese men had very great trouble with me because women didn't do t'ai-chi in those days. Most women still had bound feet, you know. I never, in all my ten years out there, I never ever saw a woman doing the t'ai-chi. Never. But men did it. You'd see them in the parks in the morning in Hong Kong. In the botanical gardens down near the governor's house there's a beautiful park and there they did the t'ai-chi. And so these two Chinese chaps, they thought, 'What can we do with this crazy Western woman? We can't possibly touch her, because that is taboo. And we can't teach her to fight, because she doesn't want to fight.' And so, what I learned in the end was not the martial art aspect of the t'ai-chi."[12]

Instruction continued until late into 1958 when she left Hong Kong. She never returned to the Far East; but China, which had been her nemesis and a source of despair, was to prove the key to freeing her stifled creativity. She did not, however, appear to change her view of living there. A diary entry from late 1956 says:

"Nearly a year has passed since I wrote my pessimistic outlook on life from Saigon. I feel as much a stranger to life in the Far East as ever."[13]

RETURN TO BRITAIN

When the tiger is in conflict with the Yang celestial dragon it becomes Yin, the quality of earth. To the t'ai-chi performer, the tiger represents all forms of energy, and it is with these energies that we have to learn to deal. We have to direct our energy in such a way that the natural healing process of the body can be enhanced. We have to use it with intelligence, not allowing it to become totally depleted but always retaining a reserve.

Gerda Geddes   *LOOKING FOR THE GOLDEN NEEDLE*, p57

During her convalescence in Europe in 1955, Gerda had sought a second opinion about her state of health. The diagnosis was blunt and to the point.

"Because I really wasn't at all well, we went to see a Harley Street specialist who looked at me from all directions and carried out many tests. He said to David… 'If you want to keep your wife alive, you should take her away from the Far East.' It was that critical really. He said that my whole system was worn out, partly by the climate and partly by childbearing and operations and miscarriages."[1]

Gerda and David took stock in the light of this serious assessment. They quickly discounted the possibility of living apart. Realistically there was little choice for them but to return to Europe. However, David's career was progressing very well: he had been made a Jardine Matheson director in April of 1955.

"So when we went back to Hong Kong after that leave, David

went to his boss, Sir John Keswick, and told him what the doctor had said. But we didn't want to be separated so he didn't want to send me home on my own. We wanted to stay together. John Keswick said: 'We might be able to help you out because at the moment there is a vacancy coming up in our head office in London and you can fill that vacancy. But it won't be forever. It'll be for maybe three or four years and then somebody else will come in and take that job.' So in 1958 we went home and that was because of my health. So in one way I ruined David's career and I felt very, very badly about that."[2]

And there was a further painful consequence to face: leaving behind their faithful 'Number One Boy', Ah Dee, and the members of his family who had looked after them so well since they had first set foot in China nine years earlier. Ah Dee had had a major impact on Gerda's life. He had been a rock of support during the turbulent Shanghai period, he had talked his way through a curfew and past armed guards to get her to hospital when Jane's birth was imminent, and he had been essential to the family's survival on the nightmare train trip to Hong Kong where, with dignity, loyalty, and style, he had managed and looked after their growing household. But he was more than that. He was in many ways her window on China, her trusted access to the land which had fascinated her but had almost killed her. When, in *Looking For the Golden Needle*, she wants the reader to reflect on the cycle of life and death, it is to Ah Dee and his family that she turns for assistance:

"Here is a Chinese saying: 'When a human being is born there is a ripple on a still pond. When that being has finished its journey there is another ripple on the pond and the spirit returns.'

To the Chinese, Cyclic Change plays an important part, and every effort is usually made to return to the place of birth when the time has come to die. We had a strange example of this when we were living in Hong Kong. All our servants came from China. They were members of the same family and came from a place called Kui Kong. We had taken great trouble to get them all exit visas from China which in those days (1951) was very difficult, and people who managed to get out of China considered themselves extremely lucky. One day, Ah Dee came to me and said, 'Just now Old Auntie very old, soon will die; Old Auntie must go home.' The old amah had bound feet and was small and frail. We tried to stop her but to no avail. She picked up her little bundle of worldly possessions and set off. Ah Dee took her to the railway station in Kowloon and she was never heard of again."[3]

And now it was time for Gerda and Ah Dee to part.

"Leaving Ah Dee and his family was devastating. But David arranged for them to get a job with a rich American who gave them a flat in New York. It was a heartbreaking farewell but, on the other hand, it made everything very good for Ah Dee because it enabled his children to have a good education and they went on to become Americans. So for that family it was the right thing. We corresponded for a long time. Ah Dee died many years ago but his girls managed to go to university, so socially they became much better off by becoming Americans."[4]

At the end of September 1958, the family began the air trip to Britain, flying with Hong Kong Airways of which David had become a Director. A publicity photograph shows the family group at the foot of the aircraft steps. Jane and Harriet are charmingly clad in matching tartan trews, simple short-sleeved blouses, and travelling shoulder bags. A favourite doll accompanies each of them. David, suited and briefcased, points to the camera. Gerda, simply clad in dark suit and string of pearls, has put on weight and is smiling. Her smile is full and radiant and she looks delighted to be travelling back to Europe. The caption, headed "Hong Kong Airways Executive Arrives" and dated 30/09/58, reads "The Hon. D.C. Geddes, Director of Hong Kong Airways and Jardine Matheson and Co., accompanied by his family, arrived in Tokyo Tuesday evening by a Hong Kong Airways plane from the Crown Colony *en route* back to London to take on a new post. They are returning home via Canada and the U.S. after a short stopover in Tokyo."

In November 1958, the family bought a flat in the Kensington area of London, next door to Holland Park.

"It was a great change. After all those years out there where I hadn't done anything, I had no strength in my fingers. When I had to start washing up, cleaning bathrooms and things, in the beginning my hands were so weak that they couldn't do it. Although I soon got stronger again, I missed Ah Dee many and many a time, I can tell you."[5]

But her return to Britain was much more a cause for celebration than lamentation. She had left behind a climate and a lifestyle that had been physically and emotionally debilitating, she was back in London which had contributed to her creative flowering in the late 1940s, and she had brought back one of China's treasures hitherto unknown in Europe: the art of t'ai-chi. She had made good progress to the point where Choy Kam-man in one of his letters to her described her as "my first and only true successor." In another letter, he catalogued the many health benefits of Chinese Shadow Boxing (t'ai-chi), asked her to promote and teach it when she returned to her own country, and criticised "narrow minded Chinese Shadow Boxers" who thought it should never be taught to foreigners. For her part, she was in no doubt that she had learned a method of moving that could be helpful to others. She understood movement through her dance training, her psychoanalysis, the therapeutic work she had carried out in Sweden, and her job for the National Theatre in Oslo. But there was something different about t'ai-chi, something valuable, something she should pass on.

"The main thing was the alignment of the body which was different. In dance, you inevitably turn your feet out, like in ballet, and the movement in your hip joints is quite different. And ballet is quite exterior somehow. Unless it is being performed by a genius like a Margot Fonteyn or some of the great dancers, ballet doesn't move me in the same way as modern dance does.

In the t'ai-chi you have to get a hold of the flow of the movement. That flow doesn't necessarily penetrate through dance where you might move abruptly, or suddenly stop. But in the t'ai-chi with its Taoist philosophy on constant change, the flow is continuous and you are changing all the time.

I felt that I had been most privileged to learn the t'ai-ch ch'uan. I practised every day, and I wanted to share my experiences with others."[6]

Then, during their first year back in Britain, David and Gerda began to have doubts about their decision to live in the middle of the city. "London is not a place for children to grow up so we wanted to get them out into the country. We looked at well over a hundred houses. We had put aside £6,000 which in those days would buy you a very suitable house. We had the money ready and waiting. After we had looked for months and months and we were nearly giving up, I one day saw an advertisement in the paper for an old farmhouse down in Kent. I said to David: 'Why don't we go and look at this house? It might be the last house we look at.'

So we went down there on a May evening when the sun was shining and we came to this old, old farmhouse with a fantastic orchard where all the apple trees were in flower. The place was in a mist of mystery and beauty. We went into the house and talked to the lady who said: 'Some other people are very interested in this house. If you want it you'll have to make up your mind very very quickly.' The price was £12,000, exactly double what we were planning to spend. And David, being David, said 'I'll put £12,000 in cash on the table tomorrow.' And we bought the house without having any surveys made, nothing at all. When I said to him: 'Shouldn't we have a little look and see?' David replied: 'If that house has been standing there for four hundred years, it'll stand there for another fifty years when we'll be living there.' And he was right. That's the sort of man David was. He jumped into this impossible position, but it worked."[7]

They had become the proud, if slightly apprehensive, owners of Oldhouse Farm.

DOMESTIC JOY, T'AI-CHI DISAPPOINTMENT

You have to discover your own talents. If you can find inside yourself something which fills you with enthusiasm and which arouses your curiosity then you must concentrate on making use of your talents, and you will find that life becomes more meaningful and there is a reason for continuing with your struggles.

Gerda Geddes   *LOOKING FOR THE GOLDEN NEEDLE*, p74

Oldhouse Farm, at Hildenborough in the Kentish Weald, was a handsome 16th century farmhouse nestling in seven acres of garden, orchard and tennis courts. The main building was a rambling affair with tall white chimneys. The white-painted ground floor, half-timbered in places, supported an upper story of hung tiles. Attic windows peeped out of the long slope of the tiled roof. An old wooden farm wagon parked in the orchard added to the storybook atmosphere.

"I very much took to life down there. I loved it and I was very happy in Oldhouse Farm where we ended up staying for twenty years. It was a house that told a story but it was a happy story. It had a priest hidey-hole and it had three buried wells around the house, we went dowsing to find out where they had been. I could find them but nothing happened for David and he was slightly irritated. He said 'I go around with these sticks and I don't feel anything. They don't move!' And mine would go so hard that my arms would shake. Oldhouse Farm was about four hundred years old so many, many people had lived there before us and by finding these wells you could almost imagine what their lives had been like. I felt that I fitted into the whole of the place. It was very leaky and in the girls' bedroom there was a hole in the wall where the light came through. So there were lots of places that were not up to the standard of modern house building. But David always said, 'Well, it's been standing for hundreds years so why should we change it?' He respected it very much for what it was."[1]

Gerda took particular pleasure from the stability and security which she felt her daughters gained from growing up at Oldhouse Farm, and contrasted their experiences with her own childhood.

"All those years in Oldhouse Farm were very harmonious years. And the children were very happy at that time. They both say those were the happy years. They both loved school and attended regularly. The year was mapped out by term-time and holidays. It was all a very regular time of life, looking after the animals and growing all the vegetables and being out in the country. It was a very fortunate background for the children to grow up in and I think they gained a great deal from it. There was an order to their lives. I think I experienced much more confusion because my childhood was more complicated. Jane and Harriet didn't have the same traumas to deal with. They obviously had their ups and downs because life is like that, it can't be even all the time, but during those fast developing years they were happy.

They went to a fairly local grant-aided school because I didn't want to send them to boarding school. I thought that as long as David and I were fairly happy it was more natural to grow up in a home than in an institution. David would have sent them off to Benenden. He had gone to boarding school; first to a very sadistic prep school where they were beaten every week just as a matter of course. It was taken for granted that they had broken some rules, so they were all beaten. That was when he was eight years old. There is a lovely photograph of David aged seven, a curly haired little boy with a big open smile on his face. Then, in another taken a year later when he had gone off to boarding school, his hair is short and his face full of tears. How parents could do that is beyond me. If we'd had a boy it might have been insisted upon because all of that was very much ingrained into life in those days. But we had daughters, and they didn't go to boarding school.[2]

I was a mum, living a country life that was suiting me down at the farm. I just loved it, and the period in my children's life was just wonderful. I loved that life: I loved to take the ashes from the Aga every morning and to be the first member of the family to go out of the house when I emptied them. That was one of my main targets that I loved doing and I was up before anybody else. The house was quiet and the day was beginning. I can remember appreciating every single day like that."[3]

And there was another major change. She had escaped the constricting social bubble of Far Eastern expatriate life and was now within commuting distance of London and its rich feast of artistic and cultural possibilities. And her charming new home was within easy reach of friends and family. Princess Peg and Prince Lu were regular visitors, and trips to their home at Schloss Wolfsgarten, near Darmstadt, helped slake Gerda's thirst for creative stimulation.

"We very often met Benjamin Britten and Peter Pears when they were at Wolfsgarten and we became very good friends. There was a sort of circle around Peg and Lu which included Laurie Lee, the writer, and his very beautiful wife. And then there was Golo Mann, the son of Thomas Mann, the writer. And Julian Bream, the guitarist, he was also a very close friend of Peg and Lu. We used to have some fascinating conversations. When the wine was flowing, the tongues loosened. We had an awful lot of laughter, because they were all such witty and wonderful company. David was also a very good raconteur and everybody loved funny stories, so it was a carefree, wonderful atmosphere. The other person who was almost always there, and one who became a very dear friend of mine, was called Tiny, the sister of the Duke of Edinburgh. And there was Heinrich Hessen, a painter who was a nephew of Lu's. Lu was very cultured, probably the most cultured person I've ever met.

And every year Peg invited us up to the Aldeburgh Festival, She had big parties up there, and all these intellectuals flocked around Peg, they just loved her. She was so charming and had such a wonderful way with people; everybody just took a look at Peg and started telling her their entire life."[4]

In 1960 Gerda, David and daughters Jane and Harriet spent a German Christmas with Lupeg at Wolfsgarten. Other guests included Julian Bream and Laurie Lee and the event turned out to be memorable for the most unexpected of reasons.

"We spent the whole of Christmas at Wolfsgarten. Laurie, his wife Kathy, and Julian were also there. Peg wanted to show them what a real old-fashioned German Christmas was like. We had a fantastic Christmas Eve dinner. Everything was wonderful and then we all went to bed. We were wakened about two o'clock in the morning with shouts of 'Fire! Fire! The house is on fire!'

At Wolfsgarten there was one huge house that had something like twenty-eight bedrooms. That was one part of the square. On two sides there were smaller houses. Peg and Lu lived in one of the smaller houses and we were staying in the other. The rest of the guests were staying in the big house; and when we looked out of our window we could see that it was ablaze, with flames whishing out through the roof.

We all got out safely. There was lots of snow and we stood around in it half dressed. The big house that was burning was full of treasures, all kinds of famous pictures and wonderful furniture. And there was a huge silver storehouse in the cellar. Because it was Christmas, the fire brigade took a long time to come and when the firemen arrived they were the worse for wear from their Christmas Eve celebrations. They put their hoses up to heaven or right over the blazing roof, they never could aim at the right place.

We had all been celebrating too but Prince Lu began organising the rescue of the treasure. David was there in his dressing gown and slippers, and Julian, and Laurie who was ill and had gone to bed earlier with a temperature before escaping from the fire. It was a very dramatic night because there were flames and drunken firemen and lots of snow. We were only half dressed. The men were running in and out and in and out and my brother-in-law was shouting; 'The silver, we must save the silver.'

The fire had a good hold and in the end it burned off the roof and the top floor. It remained fire-damaged all during that winter. There was lots of water damage too. But the silver was saved, along with most of the other important treasures.

At first it was thought that Julian had started the fire by leaving a cigarette burning in his bedroom and he felt very guilty about that possibility. But in the end they found out that the real cause was a smouldering beam in a huge old fireplace. The night before our Christmas Eve celebration, the Duke of Edinburgh had been guest of honour at a party where there was a blazing open fire and no one realised that a beam in the fireplace had started to smoulder."[5]

Julian Bream's complete innocence is confirmed in a history of the local volunteer fire brigade which identifies a defective fireplace as the cause of the 1960 fire.[6]

Gerda's return to Britain had brought important changes. Social life had become stimulating and at times glamorous; the domestic scene was idyllic and she had immersed herself in her role as homemaker and mother.

But she had brought from China plans for herself too. Her hopes lay in two directions. First, she had learned t'ai-chi and in so doing had reconnected with the creative independent spirit which had fuelled her early adulthood and led her, through dance-training and psychoanalysis, into a lifestyle peopled with original artists from the worlds of theatre, painting, dance, and design. She intended to re-open these doors, and the unique contribution of t'ai-chi would surely be the key. And, second, she had escaped a debilitating climate that had almost killed her. Now, motivated and healthy, she intended to put her creative life back on track.

During the nine months the family had lived in London, she had made sustained and determined efforts to generate interest in t'ai-chi. Within a short time of her arrival from Hong Kong she made her first television appearance after a journalist she knew, who was a Far Eastern correspondent for *The Times,* recommended her to the producer of a BBC woman's programme. Her brief slot consisted mainly of a short t'ai-chi demonstration. Then she set about knocking hard on doors she hoped would open up routes back into the worlds of dance and drama that she had previously inhabited.

"I contacted all the major theatre schools. I thought that t'ai-chi would be a wonderful way for actors and singers and dancers to go forward, to learn more about themselves. And I would teach them. My first contact was with RADA, then I contacted Guildhall, then the Central School of Speech and Drama; then I went to the ballet people at Chalk Farm, where they had their main school.

Because I'd worked in the theatre beforehand I knew a lot about actors and acting, I knew t'ai-chi would be very good for them and I thought it could be a new subject to put into their curriculum. When you've been bitten by something, you just go on, don't you? I always had the feeling that I had a little devil in the middle of my back that was pushing me forward, go on, go on, don't stop now. But I was about seven years ahead of my time. There was no understanding of it.

I placed a lot of my hopes on John Fernald, the Director of

RADA who was rather avant garde in his outlook. The whole of RADA, all of the teachers and everyone came to the theatre to listen and watch. I did my darnedest but they didn't respond. Once it was all over, the Director said to me: 'Thank you, Mrs Geddes. How very interesting.' And that was it. Total blank. I hadn't lit a spark in anybody."[7]

The only flicker of interest came from a group of Alexander Technique practitioners who invited her to give a demonstration at Leighton House, the former Holland Park studio home of the pre-Raphaelite artist, Lord Frederic Leighton; but it was small return for her efforts and she became dispirited.

Now, at home in a Wealden rural paradise, with her daughters at school and her husband up in London at the Jardine Matheson head-quarters, she gritted her teeth and continued to practise.

"So I did it on my own. Every single day I went outside on the lawn and I did the t'ai-chi. And my mother, who was rather a wise old woman, she came and she watched me, and she said 'You know, you always tell me that the t'ai-chi's about how to be relaxed, but I think you look more tense every day you do it.' And that was because I did it with my willpower. I thought 'I mustn't forget it, I must do it. It's my duty to do it every day.' And I did it, and I did it, and I did it, and I got thoroughly bored with the whole thing. I really got bored with the t'ai-chi, because it didn't give me anything. Because everyone had turned me down, I was slightly hurt."[8]

She had brought t'ai-chi from China and planned to share its treasures with Britain. Instead, alone and losing heart, she gradually tired of what was becoming an increasingly empty ritual until, as she later put it, "the t'ai-chi chuan simply dried up."[9]

And what of the second part of her plan, to return to full health, fitness and energy? To begin with she felt immediate benefits from her return to a familiar, and kinder, European climate: but the botched operation of 1954 was not yet finished with her.

Part Three
TRANSFORMATION

*It is these crutches, fashioned by our own hands, which we are to throw
away; but this means that we are asked to sacrifice something that has
become an intrinsic part of our life. This can be a frightening experience,
yet the moment we have recognised our problem for what it truly is, we enter
the freedom of a boundless… state of awareness and we realise that,
although we have left behind dead shackles, yet nothing of the living potency
of our previous mode of being has been lost. It is still with us and will
always be there as an integral part of the whole process of transformation.*

Edith Schnapper   THE SPIRAL PATH OF SPIRITUAL PSYCHOLOGY

LOSING THE LIGHT

Your real path becomes visible in the last part of the t'ai-chi ch'uan. You are told through the t'ai-chi ch'uan that there is a balance between the working of the body and the development of your spirit and it is not possible to cheat.

Gerda Geddes   LOOKING FOR THE GOLDEN NEEDLE, p79

Gerda's sense of the connectedness of dance, psychology and t'ai-chi tapped a deep stream that threaded its way through her life, a river of inner light that she had first become aware of as a small child, pedalling her tricycle through one of the many galleries in Krybbebaaken, the home of her art-collector uncle, Rasmus.

"When I was about four-and-a-half I had the experience of 'Being in the Light'. On a cold and frosty day I was racing around on my tricycle in an empty room which had a skylight. All the walls were hung with paintings and suddenly a ray of brilliant light came down and covered one of the paintings, *The Girl Sitting on the Edge of the Bed* by Edvard Munch.

I noticed the picture for the first time. A young woman is dressing, and through the window shines a clear spring light. She appears to be half dreaming and filled with excitement and expectancy, wondering what life has in store for her. The picture made a great impression on me and in later years I often identified myself with that girl. But at the time I can only remember playing with the sunbeam, racing through it, saying to myself: 'Now

I am in the light. Now I am out of the light'. This experience of 'Being in the Light' or of being illumined is something which has come back to me several times over the years, and it has always made me feel safe."[1]

Paintings were also involved in her second major experience, which happened when she was a lonely adolescent in London.

"When I was fifteen years old I came to England to attend boarding school in London. To begin with I was terribly homesick. I cried myself to sleep every night and could not say a word. One day I was taken to the Tate Gallery where I saw the Turner paintings for the first time. I was completely swept off my feet. There was that light again, and I just allowed myself to be illumined by it. My homesickness vanished; all my worries became trivial because I had been taken over by something that was greater than myself."[2]

For Gerda these numinous experiences of light and energy were as much spiritual as they were physical. The emotions and sensations that accompanied them were sometimes very intense, as happened during an incident while she was an exile in Sweden.

"Towards the end of the war, in 1945, I was living in Stockholm. One day in April I was standing in a very crowded bus with people pressed uncomfortably together. Suddenly I felt as if I had been hit by lightning. It was as if my whole body became phosphorescent. I started to perspire and shiver at the same time. I got off the bus, sat down on a bench looking out over one of the beautiful canals, and wondered what had happened to me. About ten days later I got the explanation through a letter from my mother telling me that my father had died. She mentioned the exact time of his death and it coincided precisely with the time when I went 'hot and cold' on the bus. My father and I had always been very close and I'm sure that as he died he wanted to give me some of his light."[3]

Then there was her first meeting with t'ai-chi already described in Chapter 10. In another version, which she included in an article called 'Turning Points' in Metamorphoses magazine in 1984, she emphasised the spiritual aspect of the experience.

"It was like 'meeting with the Holy', and I remember thinking: 'This is what I have been looking for all my life' – a total integration of mind and body combining psychological knowledge, physical balance, and spiritual nourishment through movement."[4]

Gerda had identified inner light and energy as defining aspects of her being from an early age. She had undergone a training analysis in Reichian therapy with its emphasis on energy flow. She was critical of Reich's later thinking and experiments in America, and she had found him most unlikeable on the one occasion she met him: but when she attended a lecture and demonstration which he gave at Oslo University, she made an immediate connection to his attitude to energy.

"He was truly clever at loosening people. It was extraordinary to see how he freed the energy of several of these professors, and also people who worked in other metiers such as the theatre. He was always talking about orgone energy. If you follow his description of orgone energy you'll see that it is the chi, the energy that the Chinese talk about, although he had no knowledge of, and no specific interest in, China. But he recognised this energy that was circulating all around in the universe, and how it got tied up in people's traumas and complexes. He said if you could free this natural energy and not leave it condensed into aggression and anger, the world would be in a much better place and a different kind of kindness and love would be allowed to come into the universe. That's really what he was talking about."[5]

Gerda recognised t'ai-chi's potential to synthesize the earlier elements and influences of her life and lead on to a new chapter; yet here she was in Kent barely able to force herself through her daily practice. What had gone wrong?

While China had shown her an ancient treasure that might hold the key to her future, it had also bequeathed her a debilitating legacy. The realities of Far Eastern life and climate had almost killed her and, along with the 1955 operation, had left her physically and emotionally depleted. She was fighting another battle too: while she worked hard at committing herself positively to the roles of mother to two growing daughters and wife of a successive business executive, she was struggling with an underlying depression.

"When I convalesced from the major operation that I had in Hong Kong, the doctor said it will take about six months and you will be right as rain. But I figured later on that I really had a sort of depression that went on for about fifteen years before it left me altogether. The hysterectomy gave me a real sideways knock. I felt that I didn't function as a woman anymore when I was in the middle of my womanhood so to speak."[6]

T'ai-chi had shown her the possibility of reconnecting with the energy and productivity that had driven her life before she met David and travelled to the Far East. More than that, it pointed towards a drawing together of what she had learned already: a fusion that would lead to greater understanding. And it offered a passport to a new life as a creative and independent woman, inspired to teach what she had learned to those she was sure would benefit from it. But all her efforts had fallen on stony ground. No-one appeared to be interested. The only future that beckoned was as homemaker at Oldhouse Farm.

Then, in May 1960, just a few weeks before her forty-third birthday, she collapsed.

"I just passed out one day. The doctor came and examined me. You'll have to go into hospital tomorrow,' he said. 'You'll have to have a major operation.' Without me knowing, a cyst the size of a grapefruit had grown inside my abdomen. I hadn't noticed, that's what absolutely baffled me. I couldn't understand, with all my awareness of my own body, how I hadn't realised that I had something alien growing inside. So I was pushed into hospital and had an operation straightaway. It turned out this cyst had grown onto a tiny bit of ovary that was left after the operation in Hong Kong, just a tiny fingernail of ovary so that the hormones could go on functioning. The doctor was very serious and said, 'Your cyst could be cancerous and it'll take ten days before we get the result of the culture.' So I was lying in the hospital for ten days thinking: 'I have cancer, I'm going to die. My children are too small, I can't possibly leave them.'"[7]

T'AI-CHI REBIRTH

We continue naming the symbols; The Snake Creeps Down Into the Water,
followed by The Golden Cock Stands on One Leg. The snake, often
associated with the dragon, represents, amongst other things, healing power,
cunning, knowledge and learning. It has the capacity, by shedding its skin,
to transform itself, and in the movement of t'ai-chi chuan it becomes a
golden cock. The golden cock signals the dawn of a new day, a new
beginning. In the context of the t'ai-chi ch'uan this is a transformation that
takes place in this life; it can happen at any time when one has reached a
certain level of awareness.

Gerda Geddes: LOOKING FOR THE GOLDEN NEEDLE, p62

Gerda lay in her post-operative hospital bed awaiting the biopsy results.
Her thoughts swirled between the challenge to her own mortality and
the potential tragedy of motherless daughters and a widowed husband.
Then, at this lowest of points, China extended its hand and offered more
of its gifts. As a distraction from her plight, she began to read a book
on Chinese thought and history. She followed with interest a summary
of the country's dynastic past. Then she began to discover references
that she knew from the names of t'ai-chi moves.

"I came across the expression, Carry Tiger To Mountain.
Suddenly a light was turned on and I thought, 'What does it mean?
This is something I will have to learn more about. The symbol
has a meaning. Where does it come from?' And then there was
also Cloud Arms. And the Monkey, Pushing Away the Monkey,

I found them in that history book. That spurred me on. I was lying there thinking: 'I'm dying but now when I'm at the end of my life I suddenly start finding out about the symbols. And the symbols belong to the movements.' That was the beginning of discovering the Allegorical Journey.

After ten days I was told that the cyst was benign; it had been taken away and I would be all right from then on. And I have been. But you see how dramatic life can be. And how a total collapse brings with it your salvation. I've experienced this so many times in my life that I can't help but believe in it. Something is mapped out for you but it doesn't happen on its own, it only happens if you take the chance; take the initiative and say, 'Ah, this is for me, I have to do something about it.'

So from that moment on it was like a huge jigsaw puzzle. I started reading. It was self-education. I found one book and it pointed to another book. And so it went on. About painting, about music, about Chinese customs. It brought a depth into the t'ai-chi ritual, and it gave me an understanding which grew, little by little, until, one day, there was the story. The Allegorical Journey has been the centre of my life ever since."[1]

This turning point brought a determination to use what she had learned about her body and its energy to make herself well again.

"I became healthy after I had the second operation. I was so determined to get well. Once you allow that healthy energy to come into your body it starts circulating quite quickly. I had to work that cyst out of my body and the more I let it go, the healthier I became.

To the end of the Sixties there were still remnants of the depression but then it disappeared altogether. I would say I had at least fifteen years of being below par in my midlife. That was difficult for my husband and for me as well. I would always start with saying. 'No I can't do it. I'm not strong enough.' He was somebody who wanted to do things and go places, so lots of time when he was full of life and full of energy and curiosity I would just trail behind and say, 'I am so tired I can't do it.' That lack of energy was not my proper nature. Before the first operation I always had lots of energy. Then I just disintegrated. But after that second operation the energy came back and I knew there was something good to work on."[2]

But for the moment t'ai-chi practice was banned on medical grounds. During the months of her convalescence, Gerda immersed herself in Chinese culture, and puzzled over her ignorance about it, despite ten years spent in the Far East.

THE TAO, CHI, YIN AND YANG

In her book *Looking for the Golden Needle* Gerda acknowledges Taoism, Buddhism and Confucianism as the great trinity of Chinese thought and culture; but it is to Taoism that she turns mostly in pursuing the Allegorical Journey. In the Taoist view of the universe, all things originate from, and return to, the Tao. Although it is the source of all creatures and objects, the Tao is not a deity. It is nameless, boundless, beyond language, and contains everything including gods and spirits. It is commonly translated as the Way or the flow of the Universe. That flow is powered by a universal energy called Chi which has two forms. Yin chi is the female aspect and associated with stillness, softness, tranquillity and receptiveness. Yang chi is the male aspect and associated with activity, strength, advancing and hardness. Yin and Yang are not seen as opposites, however, but as complimentary forces whose interaction brings everything into being.

According to Taoist cosmology, the flow of the Tao keeps the universe in a constant state of change from non-being into being, potential into actual, Yin into Yang, female into male. This model of continuous movement underlies the *I Ching (Book of Changes)* which is described on page 174. Wisdom is to be found by living in harmony with the flow of the Tao (wu-wei or the way of non-action) rather than trying to control events or resist life's impermanence.

At one level such concepts can seem paradoxical and arcane. They can also have very practical applications. When used in Feng Shui they encourage the harmonious arrangement of domestic furniture and fittings.

Traditional Chinese medicine is derived from Taoist ideas and acupuncture needles are inserted into chi meridians to clear blockages or stimulate the flow of energy around the body. And it is quite in order to compliment a Chinese cook by saying his or her wok has 'good chi'.

"I could be ashamed of how little I knew about China when I started to learn t'ai-chi. Then back in Britain, after I had my second operation, I just couldn't stop reading. I absorbed everything that I hadn't learned about when we were in China. It's as if it all had to mature before I could begin on it.[3]

One book followed another; poetry, mythology, folk tales, books on divination, on health and acupuncture, the art of painting, the art of calligraphy; everything I could lay my hands upon. The ancient world of China became part of my existence, much more so than when we actually lived there. I came across tales of Taoist monks who 'Embroidered with Golden Needles', of fair ladies who 'Worked with Shuttles', and of 'Heavenly Horses' from the Tang dynasty. I realised that these were all names connected with the t'ai-chi ch'uan. My curiosity was aroused and from then on it became like a treasure hunt.

There is a famous quotation by Confucius: 'If I give my student one corner of a subject and he cannot find the other three corners for himself, I do not repeat the lesson.' My teachers had given me one corner, and now I was preparing to find the other three."[4]

Gerda planned to use the physical practice of t'ai-chi to help her find these other three corners, and to follow the path of discovery that she was pursuing with growing excitement. But when her convalescence was over and she started to practise again, she made a devastating discovery: she could not remember all of the t'ai-chi sequence. She had forgotten most of the connecting moves that bind the individual elements into a slow flowing sequence. She had written nothing down because of her belief that the body has its own memory and that what it does not remember, it has not properly absorbed and understood. It was a serious problem. There were no t'ai-chi teachers in Britain, the old master was dead and his son, Choy Kam-man, had moved to San Francisco. Gerda wrote to him in despair, asking him to have a film made of himself in the hope that she could relearn from watching it. But when, at last, the film arrived, she discovered that she was facing a serious and frustrating challenge.

"He had made a film of the whole of the t'ai-chi, the way he had taught it to me. But one of the difficulties was he had his back to me most of the time; I could never see the arm movements in front of the body. I only saw them when they came out from the body, so I had to try to remember exactly what those arm movements were. And when he faced me and I tried to copy his movements it was like looking in a mirror. If he made a movement to the right, I had to do it to the left in order to copy what he was doing. I was so frustrated, I couldn't quite get it and I didn't quite understand it."[5]

Jane and Harriet, aged eleven and eight at the time, have clear memories of Gerda's struggle. They would come home from school to find their mother shut away in a blacked-out study, standing in front of a flickering silent screen, trying to create a mirror image of what she was viewing as she bumped into furniture in the dark. Some days there were tears. But more and more the girls would discover Gerda practising t'ai-chi on the tennis court with Nana the sheepdog and the twenty-four ducks from the orchard lined up watching her, their heads turning in unison like a Wimbledon audience.[6] Slowly but inexorably, Gerda's determination was bearing fruit.

"It proved to be an excruciating process. But eventually I mastered it, and got the t'ai-chi together again. And this time it had come to stay. My whole approach had changed. I was much more humble and the other 'three corners' were becoming visible, one by one.

Now I was beginning to feel what is meant by being 'full' or 'empty', how to use the minimum effort in a movement by finding the exact point of balance in the body at every moment, how to discover 'lightness' by first discovering 'heaviness', and how to be aware of the continuous flow of the chi."[7]

Her immersion in Chinese thought and culture was helping to fuel her t'ai-chi renaissance. She was increasingly convinced that a powerful and meaningful symbolism underlay the sequence of movements. Help was also coming from an unexpected source: her dreams. Reichian therapy focuses mainly on the body and does not make special use of dreams, but this aspect of psychoanalysis had always interested Gerda. She was an admirer of the analyst Carl Gustav Jung who emphasised the symbolic nature of dreaming, and now she began to notice changes in her own dreams.

"Slowly little bits and pieces came dropping down and started to fill in this jigsaw. Fragments of explanation came to me through reading but also through dreaming, that's what was so uncanny. During this period I had lots of strange dreams that showed me where to go. I kept thinking about Jung all the time. And slowly this Allegorical Journey built itself up until it made total sense to me, absolutely total sense. And it changed several of the attitudes in my life. It was almost like a transformation that took place."[8]

One dream was of special significance to her.

"At the time when I was beginning to discover the importance of the symbols in the t'ai-chi ch'uan, I had a dream. I call it 'The Baskets'. In my dream I was walking through a forest of beautiful trees. It was very still, no birds singing, no breeze blowing. The experience seemed to be entirely out of time. Eventually I came to a lake. The lake was like a mirror with the surrounding trees reflected in it.

I stood on a grassy bank, and, as I could walk no farther, I started 'playing' the t'ai-chi ch'uan. As I went through the sequences, every movement I made seemed perfect. My balance was perfect, my breathing was co-ordinated, the flow uninterrupted and the meaning of the sequences seemed crystal clear. I was thinking 'I understand everything I am doing, I have lived through these different phases of development, I know now how to Push Away The Monkeys, I have found my creative potential, I have learnt to be humble, I know how to regulate my energy, I am not much troubled by aggression, anger and fear, and I have found my Golden Centre, the neutral place where there is peace and harmony.'

At this point in the performance of the t'ai-chi ch'uan comes the sequence of Snake Creeps Down Into The Water, and as the movement was taking me down, the lake was suddenly covered in thick ice which I could not penetrate. I could not get down into the water, so I had to go back and start the movement again. As I was raising my left arm, a basket came sailing through the air and landed on my hand. Inside the basket were my two children. I continued the movement and the basket landed on the ice. I had to go back and start again. Another basket appeared, containing my husband. It seemed very heavy and it landed on the ice with a thump. Back I went, and baskets kept coming. One was full of cigarettes (I smoked in those days!). That was a light load, but thousands of cigarettes floated all over the ice. Next came a basket of all my favourite books, the ones that I treasure and am loath to lend to people in case they are not returned. Then came a basket with the most beautiful, expensive clothes; Parisian models, exquisite silks, luxuries which I used to long for. Next came our house in Kent, Oldhouse Farm, with Nana the sheepdog, all the old oak trees, the old apple orchard and the garden. The last basket to arrive contained Norway with its mountains and fjords and my whole childhood. By this time I had been trying to do the very strenuous movement of Snake Creeps Down Into The Water so many times that I was utterly exhausted, and was lying down on the ice unable to move. Suddenly I heard a hollow voice from under the ice, and I saw the flickering light of a candle. The voice was that of Ah Dee, our houseboy, who was a great friend of mine. He said, 'Never mind Missie, Ah Dee just now will make small hole in ice with candle and then Missie can make big hole and then ice will all go away.' So I had to start breathing as deeply as I could and eventually I melted the ice and everything that clung to the ice and to me was freed. That was the end of my dream.

I woke up feeling exhausted, bewildered and strangely elated, as if something of great importance had happened to me through the dream. My interpretation showed me not only precisely how far I had gone, but also where I had got stuck in my development and how the dream was directly connected to the Taoist teaching of 'letting go'. I had to melt the ice! I was reminded of my very Western approach to the t'ai-chi ch'uan, trying so hard to analyse, understand and explain everything intellectually, thereby using my head and not my heart. Thus the ice formed and prevented me from letting go of my baskets. I tried in my everyday life to become warmer and nicer. It helped, but in the end most of that ice had to be melted by tears. It took about two very difficult years to live through."[9]

By 1963, four years after her initial failed attempt to interest the worlds of dance and theatre in t'ai-chi, Gerda felt ready to try again. This time she sought counsel directly from ancient China: she consulted the *I Ching*.

I CHING (BOOK OF CHANGES)

This ancient scripture describes a system of thought central to Chinese cultural beliefs.

It espouses a philosophy based on the balancing of opposites, the Yin and Yang of Taoism, whilst recognising the inevitability of change. Although it is often viewed in the West as an oracle or text of divination, it is the oldest of the Chinese classics and is considered a book of wisdom. *I Ching* study was an integral part of the Imperial Examination System which, from 605AD until the end of the Qing dynasty in 1905, was used to select civil servants.

Traditionally, several stages of authorship are recognised. The first is given to the legendary figure of Fu Hsi, one of the mythical Three Sovereigns of ancient China and the reputed inventor of writing who is said to have lived around 2800 BC. Sections of the text known as Judgements are attributed to King Wen, progenitor of the Chou Dynasty in 1150BC, whose son, the Duke of Chou, also made significant additions. Confucius (551-479BC) is credited with adding important Commentaries although this, and other aspects of the traditional view, has been called into question by more recent scholarship.

Sixty-four abstract line arrangements called hexagrams lie at the heart of the book. Six horizontal lines are stacked one on top of the other. The lines are either continuous, called Yang lines, or broken Yin lines. Each hexagram is numbered, named, and described in terms of its symbolism, its significance, and the meaning of its individual lines. To consult the *I Ching,* the question or issue of concern to the person seeking guidance is held in mind while a hexagram is built up line by line using one of two methods. The first involves a scoring system based on dividing a bundle of fifty dried stalks of the yarrow plant. The second is based on throwing three coins whose heads and tails have been assigned different values. Both methods direct the consulter to a unique hexagram whose text is then considered in the light of the question being asked.

Using the method of throwing coins, she received hexagram number fifty, Ting, or the Cauldron, a ritual bronze vessel for holding offers of cooked food. In order to make sense of the *I Ching's* pronouncements to her, she adopted the approach used by Jung. When he was asked to write a foreword to Richard Wilhelm's translation, Jung consulted the *I Ching* then chose to interpret the answer as if the book was speaking directly to him. Gerda therefore treated her response as if it was the t'ai-chi itself which was replying to her two queries: Should she teach it in the west? And should she include her interpretation of its symbols in her teaching?

She studied the results with growing excitement. The general finding, or 'Judgement', was that t'ai-chi contained spiritual nourishment that would benefit those who learned and practised it and, through them, it would benefit society more generally. The outcome would be great good fortune and success. And individual lines of the hexagram gave more detail. T'ai-chi's excellent qualities were going unrecognised and unused. Hidden spiritual powers emanate from it which are most eagerly sought after by those who feel a strong need for help, but it can also be used profanely if people do not understand it fully.[10]

The oracle had spoken. It was time to begin.

A NEW LIFE BEGINS

But even after this great transformation, life goes on and the Monkeys and the Golden Needle appear again, so even if you have been so called 'Enlightened' there are still difficulties on your path. Once more we are being reminded that we are part of the whole. As one grows older this becomes much easier to accept. One instinctively feels closer to everything.

Gerda Geddes   LOOKING FOR THE GOLDEN NEEDLE, p80

Within the Eastern tradition, a great many aphorisms and verses point to the paradox that follows moments of enlightenment or illumination: everything is changed yet life stays the same. An old Chinese poem says:

Mount Lu in misty rain; the River Che at high tide.
When I had not been there, no rest from the pain of longing!
I went there and returned...It was nothing special:
Mount Lu in misty rain; the River Che at high tide.

So it was for Gerda. She remained the homemaker of Oldhouse Farm, wife to David and mother to Jane and Harriet. She and David went up to London and socialised: a society photograph from the early sixties has him resplendent in white tie and medals while she is a picture of satin clad elegance. The meticulous family albums which David kept include an April 1964 invitation to a Benjamin Britten recital at Wolfsgarten, which was a regular holiday destination for the Geddes family as was Schloss Tarasp, Lupeg's spectacular hilltop castle in Switzerland. Yet, at the same time, Gerda was immersing herself in Chinese culture, reading everything she could find and seeking out links to the Allegorical

Journey she was now certain underlay the t'ai-chi ritual that she was practising with diligence and with increasing confidence.

She was aware of changes in herself, and as her physical strength and her energy improved, so did her mood. After the 'Baskets' dream, she made a pledge to her family.

"I came down to breakfast that morning and told my dream to the family immediately. And I said: 'This is a funny dream but I've made up my mind that I'm going to change. I'm going to be

David and Gerda on the town

much kinder now, and I'm going to be much more patient.' The children and my husband all breathed a sigh of relief. That actually happened: I changed, I did become much kinder, and I didn't say no to everything, I said yes to lots of things where before I had said, 'I'm too tired, no. I can't do it.' Then life came back into me and a transformation did take place.

You can't say you've been guided because you don't know, but things certainly did happen after that dream. Everything took off, but that was only after I felt that I had got rid of all the things that were clinging to me: my books, my wonderful clothes, my cigarettes, my house, my Norway, they all went. They weren't just mine anymore."[1]

She also found herself reflecting on the years of analysis she had begun in Norway more than twenty years earlier, based on Reich's theory of 'muscular armouring', the body's reaction to, and defence against, traumatic events.

"The example Reich used was a jellyfish. The jellyfish moves freely in the water but if it comes up against a disturbance like a rock or a mountain, it will push against that with all its force until it hurts itself. If it does that many times, the natural movements will shrink so that it becomes smaller and smaller. And this is what happens to our feelings if they constantly come up against barriers and obstacles. The child shrinks and gets frightened and won't go out openly into life for fear of being hurt. If I express my feelings naturally, somebody will hurt me. That was what he worked on. He said you could get hurt or hindered in many ways, it may not necessarily be by being physically punished or by the tone of someone's voice, it may be the environment which is created by your parents, and your grandparents, and your great grandparents. And all of those things he saw pretty clearly. That became very, very clear to me during my treatment. I had a feeling of relief: thank goodness, now I don't have to be hung up by that anymore.

In retrospect, that's how it felt. You can only ever speak out from your own experiences, because they are uniquely yours. When you allow yourself to be influenced by somebody else, when you copy somebody else; that isn't actually you. The real you comes from your own experience. That's why it is very important in this life to have a good teacher, just half opening the door so you have the choice. You can stand there in the doorway getting stuck, looking out upon the paradise but not daring to go out there. Or you can take the initiative and actually go out of the darkness into the light. And if you do that then you have growth potential in yourself which is vaster than you thought it was. You push yourself out of the door, and you feel: 'I'm growing. I'm growing now.' A transformation is taking place."[2]

Gerda's rekindled energy found its way into the notebook she had received from David on her thirty-eighth birthday during the dark year of 1955 when she was convalescing in Europe. In the five years to her 1960 operation it contains only eight dated entries, often unhappy in tone. Then in 1961 there are pressed shamrocks from a holiday in Ireland and January 1962 opens with an unattributed, life-affirming quote: 'Think love and love surrounds you and all about whom you think. Think health and health comes. The physical reflects the mental and the spiritual.' Although she did not develop a regular diary habit, the notebook from then on contains lively accounts of family events as well as detailed dream narratives.

The diary also records a skiing accident in Norway in April 1963 when Gerda slipped on ice while performing a turn and suffered severe tendon and ligament damage to her knee and upper leg which required a long period of rest and healing and delayed her teaching plans. Around this time she gave a lecture on t'ai-chi at the home of an osteopath in Tunbridge Wells. Given the proximity to Oldhouse Farm, a fifteen-minute drive away, it is likely they had met as a result of treatment she needed for her damaged leg. By coincidence, one of those who attended the lecture was Eric Crozier, librettist and collaborator with Benjamin Britten. He and his wife also lived nearby, although Gerda had not previously met them.

"I remember very clearly asking him, 'Do you think I should try and start teaching?' and he said 'Yes, you should definitely start teaching because if you don't you will always be frustrated for the rest of your life. And if your teaching is good enough it'll take on, I know it will. And if your teaching is not worthwhile, the people will disappear. That's the risk you have to take.'"[3]

It is difficult to pin down exactly when Gerda started teaching t'ai-chi. She was unsure of the year but clearly remembered her first pupils: an acupuncturist called Felix Mann and his mother. In a recent letter, Dr Mann confirmed that he had t'ai-chi lessons from her 'in the early Sixties'.[4] Given the time needed to recover from her skiing injury, a 1964 date for her very first t'ai-chi classes seems reasonable. A naïve Gerda sought out teaching space in Soho where the 'studio' owners assumed her business was something other than teaching an ancient Chinese art.

"Felix Mann and his mother, they were my first students. I taught them in Soho in London. They lived in London so I thought I should teach in London. Then I looked for a studio. Innocent blue-eyed girl that I was, I thought, 'Soho is full of studios so I'll go round and look there.' And looking for a studio in Soho I can tell you was a new experience. 'What do you require? Do you want sofas? Or do you want dividing curtains?' I was obviously in the wrong place! Those shifty Soho studio owners thought I was up to no good!

But I found a studio and gave classes in it for a couple of months. Sometimes I rented for an hour and nobody came. So I thought, 'This is a wonderful opportunity for me to practise.' All on my own, in the middle of the prostitute district, I was practising t'ai-chi in an empty studio. That was how it started."[5]

Around 1965, Gerda and David began attending lectures, arranged by a discussion group they had been encouraged to join, at the College of Psychic Studies in Queensbury Place in London. According to Gerda, the group referred to itself as the College for Spiritual and Psychological Study.

"It was a tight-knit group including artists in London such as a well-known painter called Cecil Collins and his wife. The focus was philosophical and spiritual learning. They were rather upper class people and there was one woman who was a genius at finding good speakers. So David and I went once a fortnight and listened to these lectures which were absolutely top class, with wonderful lecturers."[6]

It is easy to see why Gerda, with her background, and with her feet now on a path of exploring the spiritual aspects of t'ai-chi, was attracted to such a venue and such a group of people. But David too had had experiences which drew him into this environment. In December 1944 he was travelling home from India on a troopship. When it was delayed in passing through the Suez Canal he went to visit some friends in Cairo. As he walked home to his hotel that evening, he was struck by an overpowering light which seemed to come from all directions above him. He wrote years later: "(The vision) extended in my experience over about 230 degrees horizontally and vertically. This means that I saw a much larger field than one normally sees, but also that I did not see directly behind me. The nature of what one sees has often been described. The intensely bright light which strikes from above with an electrifying force. In my case, also, an awareness of a secondary flow, the power of love blowing us along and coming from a centre located in that place which I did not see – behind me."[7] The article continues in the same crisp observational tone as befits a Cambridge-educated officer with military intelligence experience. There were three similar episodes in four days. It had not happened before and did not recur: but it changed the way he viewed his life. When he and Gerda met for the first time in Stavanger, her interest in him had been stirred by the strange, evocative pastel drawings that she saw in his flat. They were his attempts to capture the experience.

Through contacts that she made at the College of Psychic Studies, Gerda began to be invited to give t'ai-chi lecture demonstrations. In July of 1967 she was invited to a conference on healing attended by practitioners from orthodox medicine and from alternative therapies. It was held near Bristol and the participants included the artist Thetis Blacker, whose large spiritual batiks hang in Winchester Cathedral, Aberdeen's St Machar's Cathedral, Durham Cathedral, St George's Chapel at Windsor Castle, Westminster Abbey, and other places of reverence. Thetis was attending in the hope of finding a way of dealing with spinal problems that had kept her in a steel corset for twelve years, placed her in hospital on several occasions, and ensured she was seldom without pain. Earlier in her life, an orthopaedic surgeon at Guy's Hospital had told her father that she would never be able to lead a fully normal life.

According to Thetis, a battle had broken out at the conference earlier in the day. "The orthodox contingent accused the unorthodox of fraudulence and bogusness, while the unorthodox accused the orthodox of bigotry and spiritual myopia. Indignation raged on both sides, some delegates threatening to leave the conference. However, after dinner, which was partaken in seething silence, we attended what was described in our programmes as A Demonstration of Chinese Shadow Boxing by Mrs Gerda Geddes, of whom none of us had heard.

"That event altered my life. Gerda Geddes became, as it were, Orpheus pacifying the Furies of Hades. Within minutes the atmosphere of the audience was changed from antagonistic outrage to spellbound fascination. And I, as a painter of mythical creatures, was mesmerised by The Snake Creeping Down to the Water; The Big Bird Spreading its Wings; Strumming the Lute (like Orpheus himself); the Monkeys Retreat; and of course by Taking the Tiger in One's Arms and Carrying it to The Mountain..."[8]

In Gerda's performance, Thetis recognised the total concentration and complete immersion that she herself had striven for in her music (she was a trained opera singer) and her painting but that she had witnessed only rarely in performances by consummate artists like Margot Fonteyn and Yehudi Menuhin. She and her friend turned to one another simultaneously and said "I want to learn it".

Thetis and her friend Alicia Yarborough joined Gerda's small London class which by this time had moved on from seedy Soho to much larger, and much more respectable, studio space in a council-owned building near Bishopsgate tube station where fellow tenants were the London Symphony Orchestra. Then, in 1970, she learnt that a building near Euston Station was being converted into dance studios. It sounded like a more seemly environment to teach t'ai-chi. She decided to go and investigate. She had found The Place.

Gerda was influenced very much by Taoist ideas. She had several translations of one of the classic Chinese texts, the *Tao Te Ching*, and introduced it into conversations when she would quote it by heart. She sometimes consulted the divinatory text, the *I Ching*. On one of my weekly visits, I gave her a copy of a new translation. It was immediately consulted about the success of this biography. 'Great effort and great achievement' was the judgement, I'm happy to report.

Underlying Taoist philosophy is the Tao, a mysterious, primordial entity, variously translated as the Way, the Flow, or the Force. Part of the problem in describing it is the belief that the Tao has always existed and predates and subsumes everything else, including language. Perhaps the closest English adjective is 'apophatic', which, in theological terms, refers to something that can only be described by what it is not, because there are not words to describe it directly. The opening lines of the *Tao Te Ching* try to say the unsayable: translations vary but the general sense is 'The Tao that can be spoken of cannot be the true Tao'. Gerda helps a little:

"Tao, the Way, is a way of life, not a school of thought, and can only be understood by being lived – hence the small amount of written material left behind by the early Taoists. Each man must find in himself his own truth, his own beauty, his own virtue."[1]

In Taoist terms, an action is virtuous when it is in harmony with the Tao, and the advice is to live by the principle of wu-wei, often translated as 'non-action'. Puzzled readers might find a flicker of illumination in maxims like 'Don't push the river, it flows by itself', 'Go with the flow', and 'Less is more'. Gerda was sure Taoism helped explain what she saw as equivocation and fatalism in Chinese people she met during her time in the Far East. In her own life she delighted in coincidences and synchronous happenings: surely consequences of the positive flow of the Tao. And indeed, as she took me through the story of her life it seemed unusually peppered with what she described as 'extraordinary coincidences' with the middle syllables of 'extraordinary' drawn out for emphasis. 'Extraordinary coincidences' included: how, as a penniless refugee in Sweden, she quickly found both a dance teacher and a psychotherapist; how she arranged a t'ai-chi demonstration on British television within a short time of her return in 1958; and how she came to teach at The Place.

One day I asked her how she managed to have so many happy accidents.

"I've always had the feeling that I had a little devil in the middle of my back that pushes me forward: 'Go on, go on. Don't stop now. More. You have to do more'. It will be there certainly until I die, maybe even after I'm dead."

So the Yin of wu-wei was balanced by the Yang of Gerda's Little Devil. Or, as we say in the West, she made her own luck.

THE PLACE WHERE THREE STRANDS MEET

Taoism is concerned primarily with life on earth. It equates physical and mental health and insists that only a strong, healthy body can house a strong healthy spirit. It regards the physical and the spiritual as indivisible yet distinctly different aspects of the same reality, with the body serving as the root for the blossom of the mind.

Gerda Geddes   LOOKING FOR THE GOLDEN NEEDLE, p21

Gerda's destination was a Victorian building at 17 Duke's Road, just off Euston Road in central London. It had started life as the home of the Artists' Rifles or, to name it fully, the 20th Middlesex (Artists') Rifle Volunteers. Several corps of rifle volunteers were formed in 1859-60 to counter the threat of a Napoleonic invasion from France: they were self-organised and self-funded and they often recruited on professional or geographical lines. The Artists' Rifles largely consisted of painters, sculptors, engravers, musicians, architects and actors. It served with distinction in conflicts from the Boer War to World War Two, was disbanded in 1945, reformed in 1947 and now operates as the 21st SAS reserve regiment of the Territorial Army. Prominent early members were Holman Hunt, John Everett Millais and William Morris and later recruits included Noel Coward and Barnes Wallis. In 1969, the

Contemporary Ballet Trust, headed by Robin Howard, bought the regimental headquarters. A suggested new name, The Artists' Place, was quickly reduced to The Place.

ROBIN HOWARD AND THE PLACE

For almost 40 years, The Place has been a creative hub for the development of contemporary dance in Britain. It was founded by a remarkable visionary, Robin Howard. His ambition to establish a distinctive British form of contemporary dance was inspired by attending a performance by the Martha Graham Company from New York who visited London in 1954. Convinced that something important was missing from the British arts scene, he began to sponsor British dance students to attend the Graham School in New York and to invite American dance teachers to work in Britain. After he had financed a visit of the Martha Graham Company to the Edinburgh Festival in 1963, he persuaded Lord Harewood, Sir John Gielgud, Henry Moore, Ninette de Valois, Marie Rambert and Martha Graham to become inaugural patrons of Contemporary Ballet Trust Ltd, The Place's parent company.

Howard invited a close associate of Martha Graham, dancer and choreographer Robert Cohan, to become The Place's first Artistic Director. One of Howard's objectives for The Place was "to use the universal language of dance to break down social, political, linguistic and other barriers" and he urged Cohan to "form a dance company based on love".

In 1976, Robin Howard shrugged off the image of a "rich man who pottered with the arts and gave of his surplus" when he sold his land, his book collection and his shares so that The Place could buy the freehold of its buildings and secure its future. His steadfast commitment continued until his death in 1989.

Today, The Place is the UK's premier centre for contemporary dance. It works with dancers from age five upwards, brings new talent into the dance profession and guides artists through their careers. Its activities include London Contemporary Dance School, Richard Alston Dance Company and the Robin Howard Dance Theatre, as well as education, outreach, and professional development projects.[1]

Early in 1970, Gerda turned up on the doorstep and was able to book some practice space. Her small but growing band of pupils left the cavernous rooms at Bishopsgate and moved into a ground floor studio at The Place with windows onto the street. Curious passers-by could look in and watch a group of people, led by a slight woman in Chinese tunic and trousers, perform a slow dance-like ritual. They began to come in and ask questions. Some stayed, at times with amusing results.

"People actually came in from the street and said, 'What's going on here? Can we stay and watch?'

At that time, the hippy period had become an enormous wave that just got bigger and bigger. I had lots of very strange visitors. They would ask to join and I would say, 'Give it a try.' At my evening classes, some people would disappear out of the door for a few minutes, smoke hash and then come back again. At times the whole studio smelt of hash and a number of students were going around grinning in a haze of wide-eyed euphoria."[2]

Stoned students were of little interest to Gerda, and she eventually stopped evening classes to discourage them. What did excite her was a second category of curious drop-in observers: dancers and staff from The Place. Robert Cohan, the Artistic Director, and the founder himself, Robin Howard, both came along to see the strange movement class being taught by their new tenant. And gradually people from the dancing world, the world which had played such a key formative part in Gerda's earlier life, began to enrol as students. Gerda had not anticipated this development and it delighted her.

One of the first dancers to join her t'ai-chi class was Gudrun Gylling who also arrived at The Place in 1970. She had already spent three years at the Choreographic Institute in Stockholm where the head of the choreography department was Gerda's mentor and former teacher, Birgit Aakesson. There Gudrun had completed a course for dance teachers. Now, however, she wanted to continue her training as a dancer. After considering a range of possibilities including going to America or to Spain, she decided to try the new centre that had opened in London where she knew the Martha Graham technique was being taught.

When Gudrun sought out Gerda at The Place it was out of a sense of Nordic solidarity, rather than because of anything she knew about Gerda's role there. "I heard of a Norwegian woman who came to The Place regularly. And I thought I'd go and say hello because she was from Norway and I am from Sweden and there were so few Scandinavian people at the school. We could speak to one another because Norwegian and Swedish are very similar. She had lived in Stockholm during the war, and we also had Birgit Aakesson in common but I can't remember whether we found out about that then or later."[3]

During her dance training in Sweden, Gudrun had made a fleeting acquaintance with t'ai-chi when an American woman called Sophia Delza, who was a friend of Gerda's, visited the dance school (see page 192). When she discovered that Gerda was teaching t'ai-chi at The Place, Gudrun immediately enrolled in her class. "Something told me that I should learn t'ai-chi. And when I began there weren't many dancers in the class; most people came from outside The Place. There were elderly people, younger people: some were maybe studying psychology, some were working in acting; those kind of people."[4]

Gudrun found in Gerda's t'ai-chi classes a respite from the demands of dance training. Although she worked at Graham technique with sufficient tenacity to win a scholarship, it always felt to her as if she was fighting her own body to achieve positions it was not designed to achieve. She could see movement of a completely different quality in Gerda's t'ai-chi and her style of teaching could not have been more different. "She was very friendly and gentle compared to dancing teachers who could be very rough and the way they treated people could be very harsh. But she didn't have this way of teaching at all. She was also very supportive. And when she corrected you in some way it really stayed with you."[5]

About a year later, Gudrun was joined in the t'ai-chi class by another dancer who had also come to The Place to study the Martha Graham technique and who was soon having experiences similar to

Gudrun's. Eva Karczag was born in Hungary but grew up in Australia where she completed classical ballet training. "When I first came to England from Australia I started working as a ballet dancer in the London Festival Ballet but fairly quickly I began to realise that that was not how I wanted to dance. I knew I wanted to dance but that wasn't how I wanted to dance. There was a lot to see in London, and I started to get interested in other ways of dancing: for instance there was The Place and Ballet Rambert.

"I started taking Graham technique classes at the Place. These were open classes as opposed to the classes for the full-time students. At that time, I was sharing a flat with a dancer called Christopher Banner, who was a fulltime student. One evening he said to me, 'There is a woman who is doing a lecture demonstration, you should come along.' So I went, and there was Pytt doing the t'ai-chi and talking a little bit about it. I had never heard about the t'ai-chi before but something about it just said to me, 'I need to experience this'. It was an amazing meeting for me because although I had reached a point in my technical training that allowed me to work in a ballet company - I had taken it to a fairly accomplished level - still somehow I felt I was working against my body. I was always a very lyrical dancer. I have long limbs and there's a sense of fluidity in my moving that I never felt was acknowledged, really, in the balletic form. Sometimes I had to push my body to do certain things, so that I felt this isn't really what my body was meant to do."[6]

And, like Gudrun, Eva was soon enjoying the eclectic mix of t'ai-chi students. "In the open classes that I took with her, people were paying money to come, they were doing it out of interest, and wanted what Pytt was offering. In these classes some of us were dancers but there were also writers, artists, filmmakers, musicians, people off the street who found out about it and were interested – there were all kinds of people. Of course, some would fall away and others would continue coming, but overall, the level of commitment was high and the mix was inspiring."[7]

From her own experience, Gerda was in no doubt about the value of t'ai-chi in helping dancers cope with the rigours of modern dance training. As always, she expressed her views in straightforward, down to earth language.

"The dance training was so hard that most of the people who trained with Martha Graham left her as cripples because of the technique…unless you had a figure rather like Martha Graham's you ruined yourself. I started off with her teaching when I was a student in America and I only lasted for six weeks. After that I thought, if I continue with this I'll end up unable to walk. Martha Graham did something to your hips and your knees that was only for her body really. I'm very glad that I listened to my body before it had been completely ruined, because it would have been. At The Place I watched the training of the dancers and thought they were ruining their bodies just like all Martha Graham students. There had to be an antidote towards that, and it could be the tai-chi. Dancers, through studying the tai-chi, would get an understanding of their body that they could use to avoid damage or repair it. And they would develop an inner feeling for the boundaries that the body should not go over."[8]

In 1970 an American dancer, choreographer and teacher, Jane Dudley, came to The Place as Director of Graham Studies. She was able to recognise what Gerda was teaching as t'ai-chi: her brother was married to Sophia Delza, the American who had demonstrated t'ai-chi at Gudrun Gylling's dance school in Stockholm.

"This was an extraordinary coincidence. Jane Dudley's sister-in-law was a friend of mine. We met in Shanghai. Sophia Delza wrote one of the very first books in English about the t'ai-chi.[9] She was fortunate enough to find this very good Chinese teacher who was willing to teach her in spite of the animosity against Europeans and Americans. Her husband was part of an American diplomatic mission in China and he had better connections to the Chinese than my husband had. David's links were purely commercial; he spent his time in negotiations about handing over European property to the Chinese. So we approached China from different directions, Sophia and I. She was more in contact with the Chinese theatre, the Beijing opera and films."[10]

Sophia Delza (1903-1996)

By the time Sophia Delza went to China in 1948, she was already known in the U.S.A. as a modern dance performer and choreographer. During her three-year stay in Shanghai she studied with masters of Chinese theatrical dancing and she taught western modern dance technique in Chinese theatre and dance schools. She also met Master Ma Yueh-Liang who accepted her as a pupil and taught her Wu style t'ai-chi. On her return to the United States she gave lecture demonstrations of classical Chinese dance routines. She also established a t'ai-chi school in a studio at the Carnegie Hall in New York and taught regular classes at the United Nations. She published numerous articles and wrote three books on t'ai-chi in the course of her life.

Although Gerda was the first European to learn t'ai-chi and bring the art from China to Europe, she readily acknowledged Sophia Delza as the first Westerner to be taught by a Chinese t'ai-chi master. The two women stayed in contact and Gerda's daughter Harriet took classes with Sophia during a New York trip in 1974.

Despite the pleasure they took from discovering a common link in Sophia Delza and t'ai-chi, Gerda and Jane Dudley took opposite sides on the Martha Graham technique.

"She was part of the dance training which was physically very, very hard. We discussed it and we always disagreed about the rigour of what she was doing against the softness of t'ai-chi. But Jane already had arthritis by then. She had done such damage to her joints that slowly she became immobilised and later in life she could only teach sitting down. That was only just beginning when I first met her. I kept on saying to her, 'Do be careful, listen to yourself, listen to your own body. But she would say (puts on an American accent) 'Oh no, you can't be a dancer without using force, you have to use lots and lots of force, and this softness is no good.' We had endless discussions.

Then she started coming to my classes and became very enthusiastic. I think she saw something in this softness, the yielding part of my movement. It was against her way of thinking, but despite herself she saw something important there."[1]

The mutual respect between the two women grew into a lifelong relationship as colleagues and dear friends. Following Jane's death in 2001, Gerda summed up the early days at The Place with a charming story.

"Jane used to teach in Studio Three, just above me, and I would hear her shouting: 'Faster, faster, faster; jump higher, higher, higher,' whilst I would be saying: 'Slower, slower, slower; breathe deeply, sink down into the pelvis, and relax.'

At this time, in 1970, was the beginning of the hippy movement. One day six bedraggled individuals knocked on my studio door and introduced themselves as a mobile theatre company. The leader asked: 'Is there love in here?' And I said: 'Yes, there is love everywhere.' So they joined the class. We were at that moment improvising. The theme was: 'There is no beginning, there is no end.' The six actors immediately closed their eyes and started moving around and every time they bumped into someone, they would open their eyes and say: 'I love you.' After a couple of classes I became rather fed up with these people. I talked to Jane about it and she said: 'Let them come and watch one of my classes.' And when they saw what was going on there they left smartly!"[12]

But beneath the humour there was a real issue. Jane Dudley's own dancing career left her increasingly crippled with arthritis and in a wheelchair by the end of her life. She remained true to her art, however, and in 2000, a year before her death, she choreographed and performed in 'Dancing Inside', a remarkable 40 minute programme for television in which she dances while sitting in her chair and also within the supporting arms of a handsome young man.

Now that Gerda was running t'ai-chi classes at The Place, a

physical, psychological and cultural lifeline awaited those curious enough to investigate. Choreographer Tim Lamford was a Place student between 1973 and 1977, and was one of the young dancers who sought out what was on offer at Gerda's classes. "Contemporary dance technique was not what it is now. It was extraordinarily visceral and dynamic, with more than a strand of toughness in it. Students, for good or ill, were pushed physically and psychologically up to, and beyond, their limitations. To the modern sensibility, some practices would be considered very harsh indeed, crossing the boundary into bullying. But that is how modern dance was often taught by 'the old school'. Achievement was totally defined by the teacher. The majority failed. Only those with bodies most suited to the demands of the technique found the training liberating. This was, in my opinion, largely to do with the teaching styles employed rather than with any inherent bad practice in the technique per se. However, if students had weakness in the knees, hips or back, the training led to distress rather than growing freedom of expression.

"Like most dancers then, we had little idea of how to take care of ourselves. At one extreme were the ascetic few who lived on whole foods, cosmic ideas and hot water; and at the other, energy junkies thriving on adrenalin, vodka and cigarettes.

"For many young people, intellectual and artistic life in the Seventies was intensely political. Some students read Chairman Mao's Little Red Book, formed collectives and dreamed of Cultural Revolution. Photographs of Madam Mao's choreography of The Red Detachment of Women were studied for their ardent militancy. It was into this world that Pytt brought her delicate, refined work, with its scent of Ancient China.

"T'ai-chi ch'uan was not at first on the curriculum. Pytt taught a public class that coincided with our lunch break. Straight after three hours of strenuous technique classes, and before a three and a half hour highly physical afternoon, we studied with Pytt. And paid her what we could afford.

"Pytt was deeply concerned that we knew so little about how to preserve our health. She saw how we hurt ourselves though trying too hard, in inappropriate ways, and taught us, apart from the t'ai-chi, massage techniques to stimulate energy in key parts of our bodies. She caused us to question how we danced."[13]

Gerda teaching at The Place in 1990

For Eva Karczag the issues were slightly different. She had already completed her classical ballet training and had danced with the London Festival Ballet. She was dissatisfied with where this path was taking her and was looking for other ways to move. "When I started to do Graham technique, that was different, but still there was some kind of stress. But something about the t'ai-chi felt like, yes, this is organic. I don't think I even had the word organic then, but it most definitely felt right. Interestingly, learning the t'ai-chi was not like learning dance. I mean I was very good at learning dance, learning steps, but the t'ai-chi, with its circularity, and the way certain pathways return and get replayed, often a little bit differently, this was not an easy thing to learn in the way I had been used to learning. So this was somehow about letting it drop into my body by doing it and doing it. And then Pytt's way of teaching of course. She would bring in her words of wisdom, those things that she had been thinking about. It began to open my mind to a whole other world, a whole other way of looking at life really. I think that was one thing that she wanted people to begin to consider. That the eastern way of looking at the world has some very important and profound things to say also to us westerners."[14]

Gerda Geddes and t'ai-chi had gained a foothold at The Place where a new vision of British contemporary dance was being explored. She had arrived at a personal, and also at a physical, place where the three defining strands of her life, psychology, dance and t'ai-chi, were at last beginning to merge into something greater than their component parts.

PERSONAL
SEARCHES

For many years...I worked through the movements carefully, thinking: how can I open up this movement and feel that it flows through a joint and that there is no hindrance anywhere? But then the Chinese say that in order to find this openness you have to become aware of the spirit, and it is the spirit which eventually opens everything up and then when you add the spirit it is not just the physical but it is the mental as well that opens up. By discovering the spirit you will find that the body and the spirit will work together as one unit.

Gerda Geddes   LOOKING FOR THE GOLDEN NEEDLE, p74

By the time she started teaching at The Place in 1970, Gerda had already met two people who became important influences.

Father Herbert Slade, a monk with the Society of St John the Evangelist, commonly known as the Cowley Fathers, was interested in the possibilities of combining eastern and western spiritual traditions. He wrote on the subject, and had encouraged yoga practice at The Anchorhold, a contemplative community that he led in Sussex. Sometime in the mid- to late-Sixties he became a t'ai-chi pupil of Gerda's after seeing one of her demonstrations. He then introduced t'ai-chi to the Anchorhold where Gerda made regular visits to teach and also to have wide-ranging discussions with Father Slade. As a result of this relationship, three black-garmented monks and a nun sometimes attended her classes at The Place.

Edith Schnapper, a Cambridge musicologist who also had a doctorate in comparative religion, was a committed Sri Aurobindian.

SRI AUROBINDO 1872–1950

Sri Aurobindo was an Indian nationalist, poet, writer and yogi. He was born in Calcutta and educated in England at St Paul's School, London and King's College, Cambridge. By the time he returned to India in 1893, he was fluent in English, French, Greek and Latin. Between 1902 and 1910 he was active in the struggle to free India from British rule. Leadership of an extreme nationalist group and editorship of a nationalist newspaper in English led to his imprisonment in 1908 on charges of the attempted bombing of a British magistrate. He was acquitted a year later. During his time in jail, his practice of yoga and meditation brought spiritual insights and he began to base his actions on the guidance of an inner voice

In 1910 he left British India for the French colony of Pondicherry in the far southeast of the country, where he later founded the Sri Aurobindo Ashram. There he devoted the remaining forty years of his life to the realisation of his vision that a divine life could be created here on earth. According to his teachings, the conditions for this occur when the evolving life of Man meets with, and is helped by, a higher spiritual consciousness which he called Supramental.

He viewed yoga not only as a tool for personal liberation but also for engaging with the cosmic evolutionary drive that he believed was destined to take the whole of mankind on to the higher 'Supramental' stage of consciousness. Yoga in this context has a special meaning. What Sri Aurobindo called Integral Yoga aims for complete God-realisation and complete transformation of human nature. Although he gives guidelines about its practice, there is no set method to follow for a very important reason. Individuals are different and their paths will therefore also be unique.

Early in May 1968, Gerda gave a t'ai–chi lecture and demonstration at Cambridge University. Her pupil Thetis Blacker had a hand in arranging the invitation. Thetis' sister Carmen Blacker taught in the Japanese department. She and her close friend Michael Loewe, who lectured in Chinese studies, had become intrigued by Thetis' boundless enthusiasm for t'ai-chi and Gerda Geddes. At the end of the evening, many in the audience signed up for lessons. Gerda began weekly visits to Cambridge where she taught thirty new pupils in two groups, one for students and one for staff and invited guests. The academics' group also included the painter Cecil Collins, his artist wife Elizabeth Collins, and Edith Schnapper.

Gerda taught the Cambridge classes for two years and, in some ways, the classes had as much influence on her as she did on them.

"Teaching at Cambridge was very important for me. It was very much a growth period to be with all those learned people. It made me feel very humble, actually."[1]

And, more importantly, she found a guru in Edith who introduced her to the teachings of Sri Aurobindo.

"I really had nobody to guide me until I found Edith Schnapper and Sri Aurobindo. I started off with books that I discovered myself. Then I referred to the bibliography of the book I was reading and chose something that I thought looked interesting. It wasn't like following a set university course where you go from A to B and learn this and learn that. It was much more like fumbling around in the Universe.

Edith was a real intellectual. I'm much more an intuitive person. I've always had some kind of affinity or understanding of people. I think that was born in me. Edith gave an intellectual structure to that.

And she brought me Sri Aurobindo and his beliefs, his preaching. One book, *The Synthesis of Yoga*, I reread so many times I almost knew it by heart. Sri Aurobindo seemed to be so clear and so quiet. There was lots about him that I admired. He made me see many things that nobody had told me about before. Edith Schnapper and I became friends and I considered her one of my main teachers. She supplied some very important information for my development, and what I experienced through Sri Aurobindo had an important influence on my interpretation of the t'ai-chi as an Allegorical Journey."[2]

Edith Schnapper's book *The Spiral Path of Spiritual Psychology*, published some years later, explores the ideas she introduced to the intellectually hungry Gerda. The basic thesis of this densely-argued slim volume is that there exists a barely recognised branch of psychology, spiritual psychology, which casts light on the psychological processes of the spiritual life and spiritual phenomena. It also helps with the understanding of some events which otherwise can be bewildering, frightening, and treated as psychological aberrations.[3] Such notions lent an intellectual framework to experiences Gerda had undergone, had understood intuitively, and was feeding into her developing understanding of t'ai-chi. Her own copy of the book has enthusiastic underlinings or margin notes beside references to symbolic paths or pilgrimages, standing in the moment, uncovering hidden potentialities, progressing by effort of will, the potency of silence coupled to immobility, constant change and passing through stage after stage, and recurring references to circles and spirals. Here and there she notes a connection to a specific t'ai-chi move.

The two women began to meet for meditation sessions. A diary entry records a remarkable series of events that throw light on the eclectic mixture of influences affecting Gerda at this time, and her intuitive sensitivity in tuning into events around her. It began with a tragic accident on 4th December 1970. The night was dark and icy as Gerda drove her daughter Harriet to the train station. A motorcyclist, who had lost control of his machine on the slippery road, was thrown hard against the front of Gerda's car and was rushed to hospital with head and chest injuries. He died a few hours later. At the time of his death, the family sheepdog back at Oldhouse Farm was very disturbed, would not settle, and started whimpering. A few days later Gerda spotted a squirrel beside a country lane. As she drove past, the squirrel seemed to throw itself against the side of her car. She stopped. The animal was dead by the roadside, just as the motorcyclist had lain.

"A few days later a bird came into the house early in the morning. I opened all doors and windows, but the bird did not try to fly out, it only wanted to be near me. As I walked up the stairs, the bird landed on top of my head and started pecking at my scalp. I only managed to brush it off in the bathroom and it flew out of the window there.

When I talked to Father Slade about these happenings he thought it to be the dead man man's soul asking for help. His soul wanted to enter into my body. Father Slade said I must open myself and not be afraid. Edith came and we meditated together which helped a great deal. After that I felt that the man was grateful for the help he had received."[4]

A few years earlier when Gerda had consulted the *I Ching* about t'ai-chi, the main image she had received was Ting, a ritual cauldron for cooking food. Now she was adding to the pot ingredients from an Anglican monk, whose search for spiritual truth had included pilgrimage to India and the practice of yoga; and a German intellectual who had found her life's meaning in the teachings of an Indian mystic. It was a potent brew. The following account has her using visualisation, meditation, and ideas from different traditions, to deal with fatigue brought on by teaching her first class at The Place.

"Gave my first lesson a couple of days ago with ten new pupils. Felt in tremendous form, but afterwards I was utterly exhausted, like a deflated balloon with complete exhaustion accompanied by a severe pain on the right side of my solar plexus. I had given all my energy out, received no recharge, and suffered acutely from a 'leaky aura'.

I then tried to be very still and let the light flow in through the solar plexus. Eventually there was no more leak. There seemed to be a hole out of which dark matter flowed, but when the hole healed I felt filled with light. Then suddenly there was a tremendous movement as if my diaphragm was pulled upwards towards my throat and out of the diaphragm came a stream of black tadpoles. With great force they flew out of my mouth and

I felt like spitting and being sick. But some of the tadpoles moved up to my brain. In the middle of the forehead 'third eye' there was a light so strong that nothing could darken it. But the tadpoles went zooming round and round and eventually rushed to the left side of my forehead where there was an acute pain. They all wanted to get out and I tried to find an opening for this stream. The harder I tried, the worse it got. I was panic-stricken and thought if an opening was made by force, some would get out but many more would then be able to enter the head. It was only by making a great effort – or not making an effort – to be perfectly still that the evil force could get out and then the light was allowed in.

After this I gave two classes without any personal effort: everything I said and did came through me and not from me."[5]

The final sentence contains an important key to understanding Gerda's progress at this time. She was doing more than practising or teaching t'ai-chi: she was living it, caught in a flow that she simply had to follow.

"I think that my teaching was at its strongest during that period (the 1970s and 1980s). I feel that the classes I gave over that period were quite luminous: that's why so many people remember them. The atmosphere was quite extraordinary at times. That has nothing to do with me wanting to do it; it was something that came through me. And it was a peak experience over some length of time. That isn't meant to be boasting, it was just something that happened."[6]

The first meeting with her t'ai-chi had a profound effect on many people, especially those who were unable to describe what was missing from their lives, but recognised it immediately. Their reaction was frequently the same as Thetis Blacker's: "I want to learn it."

At The Place, Gudrun Gylling and Eva Karczag both felt that way, and their dancer's eyes also recognised that here was a different way of using your body. For Eva, searching for a way of escaping the physical and philosophical restraints of traditional ballet training, it felt like a homecoming. "Here was this little lady…doing something that actually had a lot of power in it. I found that very interesting. As a young dancer, I'd been taught that power was being hard and fast and yet that wasn't what I was drawn to. Some kind of lyricism or flow was what I felt my whole being wanted to engage with. And actually when I first started doing the t'ai-chi…something about it felt right, it felt like I was coming home. I was meeting up with something that I had been looking for.

"I did struggle with traditional dance techniques. My body was not happy doing those forms. I felt that I couldn't push my body in ways that were required in order to get to where I wanted to in my dancing. And I felt that was what the t'ai-chi opened up for me. A way of moving that felt right. So in terms of whether it made any difference to my dancing back then, externally I don't know. It certainly did internally. And it confirmed the connection of mind, body and spirit."[7]

Away from The Place, other early pupils were also succumbing to the impact of Gerda's t'ai-chi. Musician Sue Phipps, Peter Pears' niece, worked regularly at the Aldeburgh Festival. On the morning of 7th June 1970, curiosity took her to a lecture demonstration that Gerda was giving in the Jubilee Hall at the invitation of Pears and Benjamin Britten. "I was then thirty-nine and just reaching what I suppose people call mid-life crisis and thinking there must be something better in life. Although my life was wonderful, there was a big void in there somewhere. I was thinking, 'Well maybe I should move towards the Orient for this one. Perhaps I'll go to some yoga classes.' But I hadn't been very convinced by that and wasn't actually doing anything about it. And quite suddenly I was just hit between the eyes by this amazing woman. I was absolutely floored by her. It was a mixture of wild elation and excitement and complete and utter awe. I was certain this was exactly what I was looking for and I had to go and find it."[8] The opportunity did not present itself until two years later when she and her uncle were working on a programme for a weeklong course for promising young singers, to be held at Snape in the Britten-Pears School for

Advanced Musical Studies. When they noticed that the draft programme had the students sitting all the time, except when they stood to sing, Pears agreed to his niece's suggestion and invited Gerda. "I thought; this is not going to be comfortable for them. They must have some movement somewhere. They've got to get up, go for a walk, do something. And then I suddenly thought: Pytt Geddes. So Peter wrote to her, because he knew her pretty well, and she said yes, she'd be delighted. And so she came down and for an hour, from nine until ten every morning before the classes started we all did t'ai-chi. During that one week she was there, I learned the first part. And after that I enrolled at The Place and got on with it."[9]

Catherine Robinson was living at Taena, a community in Gloucestershire founded by George Ineson and a group of fellow conscientious objectors during the Second World War. It began as a common-ownership farming community and later evolved into a looser structure of families. George practised meditation and was greatly influenced by Sri Aurobindo. Around 1970 Catherine first met t'ai-chi when Father Slade gave a demonstration to a yoga teachers' training course she was attending. Some time later she, George Ineson, and two friends had a weekly t'ai-chi lesson for five months from a novice monk who had learned from Father Slade, an arrangement which ended when the novice took his first vows. Back at Taena they worked hard on what they had been taught, but after two years only she and George Ineson still practised t'ai-chi and there was lots they were unclear about. When they contacted Gerda in 1974, she invited them to The Place. They arrived at the height of the teaching day when the now flourishing dance school was in full swing.

"When we met her, she said the only place we could talk was in the basement corridor. And we stood in this corridor, which was pretty grotty then, with lots of to-ing and fro-ing, and sweaty dancers in their leotards walking past. But she was completely focussed as she talked about the importance of the Tao and the philosophy behind the t'ai-chi. It was as if we were in another world from all the hubbub that was going on. She was completely unfazed. She talked to us for quite a long time then she invited us to join in the next class which she was just about to hold. When we'd told her how we had learned she was very sceptical about whether we would know anything at all, because she felt it was all very second hand. But at the end of the class she looked rather surprised and said: 'Well that wasn't too bad, really. I think you'd better come to my class regularly.'"[10]

These students, like many others, responded to Gerda's stillness, focussed energy, clarity of thought and action, and to the entrancing spectacle of a woman apparently moving under the influence of some mysterious force rather than the dictates of her own ego.

THE OPEN-HANDED TEACHER

*From cradle to grave we go through a process of change, of 'becoming' and
'de-becoming'; we are, all the time, on our way towards something else.
The Allegorical Journey of the t'ai-chi ch'uan shows these natural stages of
transformation with great clarity.*

*According to Chuang Tzu, our starting point is one of original ignorance;
we have no knowledge. As we go through life we accumulate knowledge
and learning which we eventually have to shed again, so that at the end of
our life we no longer have to hold onto our knowledge.*

*Working with the t'ai-chi ch'uan is a process of learning and unlearning.
As far as learning is concerned, one has to adhere to three basic principles:
flow, balance, and clarity.*

Gerda Geddes   LOOKING FOR THE GOLDEN NEEDLE, p85

During the early 1970s, Gerda had several regular teaching commitments. She went weekly to Cambridge and taught two groups there.
In London she taught a weekly class at an Alexander Technique centre and another at the College for Psychic Studies. Catherine
Robinson attended the class there for a time and found it an atmos-
pheric venue: "Pytt taught in a room surrounded by portraits of all sorts
of people who had founded the psychic studies college. Annie Besant

(Theosophist and social reformer) was there, staring down at us with beady eyes as we did t'ai-chi.[1] Sue Phipps told a stranger tale. "I was working away in the back of this class and suddenly somebody bumped into me, nearly knocked me over. I turned round and there wasn't anybody there. When I told Pytt afterwards she said, 'Oh I'm not a bit surprised. There are masses of very unhappy spirits around that place.' "[2]

Gerda continued to hire a studio at The Place and teach three classes a week. These were open sessions, but word had spread amongst the dancers who were attending in increasing numbers. Then in the mid-1970s she was invited to join the staff and spend three days teaching t'ai-chi to all first year students as a compulsory part of their curriculum. It was a major recognition of the contribution that Gerda and her t'ai-chi were making to the training of professional dancers.

With her combined teaching programme and the increasing invitations to give lectures and demonstrations, Gerda was almost a full-time t'ai-chi teacher. She was now fifty-eight. She could have been forgiven for feeling that the struggle she had undergone to reach this point had been vindicated and it was time to appreciate her achievements and the status she had attained. But that was not the path she was on. Entries in her diary record dreams and reflections whose titles hint at the intensity of their content: The Snake Creeps Down, The Archetypal Mother Figure, The Two Bodies, The Dream of Violence (or The Defence of the T'ai-chi), The Angel with the Broken Wing, The Battle between the Destructive and the Spiritual Forces, The Holy Trinity.

An entry for 9th July 1974 records the death of her mother Lydia at the age of eighty-four. The two women had become so close that Gerda considered her mother one of her dearest friends. In a letter for Gerda's 50th birthday on 17th July 1967 Lydia had written: "In many ways I admire you. Your life has not always been easy, but you have persevered and lived with more determination and purpose than most women. Many let things slide, waste their time, give up, and achieve nothing. But I feel that you have a determination and a guiding light which seems to see you through." Lydia had gone now. Gerda, despite the success she was enjoying, still had her own light to pursue.

She was a natural storyteller and, when she taught, she also told stories of China, of the Tao, of Yin and Yang, of the Allegorical Journey she had discovered in t'ai-chi's symbolism. She was passing on not a system of movement but an approach to life. True to the wisdom of Confucius which underpinned her approach as a teacher, she was showing the students one corner of a profound teaching, then looking out for those who were capable of finding the other three. Since the days of her Reichian analysis she had prized creativity as a key to human meaning and happiness. She was equally clear that finding the suitable vehicle for one's creative expression was an individual responsibility.

"I had found that practically all the symbols in the t'ai-chi were connected with something higher. But not everyone necessarily understood that. Some people understand those sorts of things and other people don't. I can't be responsible for anybody else and I don't want to push anybody. So I did my teaching with open hands. It was there to be picked up. And if people wanted to go elsewhere, let them go."[3]

Gerda's reference to 'open hands' is a nod in the direction of t'ai-chi's early history as a monastic or temple discipline not readily available to outsiders, a world of 'closed' or 'half-open' teaching where potential students might have to knock many times and wait patiently at the gate until they were admitted. Even then, their ability and commitment might be tested at a 'door' class before they were admitted to the training hall. Once t'ai-chi had made its way into the wider community, knowledge was often held closely within families such as the Chen family from whom the servant Yang Lu-ch'an, is reputed to have learned by stealth.

Relics of such traditions can still be found within modern t'ai-chi. Some schools stress their lineage through a line of transmission going back from the current master to an important historical figure. Explicitly or implicitly, respect for the master may be invoked as a reason for not attending classes in another school or learning another style, and group membership emphasised by standardised clothing.

Gerda gave short shrift to any attempts to view her as a 'master' and firmly resisted the notion of founding or leading a school. She prized individuality, expected others to do the same, and was suspicious of collective identities wherever she found them. For her, truth did not lie in protecting the known, but rather in using it as a launching pad for the next creative leap.

"Through 'Parting the Wild Horse's Mane', we have to let go of aggression and fear before we can find gentleness in ourselves. In fact we have to discover that the important issue is letting go, not holding on to any of our acquired knowledge or emotions. If we hold on to too much, it might make us proud and we might come to think of ourselves as a guru or a great teacher which would be very much against Taoist principles."[4]

For Gerda, the teacher was on a journey as much as the pupil. Perhaps she had travelled a little further and had something to teach, but she also had a long way to go and a lot to learn. So she opened her hands and her heart, and put her trust in her pupils' judgement. As Thetis Blacker put it: "She taught all she knew with great simplicity and always treated one as an absolute equal. And when I said: 'I have learned so much from you', she would always counter it by saying: 'Well I've learned so much from you.'"[5]

Sue Phipps, another early pupil, was one of the first Gerda encouraged to become a teacher. "Pytt said, 'I've taught you all I can teach you now. The way forward for you is to start teaching, and then you will go on learning. And in fact she was right. But I also had my difficulties. I'd come back to her sometimes and say: 'Look, I've had to change this particular move. It didn't quite work for the students, the way I taught it. So I've changed it into something that does work for me and for them.' And she'd say: 'Absolutely right. That's how it progresses. You do it your own way.'"[6]

It was a lesson that stayed with her pupils and that sustained Gudrun Gylling who returned to Sweden and spent many years teaching, and following her t'ai-chi path, in relative isolation. "It's quite easy to be uncertain about what you are doing yourself. But somehow you have to explore. I changed a few things in the form. Pytt's way of giving the form to you was a great help. She never said there was only one answer, that this is absolutely the correct way of doing it. She never did that. So I felt I was free to find out other things for myself. She trusted you to do that."[7]

Catherine Robinson also went on to teach, and carried with her the fruits of Gerda's open-handed approach. "She was completely against being a sort of guru and making a name for herself, and getting us all to belong to something. She was completely against all that. And she never wanted to tie the form down and say, this is the form and no other. She was very specific and clear about what she was teaching. She very much encouraged you to go out and learn from other people, but she also said; 'Don't go trying to collect forms from lots of different people. First learn one, and then go and try others.' To her, the actual form was not so important as long as it was based on the t'ai-chi classics and principles. She was the first to say that she had only learnt one corner of t'ai-chi. Because of when she learned, and because she was a woman, she wasn't taught the martial arts applications, or Pushing Hands. She was very happy for us to go and learn them from other people.

"I learned from her that my job as a teacher is to help people discover the t'ai-chi inside themselves, not to turn them into clones of me. That was what Pytt taught. Not: 'I am the person who knows this thing and I'm going to impart it to you.' But: 'My job is to pass on this gift, and it's for you to find out how the t'ai-chi expresses itself in your body, as something unique to you.'"[8]

Gerda taught this way from a life-long conviction: the only answers that really matter, the only authentic truths, are those that we find deep within ourselves. It was a belief based on insights she had gained firstly from her psychoanalysis, then had reconfirmed through t'ai-chi. They are insights concerned with individual truth and personal clarity, and how they overcome human fear and anger.

"Fear is probably one of the original emotions. Fear is underneath and anger lies on top of the fear. If you can dissolve your anger you come to the fear. Letting go of fear in the t'ai-chi comes at the beginning of the third part, The Parting of the Wild Horse's Mane. They were very frightened of the wild horse in China and you could only approach that horse if you had no fear, because the horse would immediately sense your fear. So that is a stage forward in your development, when you can go without fear. And then the t'ai-chi becomes the whole of life, something that you have to work your way through. But you should never say to someone: 'This is the right way'. You can only say 'It's my way; it's what I have found out. It's what makes me open up and not be afraid.' The Chinese wisdom tells me that when I have no more fear in my body I can let go. Whether that is true for others or not I have no idea. You can only go by your own truth. You can learn from other people and they may from time to time help you along the way. But ultimately it is your way, and you have to go there alone.[9]

I think in life there is supposed to be a mystery. There is a divine power, but how it manifests itself I can't tell you. We are part of the stream of the whole universe, all of us. Understanding that brings a certain amount of clarity into our lives. It takes away a lot of our basic fear, because what we fear is the unknown."[10]

So she taught with open hands: not just about a way of moving, but about a way of life. How much was picked up, or how little, was a responsibility for each pupil.

During the 1970s several of Gerda's pupils started to teach. Father Slade taught at the Anchorhold and also incorporated t'ai-chi into a system of movements to aid meditation.[11] Sue Phipps taught classes in Oxford where Gerda made regular visits. Two teachers emerged from the Cambridge classes, a Vietnamese man called Chu and Bronwyn Hipkin who took over at Cambridge when Gerda began to find the seven-hour return train journey from Oldhouse Farm too demanding. Thetis Blacker also did some teaching at Cambridge. George Ineson and Catherine Robinson taught open classes together at Taena. Gudrun Gylling returned to Sweden to teach t'ai-chi. Kinthissa, a

Burmese-born woman who had come to The Place to train as a dancer, began to assist at Gerda's t'ai-chi classes and then went on to become a full-time t'ai-chi teacher.

The ripples were starting to spread.

The Biographer's Thread 9: Ask the Experts

Gerda loved conversation and was a very good storyteller. She tended towards reticence, however, when pressed for the personal information which often lies hidden behind the narrative drive of a good tale well told. My own background in psychology and t'ai-chi was invaluable in finding strategies for uncovering further information from these important areas of her life. Sadly, my knowledge of contemporary dance is woefully limited, or was until I started writing this book. It was therefore difficult for me to assess what influence Gerda and her t'ai-chi might have had on dance and dancers.

When I tried to explore this with her, she slipped deftly behind answers like: "Influence on dance? Oh, I don't know. That's for other people to say".

In the following chapter they do.

CREATIVE CIRCLES

The final circle, the 'Greater Heavenly Circulation', starts at the soles of the feet. On the in-breath it circles behind the body to the top of the head and on the out-breath circles in front of the body back to the soles of the feet. You have now filled the atmosphere around you with your awareness, so when you start moving you are conscious of the surrounding space.

Gerda Geddes　　　　　LOOKING FOR THE GOLDEN NEEDLE, p95

Gerda taught at The Place for twenty-six years. During that time, her influence spread in different directions. Creative dancers, looking for new ways to move, were the immediate and obvious beneficiaries.

CONTEMPORARY DANCE AND T'AI-CHI

Martha Graham, whose technique played such an important role at The Place, was one of a number of seminal contemporary dance pioneers. They emerged in the 1930s mainly in the U.S.A., where the grip of classical ballet was less firm than in Europe. Their rebellion against classical dance built on the work of earlier 20th century innovative dancers like the American Isadora Duncan and the Germans Mary Wigman and Rudolf Laban. Breaking out of the ballet mould allowed dancers to explore a greater range of fluidity and to push the boundaries of body movement. New dance techniques began to evolve. They included Graham Technique which uses contraction and release, fall and recovery, and is characterised by floorwork and being grounded, in contrast to the flying leaps and upward movements of classical ballet; and Cunningham Technique, named after

American dancer Merce Cunnigham, which emphasises the body's own 'line of energy' to promote easy, natural movement. The trend was shifting away from dance as a story-telling medium using forms imposed on the body, and towards a focus on the processes of dance creation and the exploration of new ways of moving from the inside of the body outwards.

By the 1960s, thanks to the work of Sophia Delza, an awareness of t'ai-chi was seeping into American contemporary dance. But it was virtually unknown in the British dance scene until Gerda Geddes walked through the doors of The Place in 1970 and began to talk about, and teach, an old Chinese form of movement based on flow, clarity, relaxation, circularity and inner energy.

Many dancers who trained at The Place, and learned t'ai-chi in Gerda's classes, went on to become important figures in the development of British and European contemporary dance where t'ai-chi, along with other innovations like release technique and contact improvisation, contributed important themes of breath and energy, skeletal alignment, groundedness, minimising tension, developing fluidity, and moving from the centre.

At a celebration of Gerda's life held at The Place in 2006, choreographer and t'ai-chi teacher Tim Lamford, one of her early pupils, summed up t'ai-chi's contribution to his, and to dance's, development. "At first I loved the t'ai-chi simply because it was so beautiful. Dancing Fair Lady Works With Shuttles, with its sense of circles breathing within a shifting kaleidoscope of squares, was like dancing a mandala.

"We began to discover things we couldn't feel in any other class. Being able to feel the floor was a new experience, to become aware of the tension in our feet was to begin to release it elsewhere in our bodies. We became more conscious of the movement of weight, which led to a realisation of the possibilities of what could be done with it. It could be held in different ways, it could be dropped, and the impulse utilised for improvisation.

"By the mid-seventies, dancers were hungry to discover new ways of moving. The old techniques that we were trained in could no longer be used for the vocabulary of dance. The movement carried no meaning for us. We had to look elsewhere for inspiration.

"Julyen Hamilton and Maedee Dupres, among many others, experimented with the t'ai-chi. Rootedness gave a new balance. Weight shifted earthwards, to be thrown with abandon into circular patterns that rippled through the body. Single weightedness led to new softer ways of turning and of touching. Julyen and Maedee worked with Rosemary Butcher, who choreographed many acclaimed works using their t'ai-chi influenced improvisations. Release technique soon came into the mix, along with capoeira, the Brazilian martial art created by enslaved Africans. Gradually through the work of a generation of dancers, these influences synthesised into a new ground of exploration. In time a fresh vocabulary developed, which is still recognisable in the way contemporary dancers move today... The revolution in dance language which grew out of the need for spontaneity, fluidity and groundedness, has penetrated every corner of artistic western theatre dance."[1]

Another early pupil, Eva Karczag, went on to become an international dancer, choreographer and educator. She too recognises Gerda's deep and fundamental contribution both at a personal level and in the wider contemporary dance context. "My lower back had been pulled into overarched-ness because of the ways I had forced my legs to turn out in ballet. I remember one class when, through the soft-knees stance of t'ai-chi, suddenly this holding tension gave way, my lower back let go, and my pelvis fell into place underneath me. Pytt came over and said: 'Yes, that's it', and rubbed her hand down my back. As I began to do more touring I would return to her t'ai-chi classes whenever I was in London. T'ai-chi had become one of the major elements of my training and taught me about respect for the body and strength through softness, about energy and how to move using energy rather than muscle force, I learned how to 'listen' to what is inside and around me, and how to move while containing an internally expansive releasing state, an integrated openness. The t'ai chi taught me subtlety and let me experience weight and buoyant suppleness. Perhaps most importantly, I found out how powerful this easeful way of moving can be.

"In New York there were dancers who practiced forms like t'ai-chi, aikido, and yoga, who were bringing those other ways of looking at movement and the body into their training and performing. Not so much of that was happening on this side of the Atlantic. Here in England, I was aware of Pytt teaching t'ai-chi to dancers; the work of Strider; Mary Fulkerson who brought release technique to Dartington College; X6, a collective making experimental dance work."[2]

Strider, the group that Eva Karczag had joined in the early seventies, was a radical, experimental dance company. Choreographer Richard Alston formed it in 1972 after he completed his dance training at the The Place. Like Eva Karczag and Tim Lamford, he had also become an early t'ai-chi pupil of Gerda's. Strider operated as a democratic company with all the performers choreographing works for the repertoire. The group investigated and extended the radical developments in dance which had emerged in America during the 1960s as a direct challenge to the approach of choreographers such as Martha Graham. The direction of change was away from narrative and towards the exploration of dance in its own right and for its own sake.

It was with Strider that Richard Alston set out on the career that has led to him being recognized as a significant and influential choreographer. His Richard Alston Dance Company is currently based at The Place where he is Artistic Director. His biography on The Place website acknowledges the influences of t'ai-chi and Gerda on his work. "Release technique, to which Alston was introduced in the 1970s, draws on the principles of Eastern movement forms such as t'ai-chi. Central characteristics of Eastern movement forms are that the weight is low and the emphasis is on a harmonious, free flow of movement. The arm gestures alternate between circular, peripheral movements and straight, direct movements from the centre. The balance of weight shifts evenly from one foot to the other, keeping the skeleton constantly in a dynamic balance. Centring the body and the energy is central to these Eastern movement forms, and to the Western movement forms derived from them. There is an emphasis on skeletal alignment and lack of muscular tension, on freely flowing movement which circles around the body, gathering the energy in order to send it out, only to gather it in again...The performer's energy and body is thus always in a dynamic balance, ready to move in any direction, at any moment."[3]

"Alston recalls that Pytt Geddes, his t'ai-chi teacher when he was a student at LCDS, argued for art which was a force for good, rather than for art which was always a force for negative criticism of life and society, a position which she considered to have been predominant in the twentieth century. This was a view with which Alston found himself in accord, then and now. Indeed, he has noted that, even now, he is interested in dance in which a sense of a harmonious community is articulated."[4]

Gerda's belief in the benevolence of art had long roots which fed on the moments of illumination which were central to her view of creativity and human development.

"It was an attitude that I had from early in my life: part of creativity was always to search for the positive. If you look at a painting, it only makes sense to you if it touches your heart. You can go through huge galleries in a sort of fog until all of a sudden there is something that shines at you and touches you; then you feel connected to the artist. That's why I was so very strongly moved and influenced by Turner in my younger days. With me, it's always something about the light. Not just in a painting: I can see the light in a building, or I can see it in nature. Certainly in a dancer; perhaps more often in a dancer than in any other artist, because the dancer experiences that light and you see it at the same time. When a dancer portrays something godlike or divine, which can happen as you watch a performance, you then find yourself in the divine light which the dancer experiences at that moment. This ephemeral, spontaneous quality of dance is so wonderful.

If you can bring a student into the light or make a student aware of that light through using your movement or your words, and it's very often words that portray it, then I feel that you've done your job. You can't do more than that."[5]

OUTWARD FLOW

If you discover the light within, you will at the same time discover the light without. Your energy can penetrate to the circumference of the circle which surrounds you, so when you become aware of an inward flowing force you will at the same time find the outward flowing energy. Through these momentous discoveries the t'ai-chi ch'uan again reminds us that we are still very much a part of the whole, but we may at this point begin to function on a higher level of awareness.

Gerda Geddes   LOOKING FOR THE GOLDEN NEEDLE, p79

The creative circles radiating out from Gerda and her t'ai-chi extended far beyond The Place and the world of dance.

"The t'ai-chi helped many dancers to avoid injuring themselves, that was an important thing. But there were also people who woke up in other directions. They found out they could alter things in their own creative discipline. Thetis Blacker was very influenced by the t'ai-chi in her work. Her batiks became very much softer than they had been before. You could see a flow coming in. And into the work of other people who were painting, and writing. I always hoped that t'ai-chi could help people discover the creativity inside themselves; that it would open up a door for them to go through and develop creatively. With many people I think that it changed their way of living: maybe they became more tolerant and not so judgmental. In the end, the concentrated point of what you come to is this extraordinary awareness. And the awareness is global."[1]

The impact of t'ai-chi on artist Thetis Blacker had literally been life changing. "It was very curious. I'd been in a steel corset for twelve years and I'd become reconciled to being permanently in pain. The orthopaedic surgeon had done everything he could think of to my spine. I'd be carted into hospital by ambulance from time to time, then they would simply tell me that nothing else could be done for me. But I never asked myself, and I never asked Pytt, whether I'd be able to do the t'ai-chi. I just knew I wanted to do it. And I found that the t'ai-chi way of relaxing my back and moving with slightly bent knees seemed to straighten my spine. Within five weeks I was no longer in pain and in five months, when I had learned the whole t'ai-chi sequence, I could do all the things that the orthopaedic surgeon at Guy's Hospital had said I'd never be able to do again. Like jumping from a height and like bending and picking up heavy things. I could do them! I threw away my steel corset. I didn't need it anymore. I was very lucky. Having been an opera singer and having been trained for the operatic stage, which also means stage movement, I had good physical memory. I could do what I was told to. I could imitate what I saw naturally, that was something I did have. So I was able to learn the sequence very easily. And I practised at home every day and night. I became obsessional about it, absolutely fascinated. Here was the answer. And of course Pytt's philosophical accompanying commentary to this was just up my street: not couched in 'religious' terms. This really dug me into the t'ai-chi very deeply.

"Within two years I was able to take over Pytt's teaching class in Cambridge, when the burden of travelling from Kent became too onerous for her. I taught two classes of about twenty pupils once a week until I went to the Far East on a Churchill fellowship. By that time of course Pytt had really become a mentor of mine in every sense.

"After I learned the t'ai-chi, I evolved a system of painting which was based on my breathing and my movement. I work on a very large scale and it requires the batik cloth to be on a large flat table. Previously, I used to have to lean over at an agonising angle to make the brush strokes and to paint the dye on. The pain would be so phenomenal that I'd have to lie down and recover from time to time. But when I began doing the t'ai-chi, I found that I could make the brush strokes from my knees. I would move the weight from the right foot to the left foot and my arm would follow. I would take the wax or the dye up on the in-breath. The wax was at three hundred degrees and had to be applied while still very hot, so one couldn't paint for more than about three seconds at a time or it would become too cool. So on the in-breath I put the brush into the pot and then on the out-breath I would make the brushstroke. And of course there was such strength and flow in it. And I also found I could reach further and I could work for much longer periods because my spine was straight. It completely transformed the appearance of my work. I got a flow and power and also a sense of space. Thanks to my deep and slow breathing, my mental concentration intensified and my imagination clarified.

"Without the discipline of t'ai-chi practice, I could never have managed to make the Winchester Cathedral Creation Banners, nor the Phoenix Altar frontals in St George's Chapel at Windsor Castle. People looking at my work can instantly tell which are my 'pre-t'ai-chi period' and which are 'post-t'ai-chi'. The best of me is in my painting, and the best of that is because of t'ai-chi, and therefore because of Pytt."[2]

And the influence of Gerda and her t'ai-chi was spreading more widely, a development aided by the small but growing number of her pupils who were now teaching. In 1973 and 1974, she taught at the Britten-Pears School for Advanced Musical Studies where, once the Aldeburgh Festival was over, six week-long master classes were held at Snape for promising young singers. She enjoyed the opportunity to work with a different creative group.

"It was very interesting. I was experienced in teaching dancers and now I had to think about the needs of singers. The professions each have their specific difficulties and problems. How could I help a singer but in a different way to a dancer? Well, they make different demands on their bodies. Dancers need help to avoid hurting their joints which are their vulnerable points. On the other hand, with singers you have to work very hard on developing movement in the diaphragm and the rib cage, and that movement has to be connected up with the rest of the body.

I met so many interesting people, top singing coaches who came from Vienna, Paris and other major singing centres. I was able to attend many of these master classes. That was exactly the same as happened at The Place where lots of famous American dancers visited and I also went as a spectator to their classes. They were both very essential and interesting places to teach."[3]

From 1975 onwards, t'ai-chi input to the Britten-Pears School was taken over by Sue Phipps. She was by then already teaching t'ai-chi in Oxford where she continued to teach classes for the next fifteen years. Between 1980 and 1991, she also taught t'ai-chi at the Guildhall School of Music.

Catherine Robinson started teaching in the late-1970s, and by the mid-1980s was playing an important role in the development of how people accessed Gerda's t'ai-chi. "I was at one of those points in life when I really could have gone in all sorts of different directions. I didn't have any real commitments; a house or a partner or a family or anything. I really didn't know what to do and I decided that I would go and talk to all of the wise people that I knew. And of course Pytt was one of them. We said to one another: 'There is something that we have to do together.' I thought at first that it meant that I had to go to her classes in London. But actually it turned out that I came to live in Kent and began to teach a class in Wadhurst, not far from where she lived. She'd had the idea that she wanted to teach local people, and not just go up to London. She started a class but by the end of the first term she realised that it was just far too much for her to take on and she couldn't keep it going. And so she handed it all over to me; I took over from January 1987."[4]

For the next ten years, Catherine, as well as teaching her own class, organised what became known as Cranbrook days. She would regularly hire the Vestry Hall in the village of Cranbrook and t'ai-chi teachers and students would meet for a day run by a guest teacher.

Gerda was regularly the guest. Between March 1988 and December 1996 she led nineteen Cranbrook days, and these were usually fully booked. Gerda's teaching was around a theme and often illustrated by stories, readings from Chinese classics, reflections on t'ai-chi and on her life. The themes ranged far and wide: flow, balance and clarity; circles within the t'ai-chi form, learning, simplicity and complexity; openness, loosening and muscular armouring; the circling breath and the healing breath; the I Ching and three kinds of change; heredity, environment, and the Spiral Path; spiritual psychology. There are references to Reichian psychology, to dreams, to Taoist classics. Her notes and the transcripts of what she said reveal a woman who is confident, assured, authoritative; whose own life journey has led to integration and knowledge that she wants to share.

Gerda also travelled to the West Country and taught similar days at the invitation of John Llewellyn who had learned t'ai-chi a decade earlier from George Ineson. One evening, Gerda had come to Taena and given a talk and demonstration of her t'ai-chi. For John Llewellyn it was an unforgettable night. "We were all absolutely fascinated by her. The clarity of the way she put things over. The beautifully fluid way she moved, the energy that just came out from her."[5] That experience drew John to Cranbrook and also to some of Gerda's classes at The Place. Once he started teaching classes himself, he arranged three days in the 1990s when Gerda came to teach in Cheltenham. As at Cranbrook, these were extremely popular and well attended by a mixture of students and teachers.

In May 1994, Catherine organised a well-attended weekend event which drew together many of the people who had been Gerda's pupils and were now teaching t'ai-chi. In the same year, Gerda made her first instructional t'ai-chi video[6] which incorporated *The Magic Bird Spreads Its Wings,* a documentary about her life and work made by Norwegian Television.

Gerda's influence was also extending into the wider world. Between 1984 and 1994 she gave at least twenty-five lectures and demonstrations at the invitation of a wide range of people including The Analytical

Psychology Club of London, The Westminster Pastoral Foundation, The Association for Dance Movement Therapy, and a lecture at Guy's Hospital. Magazine articles appeared and she made prime time television appearances including one on the Roy Castle Show.

Whatever the venue, her message was the same. T'ai-chi, beautiful and enthralling as it appeared when she demonstrated it, was not an end in itself. It was a means of making sense of one's life journey and finding one's creative centre. The Allegorical Journey was now guiding her life, and she was offering it to those prepared to pick up a corner.

PINNING DOWN THE GOLDEN NEEDLE

In order to become clear thinking and focussed you first have to push away the disturbances, the Monkeys. Then there is the image of the bird Slant Flying or Magic Bird Standing On One Leg where, through a very long in and out breathe, you receive a blessing or you receive grace which enables you to Look For The Golden Needle and bring forth your creation through Opening The Fan to show your masterpiece to the world.

Gerda Geddes   LOOKING FOR THE GOLDEN NEEDLE, p78

The ever-widening circles created by Gerda's t'ai-chi influence were reflected in the intriguing social mix which began to grace social events *chez* Geddes.

The new people in their mother's life intrigued her daughters, themselves flowering from adolescence into young adulthood. "The dancers who came down to Oldhouse Farm were wonderful, glorious, 'darling' kind of theatrical people; some very sexy men and very gorgeous girls."[1] The visitors saw a different side of Gerda as they lolled on the lawn and sipped their Pimms before lunching on homegrown salad. David enjoyed this development. He was gregarious, amusing company who regaled his new and attractive guests with his fund of stories, enjoyed his supportive role, and liked to quip that earlier in their marriage Gerda had been Mr Geddes's wife: now he was Mrs Geddes's husband. Another section of the group was her t'ai-chi people, mostly women, some of whom were already teaching, and many of whom were finding in Jane and Harriet's mother a role model of their own.

Other visitors were mentors for Gerda. Ola Raknes, the Reichian therapist from wartime Oslo, visited Oldhouse Farm on several occasions during a period when he was making regular trips to London to help with the setting up of a Reichian Centre. Father Slade visited. Edith Schnapper sometimes stayed for a few days. Edith had been to India to visit the Aurobindo group at Pondicherry. She brought Sri Aurobindian books and the two women meditated together. And if Edith looked after aspects of mind and spirit, the body was the province of another friend, Lady Rosemary Russell, a practitioner of the alternative therapy, radionics, as well as homeopathy and the Metamorphic Technique. She was a woman of diverse and esoteric leanings, once described as ranging "from Anthroposophy to Zen by way of dolphins and LSD" and including interest in Gurdjieff, Ouspensky, the *I Ching*, Subud, and Sufism.[2] Through the eyes of the Geddes daughters, there was something of the white witch about Rosemary, not least because if anything ailed them, Rosemary was likely to place a head hair or a toe-clipping into her radionics black box, turn some dials, and recommend a treatment.

In 1979 the Geddes's sold Oldhouse Farm, their family home for twenty years and bought Clayfield, a bungalow in Etchingham, Sussex. Both daughters had by now completed their university educations. Jane married just three weeks before David and Gerda moved into their new house. Harriet was busy travelling and spent five months of that year in the U.S.A. Gerda was delighted with her new modern home, a view not shared by the other family members.

"It was a beautifully big, extremely comfortable, bungalow. After Oldhouse Farm, which leaked in every orifice, this bungalow was so warm that we were always comfortable and the heating bills were halved. But the children hated the bungalow and to begin with David did as well. He said 'People like us don't live in bungalows!' and I said 'Well we do, you know, because now we are living in one.' Slowly, slowly, he came around to it."[3]

David had by now retired and planned to study for a PhD in History. Although Gerda travelled to The Place in London three days a week and had other regular t'ai-chi commitments, she saw Clayfield as their retirement home. And life there included some of the common tensions when a retired husband is suddenly at home seven days a week. Gerda wanted to gather her thoughts about what she had learned and begin writing about it. David expected them to do things together, or for Gerda to tell him what the day held. Eventually he installed himself and his record collection in the study where he enjoyed classical music at a level which threatened the house's foundations. Maybe the bungalow wasn't too bad after all! There is a bitter-sweet tone to an August 1980 entry in Gerda's diary.

"We have now lived at Clayfield for ten months. Both David and I love the place; the comfort of the house and the wonderful surroundings. Up till now I have been too busy with the house and garden and have not yet settled down to my desk. But this winter I hope I can gather my material together."[4]

In hindsight, she had a much more forthright way of describing the relationship.

"To begin with, we could hardly live in the same house. He was surrounded by tremendous sounds all the time. And I couldn't stand it. I had him around me for twenty-four hours every day. He was very restless. 'What shall we do now? Can't we go here, there, do something?' And I thought 'I've got to get away from this somehow!'"[5]

Then Gerda had a stroke of genius. She bought a wooden shed, put it in a secluded corner of the garden, and had it turned into her own private den. Simon Rickard, partner of Gerda's pupil Catherine Robinson, carried out the 'conversion'. "The small prefabricated potting-shed was an odd-looking construction with a sloping roof. A full-width angled window ran along one side and looked out over a thickly wooded slope to the valley beyond. The door was on the far end, and it was not possible to see the house once you were inside. Pytt asked if I could make the interior more habitable without compromising its basic simplicity. For insulation, I packed the walls and ceiling with slabs of polystyrene then covered them with long thin waney-edged slices of freshly sawn spruce, intended for the manufacture of fence panels. They were rough, hairy and oozing with sap, but stapled on in over-lapping rows they created a suitably backwoods atmosphere and on sunny days they filled the hut with a heady resinous aroma. I fixed up a simple desk-top inside the window and Pytt furnished the property with a couple of camping chairs, a rush mat, a spiral candlestick, a small portable typewriter and a few well-chosen artefacts to hang on the walls. The shed became retreat, study and interview-room for Pytt; over the next few years, many of her t'ai-chi friends and students spent quiet hours there in conversation with her.

"I was well aware that Pytt frequently regarded the male partners of her t'ai-chi girls as feckless, spineless or in other ways inadequate, so I was genuinely delighted to find that my part in the creation of the 'hut' seemed to earn me a permanent place in her affections."[6]

In contrast, the hideaway did not initially find a place close to David's heart: quite the opposite.

"In the beginning he looked at that hut with very unfriendly eyes. He would accuse me of not loving him any more because I shut myself away down there. Eventually he began to familiarise him-self with the idea that I wasn't available to him twenty-four hours a day. But he was slightly jealous of the hut. He said: 'Why did you think about making it? I should have thought about doing that. That hut should have been my hut!' And I said: 'But it isn't, it's mine.' It was eventually christened 'The Promised Land'."[7]

So David stayed at home with classical music and his PhD. He never quite lost his covetousness of The Promised Land. Sometimes he would tiptoe across the lawn and peep round the corner of the hut to see if Gerda was asleep. Usually she wasn't. She had started to write *Looking for the Golden Needle*.

The thoughts and ideas that Gerda set out to pin down had been gestating for the past twenty years, ever since the first surge of excitement when she began to read about Chinese culture and find references to symbols that cropped up in the names of t'ai-chi moves. Central to her teaching was what she called the Allegorical Journey. She had discovered, hidden within t'ai-chi, a powerful spiritual guide. For her, a t'ai-chi 'player' expressed in movement an allegory for the life-to-death journey of a human being. T'ai-chi could be used to understand the unfolding of an individual life; to uncover universal truths; to nourish life in all its phases; to understand existence in terms of universal energy, or chi; and to prepare for death which is no more or less than the return of energy to its universal source.

"After having worked on the t'ai-chi ch'uan for a number of years, it became increasingly clear that using it just as a ritual of callisthenics or as a health exercise was not enough. The physical movements had become absorbed into my body. My body could understand the Cyclic Change, the continuous flow of never ending circles, but in order to find further development I had to make use of the symbols. Whereas the Cyclic Change returns to its starting point, Sequent Change is an onward moving process which reveals spiritual growth represented by images and symbols."[8]

The references to Cyclic and Sequent change come directly from the Taoist thought, as expressed in the *I Ching*.

"There is a close connection between the t'ai-chi ch'uan and the *I Ching*. In the *I Ching* a distinction is made between three kinds of change. Firstly, there is None Change, the fixed point to which all change can be referred. The image of None Change is the Mountain or Keeping Still. In the t'ai-chi ch'uan we start by Keeping Still and we return to the Mountain and the Stillness at the end of each part.

Secondly, there is Cyclic Change, the four seasons, night and day, being born and passing away. Cyclic Change is represented by the body movements. The movements of the body are based on the circle, an interaction between the Yin and the Yang, a constant flow of energy, chi, waxing and waning, active and passive, full and empty.

Lastly we have Sequent Change, an onward moving process which never returns. The image of Sequent Change is the Taoist sage riding on a bird or flying through the air to the land of the Immortals where he becomes one with the Tao. The symbols of the t'ai-chi ch'uan refer to Sequent Change. They reveal a spiritual development which becomes clear through their interpretation."[9]

In the version of Yang style which Gerda had learned from her teachers, she became increasingly convinced that its three parts, comprising a total of thirteen sequences, told a coherent sequential story which was a metaphor for human life. And the story was guided by the appearance of a bird in different guises, most frequently in a move called Single Whip when the fingers of the right hand are gathered together in a manner that mimics a bird's beak. In writing the book, she drew not just on what she had learned from her reading and from her body. She also gave free rein to coincidence, dreams and the murmurings of her unconscious mind. Sometimes, as in the following conversation, it can be difficult to be sure when she is speaking imaginatively, metaphorically, telling a dream, or reporting real events. When she talks about pillars connecting heaven and earth, it is a reference to a t'ai-chi move called Fair Lady Works With Shuttles, where the 'fair lady' is Kuan Yin, the goddess of mercy and compassion.

"Every movement comes from somewhere, and it originates in a circle. You have to follow the circle. Satprem, a follower of Sri Aurobindo, talks a great deal about circles. He says that you have to fill the circle until it's at bursting point, then there's a moment when you can slip out of that circle and up to the next level. That's illustrated in each sequence of the t'ai-chi. The movement of the bird closing its beak in Single Whip is connected to that. A Chinese quotation says: 'The bird sings its song. When the song is finished, the bird closes its beak in silence'. Often after one of the little t'ai-chi sequences, you close the circle with the Single Whip. That is one little creative episode. And when you do the Single Whip, you also draw out from the bird's mouth this silken thread. You draw it gently until it stops, then you drop the silk on the floor.

Eventually, as you go on through each sequence you accumulate more and more silk and it lies there in heaps of unmade strings. Then you come to the Fair Lady's four corners…I had a dream: these things often come in dreams, which is strange. I was going into a vast room which had four big pillars, one in each corner. And on the floor there were four heaps of silk. All my students were sitting around there, and I came into the room and said: 'Why are you not spinning the silk, because that's the purpose of it all. Human beings are trying to reach towards the heavens because they want to bring the Kuan Yin, the goddess of mercy, down to earth. Why are you not doing it?' And they all looked at me and said, 'Well, these looms are not fastened to the ground. So how can we do it? You have to fasten the looms into the earth, and then we will start spinning.' I screwed these big pillars, which were the looms, into the ground so they were steady. They all started spinning to make a picture which became the connection between heaven and earth. And the Kuan Yin came down.

So when you reach that stage in life, you are opening yourself up to the four corners and widening yourself out so you see more and more of the earth, and more and more of the beauty that surrounds you. Eventually you bring all the earth and its beauty, you bring it down through the crown of your head and down into the dantien (an energy store below the navel). So there is a movement of expanding tremendously but also contracting because you have to develop the concentration that allows you to go into the sacred chamber which is the centre of balance in the body. And all we are looking for is the balance."[10]

Whatever the source of these inspirations, they led her to conclusions that were literally guides to life and to her own actions. At the heart of the book is a chapter called *Interpretation of the Allegorical Journey*. It poses three obvious and much-asked questions about the human condition.

Who am I?

What is the meaning of this existence here on earth and what should I do with my life?

Where am I finally going?

Gerda answers these questions with reference to the three-part Allegorical Journey that she found in t'ai-chi. In the first part, we move from birth to independence, accumulating energy as we go and learning how to use it. In the second part we use our accumulated energy for achievement, to find our strength, our balance, our maturity. In the third part we discover a spiritual path and a philosophy to guide us to old age. And to prepare us for our eventual departure from this life when we will Shoot Out The Arrow to send our spirit out into the universe and to return our accumulated Yang energy to the energy of the whole cosmos.

It is clear from the way the chapter is written that she has arrived at these conclusions by routes that are as much experiential as intellectual; she is not talking symbolically or metaphorically, but about real life and real death. She does not claim that she has discovered some ancient t'ai-chi arcanum, perhaps lost in history, perhaps hidden deep in the esoteric world of Taoist inner alchemy. But a whiff of oriental ambiguity drifts across the way she lets this question hang.

"It must be emphasised that the interpretation of the symbols is entirely my own, based on extensive reading of the Chinese classics, Chinese philosophy, poetry, folk tales and fairy tales.

It was through the specific order in which the images appear in the sequences of the t'ai-chi ch'uan that a hidden Allegorical Journey came to light. Whether the old Chinese Masters interpreted the movements in this way is not known, so in imposing an Allegorical Journey onto the t'ai-chi ch'uan, one can only offer observations and reflections for consideration. One can only view the creators of the t'ai-chi ch'uan from a distant perspective. One tries to enter their bodies and their minds and to comprehend their thoughts and actions, and when there is an understanding of the whole one tries to study the parts."[11]

Thetis Blacker, whose richly symbolic art appears in *Looking for the Golden Needle* and on its cover, had this to say: "She saw things in these symbolic ways and of course that did put off some people who said said: 'It's not genuine, it's her own thing.' But I felt that it was very suited to the western mind, for her teaching of western people. When she said 'I've discovered this' she didn't mean she had found it in some ancient text. What she meant was that she had discovered it by doing it herself. She realised that these names were more than mnemonic: they did have a kind of archetypal symbolism. And I quite agree."[12]

Gerda sat in The Promised Land and wrote, accompanied by aromatic pine resin in the summer, drumming autumn rain, and winter storms. As her thoughts clarified onto paper she tested them out on an enthusiastic and supportive husband.

"David was one hundred percent behind me. That was a wonderful thing. Every day I sat and wrote. In the evening he would ask about my progress, then he would listen as I read it to him. He gave me his blessing and I think that was one of the things that helped me more than anything else."[13]

Gerda and David both turned seventy-four in 1991, the year that *Looking for the Golden Needle* was published and David was awarded his PhD. The move to Clayfield, to David's study and Gerda's Promised Land, had been a creative one.

"I look back on the years of living in this bungalow really as the most harmonious, wonderful years of my life. And of course all the grandchildren had started to appear and we shared those grandchildren with equal enthusiasm. I would say they were the happiest of our married life. And I can remember David saying, 'Y'know, I don't think I've ever been as happy as I am now. But we are so happy that it can't possibly last. One of us will die and it has to be me because I can't live without you but I think you could probably exist without me.'"[14]

Biographer's Thread 10: Energy, Light and Visions

Dream, spirit, vision, death, light, energy, aura; these, and many similar words, cropped up regularly in Gerda's conversation and were often the subjects of it. They were not used as abstracts or metaphors but as ways of identifying and talking about what to her were actual experiences and topics of interest. Whether she had a radionics treatment from Rosemary Russell, or visited an acupuncturist, or discussed cranio-sacral therapy, or commented on the strange invisible presences during her t'ai-chi class at the College of Psychic Studies, or talked of protecting herself against some malign force; it was all linked as far as Gerda was concerned, and the linking mechanism was cosmic energy. She commonly referred to it as chi, the Chinese universal energy which t'ai-chi taught her to circulate around her body. It formed all things: thus the boundaries between objects, people, everything, were permeable, perhaps illusory.

She found significance in unusual events and coincidences. Several diary entries record incidents of strange interactions between birds and Gerda, or others close to her: perhaps not surprising given the significance which she attributes to the symbol of the bird in the Allegorical Journey.

She also found import in dreams, many of which she recorded in her diaries. Sometimes the boundary between dream and waking is difficult to identify in the flow of the narrative. Sometimes it doesn't seem to matter.

In the following chapter she talks about the spiritual bond that existed between her and David, cemented from the very beginning of their relationship when he shared with her the paintings in which he had tried to capture the mystical vision that he had experienced in 1944.

Three months after I started interviewing Gerda for this book, she had a folder waiting when I turned up for our weekly meeting. It contained copies of some pictures and several yellowing pages of typescript.

'I have something for you which is about David's vision, which actually changed his life altogether. And which brought us together.

He tried to write about it again and again over the years. He wrote several versions. I think this is probably the best.

'In order for you to understand me, you should know what happened to him. In one way he was really the light in the background. And I made practical what he said, what he sat and philosophised about. So he put light into me and I think that it was his light that was shining through my teaching. Maybe this will add to your understanding of my life. I want you to borrow it.'[1]

If that encourages us to find David's voice whispering between the pages of *Looking for the Golden Needle*, maybe it's a fair reward for his other role as Gerda's anchor. According to Harriet: 'He grounded her, kept her from flying away.'[2]

LOSS AND GRIEF

Man always wants to find an explanation for everything. We seem to be comforted by being given a firm guideline. In many of the major religions it is stressed that if we live 'good' lives and obey the instructions of their scriptures and do not 'sin' we will go to some Heaven or Nirvana or Valhalla and live happily there forever after. Everything is black or white, true or false, right or wrong. But maybe the truth lies somewhere in between. Maybe there has to be a mystery. In Nature, in great art, there is a mystery; something which touches our hearts, not easy to express in words.

The ancient Chinese theory is that when we die our Spirit Soul will float upwards and will join with the energy of the cosmos: according to the life we lead we contribute more or less to this living energy.

Gerda Geddes   LOOKING FOR THE GOLDEN NEEDLE, pp75-76

There were four more happy years together at Clayfield. Then, on 29th November 1995 following a series of strokes earlier in the year, David died. Gerda, Jane and Harriet were by his side.

During the years when Gerda had been exploring her t'ai-chi path, David had been following a journey of his own. In 1965, not long after Gerda started teaching her first t'ai-chi class, he received a golden handshake from Jardine Matheson. It was not something he welcomed. Like many men of his generation he had been called up immediately he graduated from university and before he could lay down any foundations for his future career. They both considered it extremely fortunate that he had landed a post with a major Far East trading company so soon after the war. He had used the opportunity to full advantage and had risen to become a director. But he was no longer wanted. He was just forty-eight. What would he do?

He had several false starts. He completed a teacher-training course; after six month's teaching, he decided it wasn't the profession for him. His lack of expertise led to the failure of a photographic shop and studio business. Then, at the age of fifty, he successfully applied to join the Civil Service and was appointed to the Department of Intermediate Technology which drew on the ideas of Fritz Schumacher, author of the influential book *Small is Beautiful*.[1] According to Gerda, David was full of enthusiasm for helping Third World countries, but the can-do approach that he had learned in his business career, and his direct manner, did not fit the committee-bound 'Yes Minister' world he had joined. His enthusiasm waned. Disillusion set in.

"That was the time when I started to go up and he started to go down. A couple start off together. When you get married you are overwhelmed with love and you can't be without each other for five seconds. You share everything. And then the everyday takes over, slowly one partner starts to go ahead and the other one is left behind. And sometimes that woman who is left behind will be permanently left behind and will always be sat upon. But another woman with initiative will then start to go forward. You go like this, in a marriage, one going ahead and then the other. And when you get to the place where you meet, that is when you are all happy again. And it's wonderful, it's all fine. Then one starts to go ahead again. I think that happens in most marriages, really. It certainly happened with us. So we were very fortunate to have sixteen very good years together at Clayfield."[2]

Inevitably, the loss of her husband and partner of forty-seven years was devastating. They had been devoted to one another throughout the eventful life they had lived since their meeting in 1947. In a very real sense they were soul mates, their relationship cemented from the start by the discovery that they had both had, in their own ways, numinous experiences. Gerda's early encounters with light had led her on a lifetime journey: in David's case, he lived his life bathed in the afterglow of a powerful mystical vision experienced over several days at the end of the war.

"The first time I met David and saw his painting of the five suns, I felt something strange happening inside me. And that was what held us together. At our first encounter, two spirits also met up there (gestures with both hands above her head). And that lasted all through our marriage until he died. But the effect of David's vision was that he never felt very comfortable in this life. He said when I first met him: 'You can't depend on me completely, because I left all my heavy luggage over on the other side and that's where I belong, that's where I'm going to live eventually. What I'm going to do with this life, I don't know'. Nothing on this earth was as important to him as the vision he had had. For years and years he was just trying to figure out what that vision was all about, what its message was and what he was supposed to be doing. He never really solved it.

As he became more ill, he almost became that light. It was extraordinary. He had to stay in a nursing home because I couldn't look after him. He had a big picture of me hanging on the wall by his bed, so he looked at me all the time. He told me, 'I feed on you, because you give me the light.' And I said, 'No, no, no, it isn't me. It's your own light that you are feeding on. And you must listen to that.' He told me, 'Well, you are giving it to me. You have found your light.' And that made him very dependent on me."[3]

David and Gerda had already decided that their ashes would be scattered in the sea at Scapa Flow in Orkney. They had developed a special relationship with Scotland's northern islands. Years earlier, David had traced ancestors to Orkney and the family made their first trip in 1965 to investigate. David was sure his family had originally come from Stromness and he believed there were family graves in an old cemetery nearby at Warbeth.

"We went up there with the children and had a bewitching grave hunt trying to find these gravestones. We had little penknives and Jane and Harriet were going 'Oooh there's a letter, come and see'. Eventually, we managed to decipher who they were. That was a very exciting journey.

There's no church there, only these very old graves and the water: the streaming water is what gets you, because the old churchyard lies down by the sea. The Vikings used to have their graveyards down by the sea because they wanted to be near water. And just at this point, at Warbeth beach in Orkney, there is a terrific current. Sometimes the water forces its way out of Scapa Flow and sometimes the Atlantic forces its way in. That goes on forever. And the tide comes in and the tide goes out and there is always, always a flow going one way or the other. And to me that flow up there is the flow of life. Everything flows, everything changes. That stream of energy is essential and important."[4]

Amid great excitement the family found three gravestones that were of David's ancestors. David had the stones restored. When he returned home he arranged for the carving of a further stone to commemorate the scattering in the sea off Warbeth beach of his ashes and those of 'My Beloved Norwegian Wife'. Names and dates of birth were shown. In the 1970s there was another exciting family trip to Orkney, this time by car and with the commemorative stone in the boot. It was unloaded and stored in an Orcadian stonemason's yard until 1996 when, with the date of David's death added, it was installed in the wall of Warbeth cemetery. David's remarkable and unusual piece of foresight had Gerda's wry approval although she wasn't entirely sure she had given him permission to include her name on the stone!

In July 1996 Gerda, accompanied by her daughters, sons-in-law and five grandsons, travelled to Orkney where they were joined by other members of David and Gerda's families as well as friends who lived locally. David's brothers were dead but his nephews attended along with his sister Peg, herself now a widow of some years since Prince Lu's death in 1968.

"On Sunday 7th July we hired a fishing boat and sailed out into Scapa Flow where I lowered David's ashes into the water. It was an unforgettable moment. To me it was returning David's Yin force back to where he started from. We precisely marked the place so one day I will be there too. It was overcast and a bit windy. When the ceremony was over we all had a mug of whisky and hot water of which David would have approved thoroughly.

Then we proceeded to Warbeth beach. When we parked the car by the cemetery we could hear the piper playing a lament. We walked to the memorial stone where a Norwegian flag had been placed over my name because, as I told everyone, I wasn't dead yet!

The piper led us from the churchyard. Then suddenly the sun came out and shone brilliantly. I felt as if David's Yang force had been contained in a birdcage, but when the sun came out he was set free and he flew right into the picture he had seen in his vision. All is now well with him and I am left behind."[5]

The inhabitants of Orkney and Shetland have well earned reputations for their ability to mark important human occasions. Weddings are known to have continued for days and funerals are not overlooked. David's good forward planning ensured that two cases of Glenmorangie malt whisky were on hand to complete his send-off at a party in a nearby hotel. When the party was over, Gerda spent a six-day holiday on the island with Harriet's family then a week at Jane's home in Aberdeenshire. By contrast, her return to an empty Clayfield was bleak.

"Coming home to the loneliness has proved very difficult. I must find a solution. This pain is unbearable and I cannot allow it to last."[6]

Thetis Blacker was a very supportive friend during David's illness. She had stayed with Gerda for a while and witnessed at first hand how difficult she found the prospect of David's death. "But then when he did actually die she took it marvellously well, wonderfully well. She had had time to be reconciled. But it was terrible pain for her. Terrible, terrible pain. I think her love of David was such…it was as if he was half of her. He was so complementary to her that after he did die, she suddenly realised what she had lost. To begin with it was very difficult for her."[7]

Gerda spent a year and a half grieving at Clayfield. She retired from The Place soon after David's death but a project of making another t'ai-chi video[8] engaged her energies and interest. Nonetheless, she found living alone after forty-seven years of marriage very taxing and, sometimes, frightening.

"Coming back into that empty house every time I went out was quite a strain. And I was also frightened down there because it was rather remote and occasionally there were break-ins and burglaries in the neighbourhood. One night when I was lying in bed I heard something moving outside my bedroom window. The bungalow windows were quite close to the ground. I heard some breathing and some very subdued coughing. I lay there absolutely rigid, stiff. Eventually I couldn't bear it any longer. I tiptoed over to the window and opened the curtain a tiny bit. There was a herd of deer eating the flowers below my window. And I thought, 'There you are. After all the fear and trembling, your worst nightmares come to nothing'. Quite soon after that I decided it was time for me to leave."[9]

To begin with, Gerda considered buying a flat in London. She loved the vibrancy and cultural opportunities of the city where she had taught t'ai-chi regularly for over thirty years and where she had many friends. But the more she mulled it over, the less certain she became.

"Then I thought, the older I get, the more difficult London is going to be. I'm going to be frightened in London, with all the crime and stuff that goes on there, and I'm not going to spend every night sitting in the theatre or looking at a dance performance."[10]

The answer lay in Scotland, and in a chance comment made to Jane Geddes. Jane lived in rural Aberdeenshire and commuted to Aberdeen University to teach in the History of Art Department . When one of her neighbours pointed out a house close by, which had been empty for two years, Jane made enquiries. Her persuasive approach to the owners prompted them to carry out necessary modernisation on the understanding that Gerda would take out a lease once the work was complete. Gerda's relief at this development is clear from her diary entry for Christmas 1996.

"Spent two weeks with Harriet and family. Wonderful, peaceful Christmas, almost like being reborn. Now feel that the right decisions have been made about the future."[11]

On 26th January 1997, Gerda had a telephone conversation with David's sister, Peg, in Germany. The two women discussed Gerda's forthcoming move north, Peg insisting that she wanted to be the first guest to sleep in Gerda's spare room. Goodbyes were said in a glow of friendly excitement at this prospect. At 4 am the following morning, Peg died of a heart attack aged eighty-three. It was the end of a friendship that began fifty years earlier when Peg lent Gerda a wedding dress that tragedy had prevented her from wearing.[12]

On 1st July 1997, Gerda moved from Clayfield to Scotland.

Gerda on 17th July 1992, her 75th birthday, with daughters Jane (left) and Harriet

THE SCOTTISH
YEARS

With Snake Creeping Down Into The Water, a major transformation takes place. Although we are changing all the time there are moments when our transformation takes a leap and we are reborn into A Golden Cock Standing On One Leg. The encouraging point is that this rebirth takes place in this life. You do not have to wait till the end of this existence, but your remaining years on this earth may be spent being surrounded by more light.

Gerda Geddes   LOOKING FOR THE GOLDEN NEEDLE, p80

Just two weeks before her eightieth birthday, Gerda moved into a small farmhouse called Kirkton of Coull in central Aberdeenshire on the edge of the area known as Royal Deeside. Kirkton of Coull is seventeen miles (twenty-eight kilometres) as the crow flies east of Balmoral Castle, built in 1856 by Queen Victoria who had fallen in love with this part of Scotland, and just four miles (six kilometres) from Aboyne, one of a series of charming towns and villages that lie on the River Dee between Aberdeen and Balmoral.

The detached granite house is built into the side of a hill. Its name tells its story. 'Kirk' is a church and the suffix 'ton' is an abbreviation of 'toun', an old Scottish word for a farm, its collection of buildings, and the surrounding arable land. Coull Parish Kirk sits on flat ground a short walk downhill from the farmhouse. It is a small eighteenth century building with no electricity, and is only used only for occasional services in the summer months. Next to it is a handsome two-story building, the former manse. In 1997 it was the home of Gerda's daughter Jane.

Two aspects of Kirkton of Coull's setting especially appealed to Gerda and put her in touch with her Norwegian childhood. Coull Hill, immediately at the back of the house, was wooded and offered forest walks almost as soon as she left her back door. The front of the house looked west across a wide valley towards the Deeside mountains: the peak of Morven was framed in the window of her study. Flanking the house were outbuildings used by a local farmer to store cattle that soon became accustomed to a new neighbour who sang to them in Norwegian and performed t'ai-chi under their soft watchful gaze.

Thanks to her daughters, everything had gone smoothly. Gerda felt at home.

"The move would have killed me if I had not had Harriet to help me. She thought of everything and we drove up here together, spending one night in the Lake District.

Everything fitted into Kirkton of Coull like magic. It was as if the house was just standing here waiting for me. Jane had filled it with flowers."[1]

She had by no means left her previous life behind. During her last weeks at Clayfield, Catherine Robinson had arranged an early eightieth birthday party for her at Cranbrook. Seventy people attended. They had all been asked secretly to send something on an A4 sheet about their response to Gerda's teachings, and these contributions were compiled into a folder of memories, poems, photographs and other expressions of thanks and appreciation. Lots of people spoke; Eva Karczag performed a dance she had choreographed specially for the occasion; there was group t'ai-chi in a field, and a huge feast shared between people from her earliest to her most recent classes. In August she went to Oslo for a week to celebrate a cousin's seventieth birthday, in September she spent a week in Ireland with Harriet and her family, and in November she returned to London for ten days during which she saw Eva Karczag dance.

She also taught some t'ai-chi lessons at The Place.

"My stay in London was fantastic. Everyday was filled with lessons, exhibitions, parties, dance, concerts. But in the end I actually enjoyed coming back here to Kirkton...

By January 1st I will have been at Kirkton for six months and it has certainly taken that time to become acclimatised. Sometimes, for fleeting moments, I have felt a very deep happiness here."[2]

Then, in January 1998, she started teaching t'ai-chi in her new local community. She noted in her diary:

"14th Jan. Today is a special day. I am starting my first class in Aboyne. Who will turn up? Maybe I will find a 'soulmate'!"[3]

One of the pupils who turned up for the class became the first of Gerda's Scottish t'ai-chi 'daughters'. Canadian Nancy Berlando, a newcomer to Scotland and Aboyne, was keen to integrate and had called in at the local community school for a programme of activities. She was attracted to the t'ai-chi class because of her background in teaching aerobics and fitness classes, although she had no previous t'ai-chi experience. And, like many of Gerda's pupils before her, her life was changed by what she met at that first class. "As the students gathered, we waited in curious anticipation for our teacher. Soon, this beautiful, elegant woman.appeared. Although none of us knew her, her presence seemed to command our respect. There was an aura and intrigue about her. After a very interesting introduction about her life in China, she began to explain the t'ai-chi to us. I was captivated by her wonderful stories and by the symbolic meaning of the movements. She then demonstrated Part One of the form so we could see more clearly what our lessons would entail for the next ten weeks.

"As Pytt did the form, it seemed to me as if she was slightly transparent. You could almost see her body, mind and spirit blending together, circling through her. I was mesmerized by the way she moved! I thought, 'If I can move like her and have that kind of presence when I'm eighty years old, then this is what I need to learn.' I was completely taken in by the t'ai-chi at that very first class. I looked forward to learning more each week. Through our common interest and discussions of movement and teaching techniques, Pytt and I slowly became better acquainted, then we became friends and then very, very good friends."[4]

By summer of 1998, Gerda's occasional diary entries made positive reading.

"I have now lived at Kirkton of Coull for nearly a year and my life has gone through a tremendous change and adjustment. I am

Gerda at Kirkton of Coull 1999

slowly learning to live alone and in many ways I quite like it. My house is so cosy and warm and welcoming. I do not feel frightened living here. It is quite reassuring to have Jane next door. Although I miss my London friends a great deal, there are many compensations. I walk a lot and being a part of this over-whelmingly beautiful place makes me feel very clean and unpolluted.

My classes have gone well."[5]

A year-end summary of 1998 specifically acknowledges the role played by t'ai-chi in changing her life around.

"The most positive step I took in 1998 was to start teaching t'ai-chi in Aboyne. I started with two full beginners' classes in January which joined into one class in the autumn term when there were also two new beginners' classes. The teaching has put me in touch with many of the local people up here and has kept me practising t'ai-chi ch'uan. My t'ai-chi has advanced, especially the breathing. I am much more aware of the true energy flow and am loose in the pelvis, the waist and the shoulders."[6]

Whenever Gerda advertised new classes they were quickly fully booked and a waiting list formed. People responded to what she was offering . Nancy Berlando, with her own background in instructing, put it down to the quality of her teaching. "I've always believed that the very best teachers are the ones who tell the best stories. Pytt's stories were absolutely fascinating. She wove this wonderful tale of t'ai-chi movement, symbolism and the Allegorical Journey. She taught us many 'life truths' through her stories. She was an outstanding and unforgettable teacher."[7]

Nancy and the other students were responding to skills that Gerda had honed keenly for forty years. Now, in her old age, they were as natural to her as breathing. "She never gave her students too much; always enough however to stimulate and motivate them to learn, grow and develop on their own. She gave us 'one corner' and encouraged us to find 'the other three'. It was because of this, that my interest in t'ai-chi developed and flourishes to this day. She gave me the knowledge and skills necessary to seek out and follow a pathway in which I can continually become more self-aware and improve and develop as I need. That's the skill of a very great teacher.

"Beauty emanated from her. She shared her beauty and her t'ai-chi journey with everyone she met. They were part of her. She had an impact on so many people from all walks of life because she touched people soul-to-soul or spirit-to-spirit. It doesn't matter what you perceive spirituality to be. It takes all forms. Whatever your perception, she had the ability to touch it and to connect with you."[8]

It was not long before Gerda began to integrate her new pupils with her wider t'ai-chi world. In the first week of August 1999, a week-long t'ai-chi course was held in Aboyne. Forty-nine people attended, including a group of sixteen from Sweden led by Gudrun Gylling. Catherine Robinson and several students came up from England and some of Gerda's newer students from Aboyne attended. The weather was wonderful and there was outdoor practice on Jane's lawn and also on the slopes of Morven. Catherine made several other visits to Aboyne to teach. In 2002 Gerda's former pupil Kinthissa, who had now changed from Yang to Chen style, came and taught some Chen basics. Gerda continued to make occasional trips south to teach, the last of these in 2000 when she went down to Catherine's early in the year, then in September she taught a day in Cheltenham at John Llewellyn's invitation. In 2004 and 2005 she was guest of honour at Tai Chi Caledonia, an international event which takes place annually in Scotland. She was delighted to be recognised this way in her adopted country, and enjoyed her new friendship with Ronnie Robinson, one of the founders of Tai Chi Caledonia and editor of Tai Chi Chuan, the journal of the Tai Chi Union of Great Britain. He later wrote: "I deeply appreciated our all too brief meetings, telephone calls and the letters that she wrote, and will always remember the grace and distinction with which she held herself. Gerda was a more than worthy recipient to carry the precious jewel of t'ai-chi from the east to west. The t'ai-chi community owes her a debt of deep gratitude."[9]

In 2002, the year she turned eighty-five, Gerda stopped teaching. There had been clues she was approaching this point. Nancy Berlando was aware from early in their relationship of being groomed to take over Gerda's classes. "Whenever she mentioned retiring she would say 'Look, I want you to learn this because you could be a teacher.' It was quite accelerated learning and I had a lot of one-on-one sessions with her. And she did that freely; it wasn't something that I had to pay for. I offered to but she said, 'No, I want you to teach ' and although she didn't say it specifically, she was going to let me step into those big shoes of hers...small feet, big shoes... four or five years down the road, which was not very long to actually learn the form and then start teaching."[10]

Although Gerda was in remarkably good physical condition for her age, time was taking its toll: in February 2002 she had a hip replacement operation which stopped her practising for many weeks. And potentially more significant health problems had been rumbling for some time. Exactly ten years earlier, in February of 1992, she had suffered what appeared to be a minor stroke at Clayfield and wakened at 5.00 am disoriented, confused, and with short-term memory problems. High blood pressure was diagnosed and a complete recovery expected. Another episode occurred in 1999 as Jane was driving her from Kirkton of Coull to Aberdeen Airport. Her awareness of her body led to a meticulous recording of the symptoms.

Waving Hands Like Clouds on Morven, 1999

"On Friday the 22nd October I had a stroke in Jane's car on the way to the airport to visit Harriet for half-term. I fell asleep in the car and when I woke up I felt a tingling all the way down my right side. But somehow I managed to get myself over to Belfast where I had a very difficult week. My whole body was in shock and I did not take much intelligent part in any conversation. I had a headache for several days which was in a spot on top of my head but to the left side. I felt this very clearly about a week after the stroke and then the pain moved downwards onto the left side. I found it difficult to write and my letters were very small. My balance was also bad. It was as if I was falling forward all the time. Very irritating. I also felt very cold as if I had ice in my veins even when I was lying in bed with a hot water bottle. Slowly my circulation began to return, but not below my knees. My legs and feet are still icy even when I walk."[11]

In April 2000, she became confused and repetitive while talking to a class of Catherine's students at Cranbrook. It was an experience that dented her confidence. In September John Llewllyn invited her to a t'ai-chi day he had organised at Cheltenham which involved his pupils, people who had learned from George Ineson, and others who had learned from Gerda herself. "She was a bit put off when I phoned to ask her. She told me she'd been down to Catherine's and had lost her way during a talk. There had been a gap in her mind. But she agreed to come. She became concerned when it was time to speak and asked if I'd come up on the stage with her. But in the end there was no problem and it was a wonderful day."[12]

Gerda started thinking about an Epilogue for *Looking for the Golden Needle*. It was completed in 2001 and is included in the third edition of the book which was published that year. In it she considers the role of t'ai-chi in growing old and preparing for death, not in a morbid way but as a guide through the last stages of the Allegorical Journey by which she had lived the second half of her life. An earlier chapter describes the last two symbols of the t'ai-chi sequence like this:

"Next you Pick Up The Lotus Flower With The Leg. The lotus is the Golden Flower of Taoism, the crystallization of the experience of light. The lotus also represents everything that is beautiful. So, before you depart from this world, you pick up the lotus as if to say 'Thank you for everything that was beautiful in this life'. Then you Bend The Bow And Shoot Out The Arrow. This is the moment of the soul's departure from the body."[13]

In the Epilogue, she achieves a much more personal resonance. "I have now reached the final stage of Shooting Out The Arrow. Every stage of development we go through is absorbed into the personality, so it is all there. I think what I enjoyed most was the stage of Picking Up The Lotus Flower when all the beauty I am surrounded by revealed itself to me. It gave me a feeling of being right in the middle so there was nowhere else to go. 'It' is right here and I am in the middle of it. The final stage, the Shooting Out Of The Arrow is the mystery. Where does the arrow go? We don't know. We just grow wider and deeper all the time and all we have to do is to climb to the top of the mountain and jump."[14]

Although she no longer taught classes, individual pupils and aspiring teachers sought her out for one-to-one lessons. She made trips south: to Edinburgh to meet up with Richard Alston when his dance troupe toured, to London to keep up with old friends, to see shows, to visit galleries. And the visitors came in the other direction. From the t'ai-chi world, Catherine, Gudrun, Kinthissa, and John Llewellyn were some of the large number who made trips north to visit. Sue Phipps and her husband called in and drove Gerda up to Orkney for the St Magnus Music Festival. Gerda's earlier life also came to call in the person of Odile who had been the family nanny during the Hong Kong years. And Gerda continued to travel further afield. During the years she stayed in Scotland she made several trips to Ireland to stay with Harriet before she and her family moved to Shrewsbury. She went to Norway, there were two holidays in the U.S.A., and she visited Prague.

And the phone played its part. Cheaper weekend rates were used for long Saturday morning calls to old friends Thetis Blacker and Jane Dudley who, despite her deteriorating mobility, also managed to visit Gerda at Kirkton of Coull.

Many people whom she knew less well, and sometimes had never met at all, sought her out for advice, for comfort, or for wise counsel. Her morning mail delivery often contained letters from ex-pupils, or people who had read her book, or who were sending a video of their t'ai-chi, or wanted to tell her about events in their lives. Some evenings, her phone scarcely stopped ringing.

"I was wondering about watching television on Saturday night (21/01/06) when the phone rang. It was a call from a woman in Canada, an ex-pupil who went on to teach but no longer does. We talked for a while. I had just settled down when the phone rang again. It was another pupil from the 1970s, a woman calling from the Carmel Valley in California. Then just before bedtime I had another call, this time from a man in Ireland who was a pupil in the 1980s. He was always full of drugs when he came to me then. Now he's a writer. 'You're my white goddess,' he said to me, 'unique in this world.'"[15]

erda was best known for her t'ai–chi life. She had other sides too. She was an excellent needleworker, capable of making quality clothes or finely-worked needlepoint. She was also a lady, and one of considerable style, always carefully groomed and tastefully dressed. Although she was a light eater, she enjoyed food and eating out. On a few occasions during the months of interviews, we lunched at The Blackface Sheep in Aboyne where she enjoyed the relaxed family atmosphere, the delicious homemade soup, and sharing a slice of one of the scrumptious cakes or gateaux. The first time I went at her invitation and she insisted on paying. A few weeks later I said I would like to return the treat. She agreed to our lunching together but not to my footing the bill. "No," she told me with crisp authority. "From now on we go Dutch!"

A trip to the busy town of Aboyne was also a chance to do some top-up shopping and Gerda usually had a few calls to make. Winters can be hard in Deeside. One of our visits coincided with a cold snap. There were icy pavements and heaps of cleared snow to negotiate: exactly the treacherous conditions when elderly people risk a fall. I felt a strong sense of responsibility for her well-being but she could be fiercely independent. I kicked my way through the kerbside slush and opened the passenger door.

"Today, Gerda," I told her, more assertively than usual "you must have 'a cleek'." She took my offered arm and listened curiously to my explanation of the Scots word.

"A cleek is a hook for holding or pulling. It's also a word for a sweetheart, someone you walk arm in arm with."

She twinkled and took me by the arm. As we slithered to the restaurant, to the bank, to the supermarket, she radiated graciousness and an elegance that would not have been out of place on a saunter through the top spots of Paris or London

An interview followed by lunch was planned for Tuesday 7th February 2006. Gerda phoned on the Monday afternoon to cancel.

And to give me worrying news. She was in bed and was feeling and sounding weak. She had collapsed the previous day with what appeared to have been an angina attack, the latest in a series of cardiovascular incidents that were happening more frequently. Her doctor had mentioned the possibility of a pacemaker which Gerda had refused. She was due to leave on Friday for a two-week winter break with her daughter Harriet in Shrewsbury. The doctor felt she would probably be able to travel and suggested carrying out further cardiac tests when she returned.

"Finding out what's wrong is one thing,' Gerda commented to me dryly. 'What can be done about it? That's another matter altogether."

We never did fulfil that lunch date.

SHOOTING OUT
THE ARROW

My old friend, Father Slade, always said it is important that we prepare
ourselves for death, not in a morbid way because it is the reality, but accept
it as a part of life. He said: 'You should look forward in hope and
backwards in gratitude, but always live in the present.' I feel the t'ai-chi
ch'uan incorporates that preparation. If we practice in the right way the
t'ai-chi ch'uan takes away our fear of the unknown and gives us the feeling
of clarity and simplicity that improves the quality of our lives.

Gerda Geddes   LOOKING FOR THE GOLDEN NEEDLE, p120

Once she stopped teaching, Gerda did not regularly practise the physical movements of t'ai-chi, not because she couldn't but because she felt
she had reached a stage where it wasn't necessary. It was enough to
focus on her clarity and simplicity. In 2001, during the time she was
writing the Epilogue, she said:

> "As you keep developing it feels as if the breath becomes the mas-
> ter and does the t'ai-chi for you. This is a great help as you get
> older and the body becomes more frail, because the breath remains
> unhindered: it can still do the t'ai-chi and guide you through the
> shrinking physical power into a more weightless psychic power. In
> China you have some wonderful examples of old, advanced peo-
> ple who might be frail and crippled but who have a lightness and
> transparency about them which is quite hard to find in the West.

So although physically you may be fading, I think you can practise the imagery of the t'ai-chi right up to the point of death. In my own practice and my own life I have reached the point of Picking Up The Lotus Flower. I can sit by my window looking towards the mountains, picking up the beauty of all the experiences I have had in my life and sifting through them. It is from this point that I will gather up the strength to Shoot Out The Arrow. That's how it appears to me anyway. I have lived through the t'ai-chi for many years: now I have a wonderful feeling that wherever I am, I carry all this with me all the time. So…I'm here. It sounds strange to say, but I feel that I am manifesting what I am."[1]

She monitored her progress in her diary, sometimes in the language of the Allegorical Journey.

"17th June 2001. I woke up in the morning feeling most peculiar as if my body had no skin and as if the body was extending outwards in all directions with no barriers. The skin that divides the 'inner' and 'outer' life had gone. Maybe at long last I have achieved the transparency which I saw in that old man in China. It has taken a long time, nearly fifty years in coming. It feels a bit strange but wonderful. Almost as if I am weightless and there is nothing to hold me down: as if I have reached 'The Seven Stars'.

30th June. Going for all these drives with Jane is like 'Picking Up The Lotus'. I am discovering all the beautiful places that surround me."[2]

And when there was another health scare in 2002, she recorded her body's reaction with precision.

"I was in the kitchen early in the morning. All of a sudden I broke out into a terrible sweat, then I felt slightly sick and a sharp pain in my heart, up the arteries of the neck, into both arms and down my legs. With all this disturbance going on in my body, my brain suddenly became crystal clear, flooded by a blue misty light. I felt absolutely no fear.

For several days after I had a slight pain, like bruising, all the way through my circulatory system, but I am now recovering."[3]

She was remarkably relaxed and comfortable talking about death. In part this was a legacy of the years of discussion between her and David about their individual experiences, years when issues of cosmic energy, visions, and the immortal soul were common fare around the Geddes's breakfast table. But it was also because of her total commitment to the Allegorical Journey she had discovered within t'ai-chi and her sense that, as the person who had made the discovery, she had a responsibility to live her life accordingly.

"There is a major transformation that happens in connection with the t'ai-chi. That is when the Snake Creeps Down Into The Water. Then you rise up out of the water, transformed like the snake when it changes its skin. And you become the Golden Cock Standing On One Leg. The golden cock symbolises the dawn, the break of a new day. That happens right in the middle of the t'ai-chi and tells us that change can happen in this life. You don't have to wait until you die. I think for most people the experience happens when they die, when they go from one existence finally into another existence. But you can live in the other existence while you are here on this earth. That's why preparation is important during the last part of your life. At that stage you have to become an example of what you believe in or what's happened to you. Without being a practical example you'll just be one of those teachers who say 'Do this because I know that it's right.' It's not the words that matter, it's the actions: what you actually do with your life. You have to come down to the nitty gritty, and somehow be an example in yourself. Which is quite difficult, quite difficult."[4]

That responsibility towards others wasn't the main issue for Gerda however. Of more importance was preparation for death itself. Her views on this didn't match the usual religious conventions.

"I think there is a force. I wouldn't like to put a being into it. I don't see the shape of a god: that isn't for me. But I can feel the force and I can't explain it. That's how I feel I have to look at it.

You shouldn't be frightened of that force, but sometimes you are because you have to give yourself over to the force but you don't know how strong it is. You don't know whether it's going to destroy you. Taking the leap, that's what dying is all about. You throw yourself into the unknown. But if through your life you've had little glimpses of it - and I think most people have, I don't think anyone is exceptional about this - that strengthens your awareness as you go on living.[5]

There comes a point when you have to find your own clarity. I feel that over fifty years I have worked through everything in my body. The Chinese stress that we should be in touch with our vital organs. I have done that many, many times. There is a way of practising the t'ai-chi where you think 'Today I'm going to concentrate completely on my liver. And I'm to find out if I can read something about the functioning of the liver.' Then you dedicate that twenty-five minutes of t'ai-chi to that organ so that every in and out breath you take passes through the liver. And slowly you develop this clarity that I talk about, which I think is so important so that when you die you are clear, although you are going to the unknown."[6]

There were several other small health scares in the autumn and winter of 2005. Following another angina attack on 5th February 2006, she agreed to go to Harriet in Shrewsbury for two weeks to recuperate and escape some of the worst of the Aberdeenshire winter. For the first week she was exhausted and spent her time sitting around quietly. Then, in the second week, Harriet had a very different mother as guest. "It was as if forty years had dropped away from her. She was full of pep, eating full meals, talking. She visited friends, shopped, bought new clothes, and visited a new coffee shop in town. On the Friday night we went to the theatre in Birmingham to see a modern ballet, *Carmina Burana*. And there she was, dressed up, out on the town having large gin and tonics, enjoying absolutely every minute of it. Everything that excited her and interested her, she did it in that week."[7]

There was t'ai-chi too. She attended Harriet's t'ai-chi class and did some teaching. Two t'ai-chi friends visited. When t'ai-ch teacher and former pupil John Llewellyn visited, they talked about the differences between Gerda's Yang style and Chen style, which John was now practising. They spent some time Silk Reeling, one of the basic Chen exercises. Nancy Berlando stayed for a few days. "We were so happy to see each other. We had no set agenda, just a time to visit, share and enjoy our time together. We simply did what life required and we were very content in one another's company. One afternoon, Pytt mentioned that she was having trouble with her hearing aid so I said, 'Lets catch the bus, go to town and get it sorted out', so off we went. While there we shopped for some stockings she needed , bought handkerchiefs for a friend in Scotland and did a little window browsing. It was a fun day filled with simple pleasures and good conversation. We finished our excursion at a lovely old coffee shop where we talked about our families and life in general. As we quickly walked back to the bus depot, for it was very cold outside, Pytt linked her arm in mine and held my hand tightly. She said laughing 'This is how we walk in Norway'. It was very special to me and we kept our hands warm.

"I can still visualise her standing in the doorway as I was leaving. She had a big smile on her face and looked at me warmly. We gave each other a long, heartfelt hug goodbye and I said: 'I love you'. She said 'I love you too.' And that was it. I never saw her again. I feel so very fortunate to have shared such a close and wonderful, relationship with her. Our time together will always be one of my most treasured memories."[8]

On Friday, after returning from her thoroughly enjoyable trip to the theatre, Gerda went happily to bed with a hot water bottle. Harriet tucked her in. Sometime during the night she had a major stroke. When Harriet entered in the morning, she thought at first her mother was dead.

Gerda's wishes in the event of a serious incapacitating stroke were clear. Give her no sustenance and leave her to die in peace. She carried written instructions to that effect in her handbag. Initially, the unconscious Gerda could do nothing to confirm her wishes. When she regained consciousness the full extent of the damage was clear: very limited movement, left side paralysis, loss of speech. When hospital staff tried to moisten her lips, she closed them tightly and turned her head away. Later when she was offered a cup, she pushed it away. She resisted all offers of food and drink for six days. Her intention was clear

Jane and Harriet's plea to have no callers and to be left in peace to share their mother's death was almost totally observed. Gerda, incapable of speaking, was conscious and alert. Although the stroke had caused severe neurological damage, she remained fresh and did not lose her bloom. She could squeeze with her right hand and move her right arm. When Jane arrived after a gruelling drive through a Scottish blizzard, Gerda raised her good hand to a missing button on her daughter's shirt: it was an old joke between Gerda the consummate seamstress and Jane the university academic. Jane replied "Yes Mum, I can fix my own buttons now."[9] As the days passed, Gerda's eyes became brighter and more penetratingly blue. Frequently she reached her right arm towards the window as if beckoning the light. Harriet brought family photographs and Gerda spent a day just looking at pictures of David. On the evening of Saturday 4th March 2006, six days after the stroke, there were three people with her: her daughters and one of her grandsons. She appeared to mark the presence of each of them by giving three, last, breaths. Then she died.

CELEBRATION

Here is a Chinese saying: 'When a human being is born, there is a ripple on a still pond. We go on our journey and when our life is over, there is another ripple on the pond, and the spirit returns.'

So we rise from the vapours of the water and return to the water.

Gerda Geddes   *Looking for the Golden Needle,* p120

Gerda was cremated at Shrewsbury Crematorium on 13th March 2006. Her nephew, Lord Euan Geddes, gave the eulogy. On 24th March, a memorial service was held in Scotland at Coull Parish Kirk, just a short distance from her home at Kirkton of Coull. Two events brightened the austerity of the small packed building. During the service, spring sunshine streamed through the three stained glass windows in the southern gable and ran glitters of colour up and down the tall brass oil lamps, the only lighting source the church possesses. And at the end of the service Lize Strachan, a Danish-born woman Gerda had befriended since coming to Scotland, regaled the congregation with tales of the antics enjoyed when these two elderly, stylish, and feisty spirits had their occasional days out in Aberdeen. She brought the service to an end by commanding everyone to their feet and leading a spirited rendition of the Norwegian national anthem. Commendably, the congregation did not allow ignorance of tune or lyric to diminish volume.

On 1st July, around two hundred people attended a celebration of

Gerda's life at The Place in London. A display of photographs from childhood to old age greeted them on arrival. In the theatre, the programme was introduced and compered by artistic director Richard Alston. As her biographer, I outlined her life before she arrived to teach at The Place. Artist Thetis Blacker, who had painted in Gerda's honour a commemorative batik of a falcon swooping to pluck a beakful of light from the sun, spoke of their friendship and the impact of t'ai-chi on her own life and work. Choreographer Tim Lamford shared the experience of being one of Gerda's students in the early 1970s and outlined her lasting influence on contemporary dance. Harriet introduced a Norwegian television documentary of Gerda talking and performing t'ai-chi. She then spoke about her mother and read from the Epilogue of *Looking for the Golden Needle*.

Richard Alston choreographed two pieces for the event. One of them had special poignancy. Two dresses survived an affair Gerda had in 1940 with a strikingly handsome dancer who also designed clothes for her – some to wear and some to dance in. A simple black one was worn by a slim, blonde dancer who performed a hypnotic dance incorporating t'ai-chi inspired movements: for a few breathtaking moments a young Gerda from avant-garde Oslo was dancing.

When the afternoon's programme was over, seventy-five people 'played' t'ai-chi in nearby sun-struck Regents Park.

Three weeks later, Gerda's ashes were taken to Orkney where an Anglo-Norwegian party of twenty people had assembled for the occasion. Her daughters Jane and Harriet led the British group of ten close family and friends. There were ten from her Norwegian family, led by her closest relative Per Anker, and lots of his children and grandchildren. Before she died, Gerda had changed her mind about her urn dropping into Brings Deep, the place in Scapa Flow where she had put David's ashes overboard eleven years earlier.

"We both agreed that Orkney was the right place for our ashes because he came up from the south, from England, and I came down from the North, from Norway. Orkney was our spiritual meeting place.

His ashes were put down into Scapa Flow in a casket. I don't know if it has rotted now or been eaten up by the fishes. When I was up there this summer (2005) I went and had a good look at Scapa Flow and the place where I had dropped his ashes from the boat. And I thought: 'I can't possibly go there, even if it's just my ashes. I don't want to live down in that icy cold water.' So I've chosen another place. Jane knows exactly where it is. They'll have to have another ceremony when I die and take my ashes up there."[1]

Throwing Gerda's ashes from Yesnaby cliffs, Orkney in 2006

Gerda wanted her ashes scattered from the top of Yesnaby cliffs, a majestic stretch of horizontally bedded sandstone, battered by the Atlantic into deep gullies and precarious stacks. As Jane reported in a joyous newsletter describing the event, there were some practical difficulties. "This simple action had exercised many engineering minds for a long time. We had the nightmare of Uncle Eric's ashes, flung heroically from an aeroplane window, only to waft back into the plane through the adjacent window, a family precedent which needed improvement. Peter and Henry were all for a catapult or trebuchet. Stuffed fireworks were an option. Perhaps an enormous sling. In the end, the ashes were put into tissue paper parcels with a small river stone. This insured they could fly through a potential onshore breeze and would explode as they hit the water. It worked perfectly."[2]

Jane, Harriet, and Gerda's five grandsons each threw a packet of ashes from the cliff top. Others in the party cast handfuls of rose petals that Jane had collected and dried a week earlier on what would have been Gerda's eighty-ninth birthday.

Rarely for such a wild and exposed place, the weather was still and warm. The northern light so loved by Gerda washed over the ash- and petal-throwers as they wound their way down from the cliffs to Warbeth graveyard.

EPILOGUE

I've never done this with anyone else before, given out my life story. I don't really want me to be in it because I'm not really that kind of person. It's very difficult. You can't write a story without me being the heroine and I don't want to be a figure of any kind at all. I've always tried to avoid that. I think the only thing of importance I've contributed is the Allegorical Journey.

Gerda Geddes
Kirkton of Coull

11th October 2005

ACKNOWLEDGEMENTS

Whatever I say here will not be adequate to the job of thanking the people who helped me in the writing and production of this book. Some were key to the story, gave of themselves and their experiences, became friends. Others stepped in, helped in small but important ways, and stepped out again. The contributions of them all made Dancer in the Light what it is.

First I must thank Gerda's daughters, Jane Geddes and Harriet Devlin. They offered me unstinting support and access to information, documents and photographs, yet left me free and unhindered to tell the story of their mother's remarkable life. I greatly appreciate the trust and confidence they placed in me, and their help in finally bringing this book into being.

Thereafter, it does not feel right to highlight some over others, so I resort to a list, by first name. My heartfelt thanks are due to: Catherine Robinson, David Boadella, Eva Karczag, Gudrun Gylling, Hugh Morton, Ian Hamilton, Iris Tomlinson, James Roose-Evans, Jane Innes, Jenny Mayhew, Julie Wyness, Kari de Koenigswarter, Michael Gilman, Nancy Berlando, Rhoda Michael, Richard Alston, Richard Ralph, Ronnie Robinson, Ruary Mackenzie Dodds, Simon Rickard, Sue Phipps, Tim Lamford, Tony Woods, Veronica Lewis, Vijay.

Sadly, two important contributors to the book, Thetis Blacker and John Llewellyn, died before it was published. I met each of them only once; they left me with special and enduring memories. Thank you.

Thanks are also due for the use of copyrighted materials: to Guro Iversen for the cover portrait painted by her mother, Ingeborg Rudi Iversen; to Janine Wiedel, www.wiedel-photo-library.com, for the use of the photograph on page 195; and to Claes Svanteson, www.claesgbg.se, for use of the photograph on page 249.

It has not been possible to trace the copyright holder of the sketch by Egon Moeller Nielsen on page 53. Anyone with information can contact the author through Psi Books.

NOTES

Prologue

1 from 'Turning Points'; article written by Gerda Geddes for *Metamorphoses* magazine, 1984
2 p51 Geddes G,. *Looking for the Golden Needle*. Mannamedia. 3rd edition 2001

1. The Beginning

1 p27 Geddes, G., 2003. A Norwegian Childhood. Unpublished memoir.
2 p27 ibid
3 p28 ibid

2. Norwegian Childhood

1 Taped interview with Gerda Geddes: Kirkton of Coull 02/02/06
2 Taped interview with Gerda Geddes: Kirkton of Coull 24/01/06
3 p8 Geddes, G., 2003. A Norwegian Childhood. Unpublished memoir
4 p16 ibid
5 From a yellowed, undated typescript found in one of Gerda's diaries.
6 Taped interview with Gerda Geddes: Kirkton of Coull 02/02/06
7 ibid
8 Separate comments by Gerda Geddes from tapes 11/10/05, 24/02/06, 02/02/06

3. Wing Spreading

1 p16 Geddes, G., 2003. A Norwegian Childhood. Unpublished memoir
2 p16 ibid
3 Taped interview with Gerda Geddes: Kirkton of Coull 13/12/05
4 letter from Mrs Fleetwood Varley to Gerda's mother 11/03/34
5 school reports signed by Mrs Fleetwood Varley and dated 26/04/34 and 20/09/34

6 p16 Geddes, G., 2003. A Norwegian Childhood. Unpublished memoir.
7 Taped interview with Gerda Geddes: Kirkton of Coull 28/10/05
8 for detailed discussion see Grytten, Ola. The Economic History of Norway. EH.Net Encyclopedia, edited by Robert Whaples. January 11, 2005. URL http://eh.net/encyclopedia/article / grytten.norway
9 Taped interview with Gerda Geddes: Kirkton of Coull 12/01/06
10 Taped interview with Gerda Geddes: Kirkton of Coull 28/10/05
11 Taped interview with Gerda Geddes: Kirkton of Coull 12/01/06
12 pp8-9 Geddes, G., 2003. A Norwegian Childhood. Unpublished memoir
13 Taped interview with Gerda Geddes: Kirkton of Coull 12/01/06
14 Taped interview with Gerda Geddes: Kirkton of Coull 07/12/05
15 Translated from the Norwegian by Gerda's daughter Harriet
16 Taped interview with Gerda Geddes: Kirkton of Coull 07/12/05
17 ibid
18 ibid
19 Taped interview, Kirkton of Coull 07/12/05

4. War and Resistance

1 Taped interview with Gerda Geddes: Kirkton of Coull 13.12.05
2 ibid
3 ibid
4 ibid
5 pp36-37 Riste, O. and Nokleby, B., 1999. Norway 1940-45: The

Resistance Movement.
Aschehoug. 5th printing.
6 p20 Geddes, G., 2003. A
Norwegian Childhood
Unpublished memoir
7 pp20-22 Geddes, G., 2003. A
Norwegian Childhood
Unpublished memoir
8 p89 Riste, O. and Nokleby, B.,
1999. Norway 1940-45: The
Resistance Movement.
Aschehoug. 5th printing.
9 Taped interview with Gerda
Geddes: Kirkton of Coull
13.12.05
10 p22 Geddes, G., 2003. A
Norwegian Childhood
Unpublished memoir

5. The Road to Psychotherapy

1 Taped interview with Gerda
Geddes: Kirkton of Coull
12/01/06
2 Taped interview with Gerda
Geddes: Kirkton of Coull
07/12/05
3 pp18-19 Geddes G., 2003. A
Norwegian Childhood.
Unpublished memoir.
4 Undated typescript in English
headed: 'Written by Rasmus
Meyer's niece, Lydia, who knew
him very well. Translated by Pytt'
5 pp16-18 Geddes G., 2003. A
Norwegian Childhood.
Unpublished memoir.
6 pp20-21 Raknes, O., 1970.
Wilhelm Reich and Orgonomy.
St Martin's Press, New York
7 Taped interview with Gerda
Geddes: Kirkton of Coull
24/01/06
8 ibid
9 ibid
10 Taped interview with Gerda
Geddes: Kirkton of Coull
12/01/06
11 ibid

6. The Road to Dance

1 See Heller, M. C., 2005 The
Golden Age of Body
Psychotherapy in Oslo.
Presentation at Oslo University
College June 2005. Available at

www.aqualide.com
2 p19 Geddes G., 2003. A
Norwegian Childhood.
Unpublished memoir
3 Taped interview with Gerda
Geddes: Kirkton of Coull
02/02/06
4 Taped interview with Gerda
Geddss: Kirkton of Coull
24/01/06
5 Taped interview with Gerda
Geddes: Kirkton of Coull
02/02/06
6 p22 Geddes G., 2003. A
Norwegian Childhood.
Unpublished memoir
7 for example see Terry, W., New
York Herald Tribune August 5
1955, and Lloyd, M., The
Christian Science Monitor August
13 1955
8 Taped interview with Gerda
Geddes: Kirkton of Coull
02/02/06

Biographer's Thread 5: Reading People

1 Taped interview Kirkton of Coull
11/04/06

7. From Theory to Practice

1 From 'Where Dancing and
Psychology Meet'. Lecture given
in Shanghai, November 1950
2 pp23 Geddes G., 2003. A
Norwegian Childhood.
Unpublished memoir
3 From 'Where Dancing and
Psychology Meet'. Lecture given
in Shanghai, November 1950

8. Drama and Movement

1 Taped interview with Gerda
Geddes: Kirkton of Coull
24/01/06
2 Taped interview with Gerda
Geddes: Kirkton of Coull
13/12/05
3 Taped interview with Gerda
Geddes: Kirkton of Coull
02/02/06
4 Taped interview with Gerda
Geddes: Kirkton of Coull
13/12/05

Biographer's Thread 6: Dancing Around Intimacy

1 pp28-29 Philipson, T., The Force of Love. Paper in Boadella, D., Editor, 1976. In the Wake of Reich. Coventure, London.
2 see Raknes, O., Life and Religion. Paper Boadella, D., Editor, 1976. In the Wake of Reich. Coventure, London.
3 Taped interview with Gerda Geddes: Kirkton of Coull 13/12/05

9. Love and Marriage

1 Taped interview with Gerda Geddes: Kirkton of Coull 13/12/05
2 ibid
3 pp25-26 Geddes, G., 2003 A Norwegian Childhood. Unpublished memoir.
4 p26 ibid
5 pp26-27 ibid

10. The Road to Shanghai

1 p28 Geddes, G., 2003. A Norwegian Childhood. Unpublished memoir.
2 p28 op cit
3 p28-29 op cit
4 Adapted from the transcript of a talk to her students by Gerda Geddes, December 1995
5 pp27-28 Geddes, G., 2001. Looking for the Golden Needle. MannaMedia

11. The Fall of Shanghai

1 See pp77-78 Barber, N., 1979 The Fall of Shanghai. Macmillan London
2 for an account of the advice being given to British Citizens, see p60 Barber, N., 1979 The Fall of Shanghai. Macmillan London
3 Taped interview Kirkton of Coull 07/12/06
4 see p284 Dong, S., 2000 Shanghai: The Rise and Fall of a Decadent City. Harper Collins New York
5 p29 Geddes, G., 2003 A Norwegian Childhood. Unpublished memoir.

6 Taped interview Kirkton of Coull 07/12/06
7 Taped interview Kirkton of Coull 07/12/06
8 see pp149-150 Barber, N., 1979 The Fall of Shanghai. Macmillan London

12. Hostages of Mao Tse-tung

1 see pp160-161 Barber, N., 1979 The Fall of Shanghai. Macmillan London
2 Taped interview with Gerda Geddes: Kirkton of Coull 02/02/06
3 ibid
4 ibid
5 p29 Geddes G., A Norwegian Childhood. Unpublished memoir
6 p29 ibid
7 p29 ibid
8 p30 ibid

13. Escape to Hong Kong

1 p30 Geddes G., A Norwegian Childhood. Unpublished memoir
2 Taped interview with Gerda Geddes: Kirkton of Coull 07/12/05
3 ibid

14. Hong Kong Life

1 Taped interview with Gerda Geddes: Kirkton of Coull 21/10/05
2 ibid
3 ibid
4 ibid
5 ibid
6 ibid

15. Treasured Guests

1 Taped interview with Gerda Geddes: Kirkton of Coull 14/11/06
2 Taped interview with Gerda Geddes: Kirkton of Coull 28/10/05
3 ibid
4 ibid
5 ibid
6 Taped interview with Gerda Geddes: Kirkton of Coull 14/11/06

7 ref FP/2/8/7 Britten Pears library,
   Aldeburgh

16. The Path to T'ai-chi

1 Taped interview with Gerda
   Geddes: Kirkton of Coull
   11/10/05
2 Taped interview with Gerda's
   dughters Jane and Harriet:
   Kirkton of Coull 11/04/06
3 Gerda Geddes's diary entry
   20/07/55
4 Gerda Geddes's diary entry dated
   'Sept. 55.'
5 Telephone conversation with Jane
   Geddes: 04/10/06
6 Gerda Geddes's diary entry
   11/01/56
7 Taped interview with Gerda
   Geddes: Kirkton of Coull
   11/11/05
8 pp 28-30 Geddes, G., 2001.
   Looking for the Golden Needle.
   MannaMedia
9 ibid p27
10 Taped interview with Gerda
   Geddes: Kirkton of Coull
   21/10/05
11 ibid
12 Gerda Geddes: transcription of
   talk to a gathering of her students
   in December 1995
13 Gerda Geddes's diary entry dated
   'December 1956'

17. Return to Britain

1 Taped interview with Gerda
   Geddes: Kirkton of Coull
   21/10/05
2 ibid
3 pp65-66 Geddes, G., 2001.
   Looking for the Golden Needle.
   MannaMedia
4 Taped interview with Gerda
   Geddes: Kirkton of Coull
   21/10/05
5 ibid
6 ibid
7 Taped interview with Gerda
   Geddes: Kirkton of Coull
   11/10/05

18. Domestic Joy, T'ai-chi Disappointment

1 Taped interview with Gerda

   Geddes: Kirkton of Coull
   22/11/05
2 ibid
3 ibid
4 Taped interview with Gerda
   Geddes: Kirkton of Coull
   28/10/05
5 Taped interview with Gerda
   Geddes: Kirkton of Coull
   24/01/06
6 www.feuerwehr-
   langen.de/cms/htdocs/ffl.php/
   verein_jubilaeum/230/
7 Taped interview with Gerda
   Geddes: Kirkton of Coull
   21/10/05
8 ibid
9 p31 Geddes, G., Looking for the
   Golden Needle, Mannamedia
   1995

19. Losing the Light

1 pp5-6 Geddes, G., A Norwegian
   Childhood. Unpublished memoir
   2003
2 from 'Moments of Illumination';
   article written by Gerda Geddes
   for Light magazine, spring 1994
3 ibid
4 from 'Turning Points'; article
   written by Gerda Geddes for
   Metamorphoses magazine, 1984
5 Taped interview with Gerda
   Geddes: Kirkton of Coull
   22/11/05
6 Taped interview with Gerda
   Geddes: Kirkton of Coull
   28/10/05
7 Taped interview with Gerda
   Geddes: Kirkton of Coull
   21/10/05

20. T'ai-chi Rebirth

1 Taped interview with Gerda
   Geddes: Kirkton of Coull
   22/11/05
2 ibid
3 Taped interview with Gerda
   Geddes: Kirkton of Coull
   22/11/05
4 p32 Geddes, G., 2001. Looking
   for the Golden Needle.
   Mannamedia
5 Taped interview with Gerda

Geddes: Kirkton of Coull
22/11/05
6 Taped interview with Jane
Geddes and Harriet Devlin,
Kirkton of Coull 11/04/06
7 p33 Geddes, G., 2001. Looking
for the Golden Needle.
Mannamedia
8 Taped interview with Gerda
Geddes: Kirkton of Coull
22/11/05
9 pp61-63 Geddes, G., 2001.
Looking for the Golden Needle.
Mannamedia. With minor
amendments from 22/11/05
interview
10 For a fuller description see pp 37-
42 Geddes, G., 2001. Looking for
the Golden Needle. Mannamedia.

21. A New Life Begins

1 Taped interview with Gerda
Geddes: Kirkton of Coull
22/11/05
2 ibid
3 ibid
4 Letter from Dr Felix Mann to
Frank Woods 13/12/05
5 Taped interview with Gerda
Geddes: Kirkton of Coull
22/11/05
6 ibid
7 Geddes, D., A Vision and Some
Speculations. Light magazine,
winter 1979
8 Spoken contribution by Thetis
Blacker to a Celebration of The
Life of Gerda 'Pytt' Geddes. The
Place. 01/07/06

Biographer's Thread 8: Gerda's Little Devil

1 Geddes G., Looking for the
Golden Needle. Mannamedia. 3rd
Edition 2001

22. The Place Where Three Strands Meet

1 A detailed biography, and an
account of Robin Howard's work
at The Place, can be found at
www.theplace.org.uk
2 Taped interview with Gerda
Geddes, Kirkton of Coull
29/11/05

3 Telephone interview with
Gudrun Gylling 13/11/06
4 ibid
5 ibid
6 Taped interview with Eva
Karczag, Foresterseat 15/05/06
7 ibid
8 Taped interview Kirkton of Coull
29/11/05
9 Delza, S., 1961. Body and Mind
in Harmony. David McKay Co.,
Inc. New York
10 Taped interview Kirkton of Coull
29/11/05
11 ibid
12 Eulogy given by Gerda Geddes at
a celebration in honour of Jane
Dudley at The Place, 2001
13 Spoken contribution by Tim
Lamford to a Celebration of The
Life of Gerda 'Pytt' Geddes. The
Place. 01/07/06
14 Taped interview with Eva
Karczag, Foresterseat 15/05/06

23. Personal Searches

1 Taped interview with Gerda
Geddes. Kirkton of Coull
13/12/05
2 ibid
3 Schnapper, E.B., 1985. The Spiral
Path of Spiritual Psychology. The
C.W. Daniel Company Ltd.
4 Gerda Geddes. Undated diary
entry.
5 Diary entry 23/04/70
6 Taped interview with Gerda
Geddes: Kirkton of Coull
29/11/05
7 Taped interview with Eva
Karczag: Foresterseat 15/05/06
8 Taped interview with Sue Phipps:
Alderton 16/09/06
9 ibid
10 Telephone interview with
Catherine Robinson 10/12/06

24. The Open Handed Teacher

1 Telephone interview with
Catherine Robinson 10/12/06
2 Taped interview with Sue Phipps:
Alderton 16/09/06
3 Taped interview with Gerda
Geddes: Kirkton of Coull
14/11/05

4 p79 Geddes, G., 2001. Looking for the Golden Needle. Mannamedia

5 Taped interview with Thetis Blacker: The Place, London 01/07/06

6 Taped interview with Sue Phipps, Alderton 16/09/06

7 Telephone interview with Gudrun Gylling: 13/11/06

8 Telephone interview with Catherine Robinson 10/12/06

9 Taped interview with Gerda Geddes: Kirklands of Coull 14/11/05

10 Taped interview with Gerda Geddes: Kirklands of Coull 21/10/05

11 see Slade, H., 1977. Contemplative Intimacy. Darton, Longman and Todd.

25. Creative Circles

1 Spoken contribution by Tim Lamford to a Celebration of The Life of Gerda 'Pytt' Geddes. The Place. 01/07/06

2 Taped interview with Eva Karczag: Foresterseat 15/05/06

3 pp8-9 Essential Alston Teacher's Booklet available from www.theplace.org.uk/

4 p7 ibid

5 Taped interview with Gerda Geddes: Kirkton of Coull 29/11/05

26. Outward Flow

1 Taped interview with Gerda Geddes: Kirkton of Coull 29/11/05

2 Taped interview with Thetis Blacker: The Place, London 01/07/06

3 Taped interview with Gerda Geddes: Kirkton of Coull 02/02/06

4 Telephone interview with Catherine Robinson 10/12/06

5 Taped interview with John Llewellyn: Bodenham 17/09/06

6 Geddes, G., 1994 Understanding T'ai-chi Ch'uan. Beckmann Visual Publishing

27. Pinning Down the Golden Needle

1 This paragraph draws heavily on a taped interview with Jane and Harriet: Kirkton of Coull 11/04/06

2 Drawn from Tribute to Rosemary Russell by Julian Bond, 1986: Radionic Quarterly vol 32(2)

3 Taped interview with Gerda Geddes: Kirkton of Coull 11/10/05

4 Gerda Geddes diary entry 14/08/80

5 Taped interview with Gerda Geddes: Kirkton of Coull 29/11/05

6 email from Simon Rickard 06/12/06

7 Taped interview with Gerda Geddes: Kirkton of Coull 29/11/05

8 p71 Geddes, G., 2001. Looking for the Golden Needle. Mannamedia. 3rd edition

9 p43 ibid

10 Taped interview with Gerda Geddes: Kirkton of Coull 28/10/05

11 p49 Geddes, G., 2001. Looking for the Golden Needle. Mannamedia. 3rd edition

12 Taped interview with Thetis Blacker: The Place 01/07/06

13 Taped interview with Gerda Geddes: Kirkton of Coull 11/10/05

14 ibid

Biographer's Thread 10: Energy, Light and Visions

1 Taped interview with Gerda Geddes: Kirkton of Coull 12/01/06

2 Taped interview with Harriet Devlin: Shrewsbury 17/09/06

28. Loss and Grief

1 Schumacher, E.F., 1975. Small is Beautiful: a study of economics as if people really mattered. Sphere.

2 Taped interview with Gerda Geddes: Kirkton of Coull 11/10/05

3 Taped interview with Gerda
Geddes: Kirkton of Coull
14/11/05
4 ibid
5 Gerda Geddes diary entry:
04/08/96
6 ibid
7 Taped interview with Thetis
Blacker: The Place, London
01/07/06
8 Geddes G., 1996. T'ai-chi: Fitness
for Life. Beckman Visual
Publishing
9 Taped interview with Gerda
Geddes: Kirkton of Coull
14/11/05
10 Taped interview with Gerda
Geddes: Kirkton of Coull
11/10/05
11 Gerda Geddes diary entry dated
'Christmas 1996'
12 drawn from Gerda Geddes diary
entry 26/01/97

29. The Scottish Years

1 Gerda Geddes diary entry
31/09/97
2 Gerda Geddes diary entry
20/12/97
3 Gerda Geddes diary entry
14/01/98
4 Taped interview with Nancy
Berlando: Aberdeen 12/11/06
5 Gerda Geddes diary entry
18/06/98
6 Gerda Geddes diary entry
'Summary of Year 1998'
7 Taped interview with Nancy
Berlando: Aberdeen 12/11/06
8 ibid
9 Tribute in Tai Chi Chuan
magazine no 22 2006 p32
10 ibid
11 Gerda Geddes diary entry undated
12 Taped interview with John
Llewllyn: Bodenham 17/09/06
13 p65 Geddes, G., 2001. Looking
for the Golden Needle
Mannamedia 3rd Edition
14 p125 ibid
15 Taped interview with Gerda
Geddes: Kirkton of Coull
24/01/06

30. Shooting Out the Arrow

1 Taped interview with Gerda
Geddes: Kirkton of Coull
27/06/01
2 Gerda Geddes diary entries 2001
3 Gerda Geddes diary
entry18/09/02
4 Taped interview with Gerda
Geddes: Kirkton of Coull
12/02/06
5 Taped interview with Gerda
Geddes: Kirkton of Coull
29/11/05
6 Taped interview with Gerda
Geddes: Kirkton of Coull
03/01/06
7 Taped interview with Harriet and
Jane: Kirkton of Coull 11/04/06
8 Taped interview with Nancy
Berlando: Aberdeen 12/11/06
9 Details drawn from taped
interview with Harriet and Jane:
Kirkton of Coull 11/04/06

31. Celebration

1 Taped interview with Gerda
Geddes: Kirkton of Coull
14/11/05
2 Letter by Jane Geddes dated
24/07/06

BIBLIOGRAPHY

Selected References

Books

Barber, N., 1979. The Fall of Shanghai. Macmillan, London

Boadella, D., (Editor), 1976. In the Wake of Reich. Coventure, London

Delza, S., 1961. Body and Mind in Harmony. David McKay Inc., New York

Dong, S., 2000. Shanghai: The Rise and Fall of a Decadent City. Harper Collins, New York

Geddes G,. 2001. Looking for the Golden Needle. Mannamedia. 3rd edition

Gia-Fu Feng, English, J. (translators), 1999. Tao Te Ching. Wildwood House Ltd., Aldershot

Raknes, O., 1970. Wilhelm Reich and Orgonomy. St Martin's Press, New York

Riste, O. and Nokleby, B., 1999. Norway 1940-45: The Resistance Movement. Aschehoug. 5th printing

Satprem, 1970. Sri Aurobindo or the Adventure of Consciousness. Sri Aurobindo Ashram, Pondicherry

Schnapper, E., 1985. The Spiral Path of Spiritual Psychology. The C.W. Daniel Co., Saffron Walden

Slade, H., 1977. Contemplative Intimacy. Darton, Longman and Todd, London

Wilhelm, R (English translation by Baynes, C.F.). I Ching. Routledge and Kegan Paul, London 3rd edition, reprinted 1984

Wong, E., 1997. The Shambala Guide to Taoism. Shambala Publications, Inc., Boston

Websites

Heller, M. C., 2005 The Golden Age of Body Psychotherapy in Oslo. Presentation at Oslo University College June 2005. Available at www.aqualide.com

www.theplace.org.uk

www.brittenpears.org

DVDs

Geddes, G., 1994 Understanding T'ai-chi Ch'uan. Beckmann Visual Publishing

Geddes G., 1996. T'ai-chi: Fitness for Life. Beckman Visual Publishing

INDEX

Aakesson, Birgit: 72, 74, 188, 189;
New York debut, 72; style of
dance, 72; GG's indebtedness to,
72-73
Aastvedt: 14, 60, 96; detailed
description, 31-32; occupied by
German officers, 41
Aboyne, 246-247, 248, 253
acknowledgements, 266
acupuncture, 169-170
Ah Dee, 100, 115, 117-119, 121-122,
143, 149-150, 173
Aldeburgh Festival, 131, 156, 221
Alexander Technique, 159, 206
Alexandra, the last Czarina, 132
Allegorical Journey, The, 4, 168, 172,
178, 208, 224, 229, 232, 234,
247, 250, 256, 265
Alston, Richard: 217-218, 251, 262;
Richard Alston Dance Company,
187, 217
Amethyst, HMS, 107
Anchorhold, The, 197, 211
Artists' Rifles, 186
Balmoral Castle, 243
Barber, Noel, 110
Bergen, 13, 18, 43, 128, 139
Berlando, Nancy, 245, 247, 248, 259
Besant, Annie, 206
Blacker, Carmen, 199
Blacker, Thetis, 182-183, 198, 199,
202, 209, 211, 219-221, 233, 240,
251, 262
Bream, Julian, 155-157
Britten, Benjamin: 155, 177, 180, 203;
in Hong Kong, 131; in Japan,
133; Curlew River, 133; gift of
records, 134
Britten-Pears School for Advanced
Musical Studies, 203, 221, 222
Bruun, Gerdt Meyer (GG's father):
14, 15, 61-63; rope works,
Bergen, 16, 29, 30; bullet wound,
16, 23; plans for Gerda, 28; death,
62, 82, 163
Bruun, Lydia Meyer (GG's mother):
14, 15, 61-63, 139; trains as
physiotherapist, 16; hostess for
Rasmus Meyer, 18; lives in

U.S.A., 16; visits Hong Kong and
Macau 129-130; death, 207
Butcher, Rosemary, 216
capoeira, 216
Carmina Burana, 258
Central School of Speech and Drama,
158
Cheng Man Ch'ing, 8
chi, 3, 164, 169-170, 234
Chiang Kai-shek, 104, 105, 107, 108
Chinese Civil War, 103, 104-106
Choy Hawk-pang, 135, 142, 143,
144, 145
Choy Kam-man: 135, 145, 146, 151,
170; touches GG, 145; sends GG
film of t'ai-chi, 171
Clayfield, 226-228, 236, 240
Cohan, Robert, 187, 188
College of Psychic Studies, 181, 182,
206, 234
Collins, Cecil, 181, 199
Collins, Elizabeth, 199
Communist soldiers: mistreatment by,
118, 119
Confucius, 169, 175
Contemporary Ballet Trust, 187
Coull Parish Church, 243, 261
Coward, Noel, 186
Cranbrook, 222-223, 244, 250
Crozier, Eric, 180
Cunningham, Merce: 215;
Cunningham technique, 214
dance: 68, 151; merges with
psychology, 74, 76, 77, 83, 115,
194; GG's training, 40, 73, 74;
and t'ai-chi, 191, 207, 216, 217-
218
Delza, Sophia, 189, 191, 192, 215
de Valois Ninette, 187
Devlin, Harriet (GG's daughter), 38,
75, 127, 130, 138, 139, 150, 154,
171, 177, 200, 226, 236, 239,
244, 249, 251, 262, 264
Doscher, Emma, 15
Dudley, Jane: 191-193, 251; Dancing
Inside, 193
Duke of Edinburgh, 156, 157
Duncan, Isadora, 214
Dupres, Maedee, 216
energy, 64, 164, 168-169, 257

Freud, Sigmund, 56, 63
Fulkerson, Mary, 217
Geddes, Alexander Campbell, 94
Geddes, David Campbell (GG's
husband): 126, 139, 150, 152,
154, 156, 177, 225-228; GG
meets, 85, 91; paintings, 91; visits
Aastvedt, 91; GG's engagement
to, 92; wedding, 11, 94-96; self
portrait, 92; job in Shanghai, 97;
mystical vision, 181-182, 234,
238; military intelligence, 182;
Civil Service, 237; death, 236;
ashes in Scapa Flow, 238-240
Geddes, Enid Campbell, 92
Geddes, Gerda 'Pytt' (née Meyer
Bruun): spiritual dimension, 2,
181, 238; practical skills, 2, 34,
253; demonstrates t'ai-chi on TV,
3, 158, 224; teaches first t'ai-chi
class, 3; experience of light,
illumination, 10, 164; wedding,
11; mother, relationship with, 33,
61, 83, 84, 95, 130, 207; father,
relationship with, 28, 29, 62;
parents, disparities, 14, 23, 70;
parents, marital tensions, 17, 23,
61-63; origins of 'Pytt', 25, 39;
sensitive child, 26; education, 26,
27, 28, 33, 58; boarding school in
London, 27;domestic science
skills, 28; sails to U.S.A., 32;
scholarship to Pennsylvania
College for Women, 33, 34;
dance training, 40, 73, 74;
threatened by German soldiers,
41, 43; joins Resistance, 42, 44,
45, 74; escapes Gestapo trap, 46-
47, 51; flees to Sweden, 47-50;
love affairs, 36, 58, 67, 87, 89;
psychology training, 58, 70;
psychoanalysis training, 67, 164;
practises as therapist, 67, 85, 94;
avant-garde lifestyle, 69-71; ability
to read people, 67, 75; works in
asylum, 76; therapy with
concentration camp survivors, 77,
115; therapy with traumatised war
victims, 79, 115; works with
actors, 83-84; wedding, 95-97;
illness and health problems, 98,
137-141, 148, 158, 164-165, 167-
169, 180; hostage in Shanghai,
111, 117; learning about Chinese
culture, 121-123; body/mind

synthesis, 135, 164, 265;
depression, 138, 141, 165; leaves
the Far East for Europe, 148, 157;
connectedness of dance,
psychology and t'ai-chi, 162, 164,
194, 196; skiing accident, 180;
Gerda's little devil, 184-185;
influence on contemporary dance,
191, 207, 213, 214-218; open-
handed teaching, 206-212; The
Promised Land, 228, 233; move
to Scotland, 241-251; hip
replacement, 248; minor stroke,
249; angina, 253, 258; preparation
for death, 255-258; transparency,
255, 256; clarity, 211, 258; death,
259-260; memorial, 261-264 ;
scattering ashes, 263-264
Geddes, Jane (GG's daughter), 38, 75,
115, 117-119, 128, 137, 140, 149,
150, 154, 171, 177, 226, 236,
239, 244, 248, 249, 260, 262, 263
Geddes, Lady, 94, 97, 128, 130
Geddes, Ross Campbell, 92
Geddes, Sir Auckland Campbell, 92
Gielguid, Sir John, 89, 187
Graham, Martha: 187, 214; Graham
technique, 189, 191, 192, 195,
214, 217
Guildhall School of Music and Drama,
158, 222
Gylling, Gudrun, 188, 190, 191, 202,
209, 211, 247, 251
Hamilton, Julyen, 216
Harewood, Lord, 187
Hesse Students Fund, 131
Hipkin, Bronwyn, 211
hippies, 188, 193
Hong Kong: 120-121, 128, 142;
escape to in 1951, 117-119; house
on The Peak, 120; lifestyle, 123-
126; hiring fishing boat, 124; GG
opens nursery school, 127; effect
of climate, 137-141; Odile,
nanny, 251
Howard, Robin, 187, 188
Hunt, Holman, 186
I Ching, 174-176, 184, 201, 223, 226,
229
Ineson, George, 204, 211, 223
information gathering for biography,
38
Jardine, Matheson and Co., 11, 100,
102, 110, 113, 115, 117, 148,
159, 236

Jung, Carl Gustav, 172
Karczag, Eva, 190,195-196, 202-203, 216-217, 244
Keswick, Clare, 100, 115
Keswick, Sir John, 12, 100, 115, 149
King Haakon of Norway: 19, 20, 41, 82; GG gives flowers to, 19, 20
Kinthissa, 211, 251
Kirkton of Coull, 243-246, 249, 251
Krybbebakken, 13, 14, 18, 60, 162
Kuan Yin, 230-231
Laban, Rudolf, 214
Lamford, Tim, 194-195, 215-216, 217, 262
Landmark, Ole, 18
Lee, Laurie, 155-157
light: moments of illumination, 10, 238; inner light, 135, 162-164, 218, 234, 238, 255
Lindenberg, Elsa (Reich's girlfriend), 69; creates dance psychotherapy, 70
Llewellyn, John, 223, 248, 250, 251, 259
Loewe, Michael, 199
London, 11, 27, 73, 88-90, 94, 97, 128, 149, 151, 152
London Contemporary Dance School, 187
London Festival Ballet, 190, 195
Looking for the Golden Needle: 38, 149, 228, 233; Epilogue, 250-251, 255, 262
Lupeg, 131, 177
Ma Yueh-liang, 192
Macau: 129; visit opium den, 130
Malleny House, 92
Mann, Felix, 180-181
Mann, Golo, 155
Mao Tse-tung: 104, 105, 108; The Long March, 105
meditation, 200-201, 211, 226
Meyer, Conrad (GG's grandfather): 31, 144
Meyer, Gerda ('Tante Gerda'): 92; couturier gowns, 12, 13; entertains royalty, 20, 21
Meyer, Rasmus: 13, 60; art collection, 14, 18, 162; death, 18, 60
Middleditch, David, 110
Millais, John Everett, 186
Moore, Henry, 187
Morris, William, 186
Morven, 244, 248, 249
Munch, Edvard, 18, 162

Nanking, 107
Nansen, Fridtjof, 21
Neill, A.S., 70
Norway: German invasion, 40; German occupation, 44, 45; Operation Weserübung, 40; liberation of, 81; GG returns to after WW2, 83
Norwegian Childhood, A, 2, 38
Norwegian National Theatre, 11, 83, 84, 88, 92
Old Vic, 88
Oldhouse Farm, 152, 153-155, 165, 173, 177, 180, 200, 211, 225-226
Olivier, Laurence, 89
Oslo: 56, 69, 92, 244; University, 40, 58, 70; students rounded up by Nazis, 44;'The Golden Age of Body Psychotherapy in Oslo', 69
Pears, Peter, 131, 133, 203-204
Philipson, Tage, 72, 74, 77, 86
Phipps, Sue, 203-204, 207, 209, 211, 222, 251
Pisk, Litz, 88-89
Place, The: 123, 183, 203, 222, 241, 262; t'ai-chi classes, 185, 186-196, 204, 207, 211, 215, 218, 223, 244
Poland: German invasion of, 37
Prince Ludwig ('Lu') of Hesse and the Rhine: 95, 131-134, 139, 155-157, 239
Princess Margaret ('Peg') of Hesse and the Rhine: 131-134, 139, 155-157, 239; air crash tragedy, 95; wedding dress, 95; close bond with David Campbell Geddes, 95; death, 242
psychoanalysis: 54, 56, 58, 178, 210 Reichian analysis, 56, 61, 63, 64, 65, 66, 67, 84, 86, 172, 208, 223
psychology: merges with dance 54, 76, 83, 84, 115 ; classes, 34, 76
psychotherapy: body psychotherapy, 63, 69
Queen Maud of Norway: 19, 41; puts GG to bed, 20
RADA, 158-159
Raknes, Ola, 56, 63, 64, 66, 67, 70, 87, 226
Rambert, Marie, 187, 190
Redgrave, Vanessa, 89
Reich, Wilhelm: 56, 63, 69, 70, 71, 86, 94, 164, 172 The Function of the Orgasm, 57; The Mass

Psychology of Fascism, 57; The Cancer Biopathy, 57; orgone energy, 57, 164; orgone accumulator, 57; jailed, 58; death in jail, 58; Character Analysis, 63; muscular armouring, 64, 179; vegetative streamings, 64; Vegetotherapy, 64, 70; sexual reformer, 56, 69; Communist, 57, 69

Resistance: 42, 74, 78; Underground newspapers, 44; casualties, 50
Richardson, Ralph, 89
Rickard, Simon, 227-228
Ring, Gerda, 71, 84
Robinson, Catherine, 204-205, 206, 210, 211, 222, 227, 244, 248, 250, 251
Robinson, Ronnie, 248
Rudi, Ingeborg, 70
Russell, Lady Rosemary, 226, 234
Sachsenhausen concentration camp, 78
Satprem, 6, 53, 230
Scapa Flow, Orkney, 238-240, 262
Schnapper, Edith, 6, 161, 198, 199-200, 226
Schumachar, Fritz, 237
Shanghai: 12, 98, 106, 110; lifestyle, 12, 100-102; Bund, the, 12, 102; Hungjao, 102-103, 108, 112, 122; Fall of Shanghai, 110; hyperinflation, 107; executions, 108, 111; Bamboo Curtain, 109, 112, 115; Communist changes to, 112, 113; curfew, 112; effect of climate on GG,137; naval blockade, 114; Shanghailander, 100, 106, 108, 115
Slade, Father Herbert, 197, 201, 204, 211, 226
Sri Aurobindo, 5, 7, 198-200, 204, 226, 230
Stockholm: 49, 70, 72, 76, 163, 189; Choreographic Institute, 188
Storhaugen, 18, 22, 31, 71
Strachan, Lize, 261
Strider, 217
Sweden, in exile, 49, 66, 71, 76, 81, 163
T.T. Liang, 8
t'ai-chi: GG's first meeting with, 2, 10, 107, 135, 164; hidden layer of meaning, 3; names of moves, 3, 167, 170; symbolism, 3, 167-168, 172, 208; as martial art, 4;

Chinese Shadow Boxing, 4, 151, 183; for personal growth, 4; for health and fitness, 4; GG's first lesson, 135, 143; brief explanation of, 142; Western woman and, 145, 147; GG demonstrates on television, 3, 185; GG forgets the sequence, 159, 170; rebirth 167-176; early classes in Soho180-181; and dancer training, 188-196; Cambridge classes, 198-199, 206, 211; GG's teaching style, 67, 202; pushing hands, 210; Aboyne classes, 245-247; memorial in Regents Park, 262
Taena, 204, 211, 223
Tai Chi Caledonia, 248
Tai Chi Chuan magazine, 248
Tai Chi Union of Great Britain, 248
Tang En-po, General, 108
Tao Te Ching, 184
Tao, Taoism, 3, 142, 143, 151, 169, 184, 204, 208, 209, 223, 232
Turner paintings, 163
visualisation, 201
Wall Street Crash: 29; effect on GG's life, 29, 30, 33
Wallis, Barnes, 186
Warbeth beach and cemetery, Orkney, 238-240, 264
Wigman, Mary, 71, 214
Wolfsgarten, Schloss, 131, 139, 155, 177
Wolfit, Donald, 89
wu-wei, 184-185
X6, 217
yang, 3, 169-170, 175, 208, 229, 232, 240
Yang Cheng-fu, 142, 143
Yang Lu-ch'an, 142, 143, 208
Yangtze Incident, 108
Yesnaby cliffs, Orkney, 263
yin, 3, 169-170, 175, 208, 229